Understanding Pragmatics

'This is easily the most useful, and engaging introduction to pragmatics that is currently available. Senft discusses the canonical topics of the discipline but he discusses them, always in an exemplary and rigorous manner, against their wider intellectual backgrounds. This combination of sympathetic, critical and illuminating exposition of the central topics and their relationships makes this book a terrific companion for all undergraduate and postgraduate students (and some of their teachers too).'

Ken Turner, *University of Brighton, UK*

'Gunter Senft's *Understanding Pragmatics* is highly systematic and orderly, with a new principled approach to the major themes of pragmatics and the central topics that have paraded under that banner. Arrayed against the familiar texts in the field, the book is more heavily grounded in anthropological fieldwork and splendidly provided with suggested and potentially thought-provoking exercises for ambitious students at all levels. I am eager to try it out with some of my own.'

John Haviland, *University of California, San Diego, USA*

Understanding Pragmatics takes an interdisciplinary approach to provide an accessible introduction to linguistic pragmatics. This book discusses how the meaning of utterances can only be understood in relation to overall cultural, social and interpersonal contexts, as well as to culture-specific conventions and the speech events in which they are embedded. From a cross-linguistic and cross-cultural perspective, this book:

- debates the core issues of pragmatics such as speech act theory, conversational implicature, deixis, gesture, interaction strategies, ritual communication, phatic communion, linguistic relativity, ethnography of speaking, ethnomethodology, conversation analysis, languages and social classes, and linguistic ideologies
- incorporates examples from a broad variety of different languages and cultures
- takes an innovative and transdisciplinary view of the field showing that linguistic pragmatics has its predecessor in other disciplines such as philosophy, psychology, ethology, ethnology, sociology and the political sciences.

Written by an experienced teacher and researcher, this introductory textbook is essential reading for all students studying pragmatics.

Gunter Senft is senior investigator at the MPI for Psycholinguistics in Nijmegen and extraordinary professor of general linguistics at the University of Cologne, Germany. His main research interests include Austronesian and Papuan languages, anthropological linguistics, pragmatics and semantics.

Understanding Language series

Series Editors:

Bernard Comrie, Max Planck Institute for Evolutionary Anthropology, Leipzig, Germany
Greville Corbett, Surrey Morphology Group, University of Surrey, UK

The Understanding Language series provides approachable, yet authoritative, introductions to major topics in linguistics. Ideal for students with little or no prior knowledge of linguistics, each book carefully explains the basics, emphasizing understanding of the essential notions rather than arguing for a particular theoretical position.

Other titles in the series:

For more information on any of these titles, or to order, go to www.routledge.com/linguistics

Understanding

Pragmatics

Gunter Senft

Routledge
Taylor & Francis Group

LONDON AND NEW YORK

First published 2014
by Routledge
2 Park Square, Milton Park, Abingdon, Oxon OX14 4RN

and by Routledge
711 Third Avenue, New York, NY 10017

Routledge is an imprint of the Taylor & Francis Group, an informa business

British Library Cataloguing in Publication Data
A catalogue record for this book is available from the British Library

Library of Congress Cataloging in Publication Data
Senft, Gunter, 1952–
Understanding pragmatics : an interdisciplinary approach to language use / Gunter Senft.
pages cm. -- (Understanding Language Series)
Includes bibliographical references.
1. Pragmatics. 2. Linguistics. I. Title.
P99.4.P72S48 2014
401'.45--dc23
2013027996

ISBN: 978-0-415-84056-9 (hbk)
ISBN: 978-1-4441-8030-5 (pbk)
ISBN: 978-0-203-77647-6 (ebk)

Typeset in Minion Pro
by Saxon Graphics Ltd, Derby

MIX
Paper from
responsible sources
FSC
www.fsc.org   FSC® C013056

Printed and bound in Great Britain by
TJ International Ltd, Padstow, Cornwall

Contents

Abbreviations

Note that the glosses in some of the examples quoted were changed (following the Leipzig Glossing Rules as closely as possible) for the sake of standardization.

1	first person
2	second person
3	third person
ABS	absolutive
ACAUS	anti-causative
ACS	achieved change of state particle
AN	animate
ASP	neutral aspect
CLF	(numeral) classifier
CNJ	conjunction
COP	copula
CRA	cross-reference set A (>ergative=, possessor)
CRB	cross-reference set B (>absolutive=)
Dat	dative
DEF	definiteness marker, definite determiner
DEIC	deictic
DEM	demonstrative
DF	disfluency
DIM	diminutive
DIR	directional
DIST	distal
E	experimenter
EXCL	exclusive

EXIST	existential predicate
FP	final particle
FUT	future
H	hearer
HON	honorific prefix
IMPF	imperfective
INC	incompletive
INCL	inclusive
LOC	locative
M	masculine
MED	medial
ms	milliseconds
NMLZ	nominalizer
N	proper name (Moerman transcript, subsection 5.4)
NOMP	nominative particle
OBL	oblique
P	particle
PAST	past
(p.c.)	personal communication
PL	plural
PP.IV	possessive pronoun series IV in Kilivila, marking inalienable possession
POSS	possessive
PRS	present
PRN	pronoun
PROG	progressive
PRT	unanalysed sentential particle
PT	discourse/evidential particle
PRV	pro-verb
QPRT	question particle
QUOTP	quotative particle

S	subject (in an experiment)
	speaker
SG	singular
T	title
TCPs	turn-completion points
TCUs	turn-constructional units
TRPs	transition-relevance places

Acknowledgements

Writing this book involved the help of many people. First of all I would like to thank Bernard Comrie and Greville Corbett for inviting me to write this introduction to linguistic pragmatics as a contribution to their Understanding Language series. I also owe thanks to them as well as to three anonymous reviewers for constructive and insightful comments on my book proposal. In addition, Grev and Bernard accompanied the writing process and gave me very useful editorial advice at various stages.

My friends and colleagues Mark Dingemanse, Ad Foolen, Elma Hilbrink, Ingjerd Hoem and Pieter Seuren read the first draft of the book. I thank them for their detailed, insightful and extremely helpful comments and recommendations for further reading. In addition, Pieter Seuren has carefully corrected what the author supposed to be English.

I thank the students of the Promotionskolleg Sprachwissenschaft der Universität Münster, especially Rahel Beyer, Elisa Franz, Katharina König, Ilka Pescheck, Verena Wecker and Qiang Zhu for reading various chapters of the book with the critical eye of the readership this book wants to address and for their feedback. (It goes without saying that all remaining shortcomings are mine.)

I am also indebted to Kristin Andrews, Susan Millership and Lucy Winder from Hodder Education and Isabelle Cheng, Rachel Daw, Nadia Seemungal and Louisa Semlyen from Routledge, project manager Rob Brown at Saxon Graphics and copy editor Lorna Hawes for their helpfulness, editorial advice and expertise.

I would like to thank Pacific Linguistics, the University of Hawai'i Press and Mouton de Gruyter for their permission to reprint parts of my own papers and books (Senft 1995; 2004a and b; 2010a).

And last but not least I would like to thank my wife Barbara for sharing work and life.

Introduction

AN ILLUSTRATIVE ANECDOTE ON WHAT THIS BOOK IS ABOUT

In 1982 I started my field research on the language and culture of the Trobriand Islanders in Papua New Guinea. Here is my record of an early experience there:

Every morning after I had gotten up and brushed my teeth, I would grab my towel and the little box that contained my soap, shampoo, hair brush and other articles we West-Europeans think to be absolutely necessary for having a bath and walked through the village to the path that leads to a fresh water grotto, about a ten-minute walk into the bush southeast of Tauwema. Although everyone could infer from the things I carried where I was going, and although all the villagers knew after some time that this was part of my morning routine, people always asked me in the village or on the path to the grotto *Ambe?* – "Where?" – implying "Where are you going to?" At first I reacted with a smile and answered with the name of the grotto: *Bugei*. However, after some weeks – having made some progress in my language acquisition, I responded somewhat impatiently by either waving with my towel to the people who asked this (for me then rather silly) question or by simply answering *O, kunukwali, bala Bugei makala yumyam* – "Oh, you know, I will go (to the) Bugei like every day". After having responded to this question in this way for a few days, Weyei – my neighbor and one of my best informants and friends – approached me and told me that I should always answer this question as exactly as possible. Thus, after some further progress in learning the language I could react to the question *Ambe?* in the appropriate Trobriand way, answering for example: *Bala bakakaya baka'ita basisu bapaisewa* – "I will go, I will have a bath, I will return, I will stay (in the village), I will work".

With Weyei's help I came to understand that this question was in fact a greeting formula. People who meet in the Trobriands and who want to indicate that they care for each other do not use greeting formulae ... such as *Bwena kaukwa* – "good morning", but instead ask each other where they are going. This question is always answered as truthfully and as comprehensively as possible (as in the example given). This has a practical reason: all paths on Kaile'una Island and most paths on the other islands belonging to the Trobriand group are just small trampled paths that often lead over sharp coral rocks where it is quite easy to hurt one's foot or leg. Also, sometimes the paths cross a grove of coconut trees, and it has also happened that people on these paths have been rather severely hurt by falling coconuts. Moreover, Trobriand Islanders are very much afraid of the *kosi*. According to their belief the *kosi* are ghostly spirits of dead persons, who were not properly mourned immediately after their deaths, and who therefore terrify the living. The apparition of a *kosi* may frighten someone in the jungle in such a way that they might lose their orientation. Therefore, the answer to this form of greeting functions to secure one's way and one's safe arrival at one's destination. If people do not show up after a certain time at the places mentioned in their answers to the greeting question, their fellow villagers and friends will look for them. Thus, being greeted with this question is a sign that the community cares for the person. It is a daily routine that serves the function of social bonding. And it is considered so important, that Trobrianders who are not greeted in this way at least by their fellow villagers will conclude that they must have committed some serious offense against the community. A village community that does not greet one of its fellow villagers with this question indicates that it no longer cares for this person. So it was a completely inappropriate reaction when I – sometimes quite conceitedly – smiled about what I first thought to be a silly question. On the contrary, being greeted with this question by the people of Tauwema after only a few days in their village was a first sign of their good will and intention to integrate me into the community.[1]

This misunderstanding shows just what this book is about: As a newcomer in the Trobriand speech community I hardly knew anything about the conventions, rules and regulations with respect to how the Trobriand Islanders use their language Kilivila in social interactions, what kind of meanings their words, phrases and sentences convey in what kind of contexts and what kind of functions their use of language fulfils in and for its speakers' communicative behaviour. To gain this kind of knowledge requires the study of the culture-specific forms of the Trobriand Islanders' language use. In linguistics, the study of language use is called 'pragmatics'.[2] This book provides a general introduction into this field.

Pragmatics is the discipline within linguistics that deals with actual language use. Language use is not only dependent on linguistic, that is grammatical and lexical knowledge, but also on cultural, situative and interpersonal context and convention, and one of the central aims of pragmatics is to research how context and convention – in their broadest sense – contribute to meaning and understanding (as the anecdote presented above illustrates). Thus, the social and cultural embedding of meaning will be in the focus of this introduction to pragmatics.

THE PRAGMATIC TURN!?

Jacob Mey, one of the pioneers and leading figures in modern linguistic pragmatics, refers to this field as 'the youngest subdiscipline of the venerable science called *linguistics*' (Mey 1994: 3261; see also Mey 1993: 3, 18). Mey and many others see the rise of pragmatics and its growing popularity and influence ever since the 1970s at least in part as a reaction to the development of American structural linguistics that culminated in Noam Chomsky's proclamation of the 'ideal speaker/listener in a completely homogeneous speech community' (Chomsky 1965: 3) whose language competence linguists describe and analyse on the basis of introspection data. The more the

Chomskyan paradigm gained influence in linguistics, the more linguists gradually realized that the general abstractions of this paradigm neglected the reality of language that is realized in speech produced by speakers in various social, cultural and political contexts with various goals and intentions. Indeed, language is much more than a grammatical algorithm with a lexicon; it is a tool speakers use to interact socially and communicate with each other. Research in linguistic pragmatics deals with how speakers use their language(s) in various situations and contexts: what speakers do when they speak and why they do it. In the focus of pragmatics are the actual language users, their communicative behaviour, their world and their point of view, in short, 'the total human *context of* [language] *use*' (Mey 1994: 3265).

This implies that pragmatics serves a kind of 'umbrella' function, as Jan-Ola Östman (1988: 28) put it – not only for 'sociolinguistics ... and other (semi-) hyphenated areas of linguistics' but also for the other traditional subdisciplines of linguistics. As Mey (1994: 3268) wrote: 'The problems of pragmatics are not confined to the semantic, the syntactic or the phonological fields, exclusively. Pragmatics ... defines a cluster of related problems, rather than a strictly delimited area of research'. Pragmatics studies language and its meaningful use from the perspective of language users embedded in their situational, behavioural, cultural, societal and political contexts, using a broad variety of methodologies and interdisciplinary approaches depending on specific research questions and interests.

The issue of interdisciplinarity brings us back to the claim that the 1970s was the decade in which the 'pragmatic turn' in linguistics had its origin. The first volume of the *Journal of Pragmatics* was published in 1977; John Benjamins started a book series with the title Pragmatics and Beyond in 1979; the International Pragmatics Association (IPrA) was founded in 1986; and its journal *Pragmatics* started under the name *IPrA Papers in Pragmatics* a year later. However, if we look at core domains of the discipline we realize that linguistic pragmatics is relevant for, and has its predecessors in, many other disciplines such as philosophy, psychology, ethology, ethnology, sociology and the political sciences.

It will be shown in this volume that pragmatics is not only an inherently interdisciplinary field within linguistics, but that it is indeed a 'transdiscipline' that brings together and interacts with a rather broad variety of disciplines within the humanities which share the fundamental interest in social action. This interest constitutes a leitmotif for this volume, based on the conviction that 'the heart of the pragmatic enterprise [is] the description of language as social action' (Clift *et al.* 2009: 50).

The volume has three central threads that bind the chapters into a complex whole:

1. Languages are used by their speakers in social interactions; they are first and foremost instruments for creating social bonds and accountability relations. The means with which languages create these bonds and relations vary across languages and cultures.

2. Speech is part of the context of the situation in which it is produced, language has an essentially pragmatic character and 'meaning resides in the pragmatic function of an utterance' (Bauman 1992: 147).

- Speakers of a language follow conventions, rules and regulations in their use of language in social interactions.

- The meaning of words, phrases and sentences is conveyed in certain kinds of situative contexts.

- The speakers' uses of language fulfil specific functions in and for these speakers' communicative behaviour.

3. Pragmatics is the transdiscipline that studies these language- and culture-specific forms of language use.

THE STRUCTURE OF THE BOOK

It was pointed out above that linguistic pragmatics is relevant for, and has its predecessors in, other disciplines such as philosophy, psychology, ethology, ethnology, sociology and the political sciences. The chapters of this book are based on this insight. Each chapter discusses a selection of core issues of pragmatics that were introduced into the field via these six disciplines. The chapters start with a reference to one or more famous scholars who introduced the issues in focus to pragmatics. Then the contents of these issues and the latest developments within these areas of pragmatics are discussed from a cross-linguistic and cross-cultural perspective. At the end of each chapter a brief summary is followed by a discussion that picks up the threads provided by the anecdote presented at the beginning of this introduction. This discussion aims not only at answering questions raised with this example with respect to cultural differences in language use and understanding, but also at illustrating how cultural, situative and interpersonal context and culture-specific conventions contribute to meaning in actual language use. Each chapter ends with an exercise/work section and suggestions for further reading. These publications are marked in the list of references with an asterisk (*).

Chapter One Pragmatics and philosophy: What we do when we speak and what we actually mean – speech act theory and the theory of conversational implicature

The first chapter looks at the relationship between pragmatics and philosophy. One of the central questions of philosophy is how we interpret our world and our lives as being meaningful, or more generally, how we generate 'meaning'. One of the most important tools we use to do this is language. And one of the most fascinating fields in linguistics is to study how speakers use their language to generate specific meanings in specific contexts. This is the interface where philosophy meets semantics and pragmatics. This chapter first deals with the general question *What do we do when we speak?*, presenting the theory of *speech acts* put forward by John L. Austin (1962) and John R. Searle (1969). In his book *How to Do Things With Words* Austin developed his general conception of speech as action and his classification of speech acts into *locutions* –

which have meaning, *illocutions* – which have a certain force and *perlocutions* – which achieve certain effects. Searle systematized Austin's theory of speech acts. He understands speaking as performing *illocutionary acts* which have both a specific function-indicating element, the *illocutionary force* and a proposition-indicating element, the *propositional content*. Speakers perform illocutionary acts in a rule-governed form of behaviour. This idea is illustrated with Searle's analysis of the illocutionary act of 'sincere promising' and its propositional content conditions. It is shown how – on the basis of such content conditions – Searle formulates constitutive rules for illocutionary acts. Then his classification of speech acts is presented. After a brief discussion of speech act theory from a cross-cultural perspective which shows that research by other scholars refutes possible claims of its universality, this first part of the chapter ends with some of Pieter Seuren's thoughts on speech acts and their socially binding force.

The chapter then discusses H. Paul Grice's theory of *implicature* and *conversational maxims*. Grice saw conversation as being guided by a system of expectations – by maxims – that are mutually shared by interactants. In his *theory of conversational implicature* Grice formulates the *Cooperative Principle* and its subcases – the four maxims of conversation. First, it is illustrated how these maxims can be violated or 'flouted', and then characteristic properties of implicatures are discussed. The chapter ends with a brief look at Grice's theory from an anthropological-linguistic point of view.

This chapter presents philosophical perspectives on language and speech which understand speech acts as manifestations of language as action that – driven by intentions of speakers – causes effects and thus has psychological and behavioural consequences in speaker–hearer interactions. It is shown that there is a difference between the way in which an utterance is used and the meaning that is expressed by this utterance in certain contexts and that speakers may say one thing that has a specific meaning but that also means something else in certain circumstances because of certain social conventions that are valid within a specific speech community. And it is pointed out that speech acts create accountability relations; thus they can be seen as a social pact between speaker and hearer which is based on conventions and requires social competence of the interactants.

Chapter Two Pragmatics and psychology: Deictic reference and gesture

How do speakers of different languages refer to objects, persons, places, periods of time and even texts or text passages? When speakers do this, they communicate in certain contexts, and these contexts shape our utterances. Natural languages are context-bound, and the subdiscipline of linguistics that concerns how languages encode features of the context of utterances is called '*deixis*'. Thus, when someone wants to know what is meant by a sentence like *He gave me this book yesterday* s/he needs to know who uttered it, when and where, and to which book the speaker refers. *Deixis* is the name given to the system of indexical forms and means that make these references, and, as illustrated by the sentence above, these indexicals are characterized by the fact that their use and meaning is completely context-dependent. The most influential contribution on the topic of deixis was presented by the German psychologist Karl Bühler in the first half of the last century, and ever since Bühler the study of deixis has been an important research domain within pragmatics. In the first part of this chapter the phenomenon of deixis is presented and discussed. After a general introduction to the topic, a cross-linguistic comparison of language-specific forms of spatial deixis illustrates the broad variety of the means languages offer their speakers for this kind of deictic reference. This part of Chapter Two ends with an illustration of the system of spatial deixis in the Oceanic language Kilivila.

The term deixis is borrowed from the Greek word for pointing or indicating. We not only point with words, but also with gestures. The second part of this chapter deals with the question *What forms of gestures do people make and what is their function?* At the beginning of the last century the psychologist Wilhelm Wundt laid the foundations and set standards for the study of gestures and sign languages in his seminal work *Völkerpsychologie*. Wundt's insights were taken up by psychologists like Adam Kendon, David McNeill and Susan Golden-Meadow who became pioneers of modern gesture research. The second part of this chapter provides a definition of gesture, presents the classification of gestures into different types, including co-thought and co-speech gestures, and discusses their functions and the interrelationship between gesture, language and mind. After a survey of the cross-cultural variation of gestures the chapter ends with a discussion of so-called pragmatic gestures. The study of deixis and gesture provides direct evidence for the fact that human interaction is multimodal.

Chapter Three   Pragmatics and human ethology: Biological foundations of communicative behaviour

Gestures are not the only expressive movements that function as communicative signals. This chapter first presents and discusses some other forms of expressive behaviour that are used in human communication. Human Ethology is a subdiscipline of biology that deals among other things with the communicative functions of all kinds of expressive behaviour. Among the most communicative of such behavioural signals are facial expressions. The chapter first reports on research about facial expressions, highlighting the so-called 'eyebrow flash' and its communicative functions. It then describes how territorial behaviour of humans expressed in personal distance, posture behaviour and body motion is another means of expressing communicative and interactional signals. It is shown that territorial behaviour is different in different cultures.

Human ethologists argue that expressive movements like those presented and discussed in the first part of this chapter have undergone distinctive differentiation in the service of signalling in phylogenetic and cultural ritualization processes. Thus, the second complex question asked in this chapter is: *Why are forms of verbal and non-verbal expressive behaviour ritualized, what is the function of ritual behaviour and can rituals and forms of ritual behaviour be referred back to some basic underlying strategies of interactive forms of behaviour?* After a brief discussion of the concepts *ritual* and *ritual communication*, the chapter discusses Irenäus Eibl-Eibesfeldt's claim that rituals and forms of ritual communication can be referred back to so-called *basic interaction strategies.* The concept of basic interaction strategies and their communicative functions are presented and illustrated with analyses of the rituals of requesting, giving and taking of the Eipo in West Papua and with complex forms of ritual communication observed during a festival of the Yanomamö in the Amazon rainforest. Finally, Eibl-Eibesfeldt's concept is discussed in connection with Stephen Levinson's recent proposals about a *universal systematics of interaction* and *building blocks for cultural diversity in social interaction,* provided by what he calls *the interaction engine.*

Chapter Four Pragmatics and ethnology: The interface of language, culture and cognition

This chapter deals with the interrelationship of language, culture and cognition in human interaction. One of the anthropologists whose linguistic insights became extremely influential in pragmatics was Bronislaw Malinowski. The first part of this chapter introduces Malinowski's ethnographic theory about meaning and language. For him, too, language was a mode of behaviour, a mode of action in which the meaning of a word or an utterance is constituted by its function within certain contexts. He was especially interested in answering the question: *What are the essential forms of language?* One of these forms is realized in what Malinowski calls *phatic communion,* a form of language use that has exclusively social bonding functions and thus does not serve any purpose of communicating ideas and expressing thoughts. The first part of this chapter presents and critically assesses this concept and its functions and illustrates it with examples from Korean. However, the concept of phatic communion highlights only one aspect of Malinowski's linguistic thinking. He was also very much interested both in universal features of language as well as in the interrelationship between language, culture and cognition that is expressed in culture-specific features and phenomena of languages.

This interest was shared by the linguist Franz Boas, one of Malinowski's contemporaries. Boas's student Edward Sapir took up his teacher's cautiously formulated ideas about this interrelationship and together with his student Benjamin Lee Whorf he formulated the so-called Sapir-Whorf hypothesis about linguistic relativity with which they claim to answer the question: *What is the relationship between language and thought?* Whorf came up with two versions of the linguistic relativity principle; the strong version claims that language determines thought, whereas the weak version claims that language influences thought. After the presentation of the linguistic relativity principle the second part of this chapter discusses, illustrates and critically assesses the hypothesis mainly on the basis of cross-linguistic/cross-cultural research on the conceptualization of space and spatial reference. This research highlights the strong interrelationship between language, culture and cognition. Its results support the hypothesis that language contributes in shaping thinking for non-verbal problem solving instances.

Malinowski, Boas and Sapir emphasized that language must be studied in its social context. Thus, it goes without saying that whoever wants to investigate the interrelationship between language, culture and cognition must know how the speech community being researched constructs its social reality. Researchers need to be on common ground with the communities being researched. To achieve this aim, the *ethnography of speaking* approach provides a useful, though complex framework. The third part of this chapter presents a critical discussion and assessment of the ethnography of speaking paradigm with illustrations from Joel Sherzer's research published as the *Kuna Ways of Speaking*. These include ways of greeting and leave-taking, curing magic and the shouting of specific texts during the girls' puberty rights.

Chapter Five   Pragmatics and sociology: Everyday social interaction

In the 1960s and 1970s the research of three North American sociologists had a strong impact on the understanding of human everyday face-to-face interaction in general and on the understanding of communicative behaviour and language use – especially in conversation – in particular.

The first part of this chapter features Erving Goffman, his insights in, and ideas about, the presentation of self in everyday life, social encounters and forms of talk. He proposed to call this subarea of sociology which studies social interaction *the interaction order*.

The second part of this chapter deals with Harold Garfinkel's so-called *ethnomethodological* studies on social order, on everyday 'common sense' knowledge about social structures and on reasoning in social action and communication; in short, on how we make sense of our social world. His famous 'breaching experiments' are highlighted and it is explained why we react aggressively when somebody responds to a greeting like *How are you?* with the question *How I am in regard to what? My health, my finance, my work...*

Influenced by Garfinkel, but also by Goffman, Harvey Sacks developed the field of *Conversation Analysis* (CA) – in close cooperation with Emanuel A. Schegloff and Gail Jefferson – to research how conversation is ordered and structurally organized. The field of CA has been developed in sociology departments and still seems to be more strongly rooted in this discipline than in departments of linguistics (although this has changed somewhat in recent times). The third part of this chapter provides a basic introduction to main topics of CA and illustrates the most recent developments of CA research.

Chapter Six   Pragmatics and politics: Language, social class, ethnicity and education and linguistic ideologies

This chapter tries to answer the question about the relationship between pragmatics and politics and the relevance and impact of politics for pragmatics. The 1960s were a highly politicized decade which saw a strong rise of Marxist ideas and other left-wing ideologies. Social inequalities and clashes between social classes came to the fore of the general political discussion and they were taken up in the scientific discourse, especially within the humanities. In 1959 the British sociologist and former teacher Basil Bernstein published a paper in which he differentiated between a *'public'* and a *'formal language'*; later he used the expressions *'restricted'* and *'elaborated code'* which children learn in their sociocultural environment. He claimed that children who are only socialized in a restricted code are limited in their communicative skills; usually these children are members of the lower classes; on the other hand, children who acquire and are socialized in an elaborate code are verbally skilled speakers who can deal with all kinds of communicative situations; usually these children grow up in middle class families. Bernstein's research had not only political but also pedagogical consequences, both in Europe and in North America. A number of so-called 'compensatory' education programmes were developed and carried out, like the Operation Headstart programme in the USA. Throughout the 1960s and 1970s Bernstein's theory on the interrelationship between language, social class and education and the compensatory education programmes were heavily criticized. This theory, which was referred to as the *deficit hypothesis*, was confronted with sociolinguistic approaches that were referred to as the *difference hypothesis*. The most prominent representative of this latter approach was William Labov. Labov argued that compensatory programmes were doomed to fail because they were 'designed to repair the child, rather than the school'; on the basis of his linguistic research he pleaded to change the institution 'School' so that school education could offer equal opportunities to all pupils, regardless of their social class background. He emphasized that a proper understanding and assessing of the verbal skills of lower class children, especially of Black lower class children in the urban centres of the USA, needed research into how they use their language in their social contexts. It is only there that one can gather adequate cultural knowledge based on participant observation and proper linguistic data which enable linguists to detect the rule-governed grammatical structure of these children's vernacular.

The first part of this chapter presents the research by Bernstein on the one hand and Labov on the other and the deficit versus difference hypothesis controversy that had strong implications for linguistic pragmatics.

The discussion of Bernstein's and Labov's contributions to sociolinguistics illustrates how linguistic research contributed to increase researchers' awareness of the political impact of their studies. This observation is taken up in the second part of the chapter which discusses the topic of linguistic ideologies and its role for linguistic pragmatics. After a brief discussion of the concept this part of the chapter presents two exemplary case studies of research on language ideologies in Pacific speech communities in Honiara on the Solomon Islands and on Rapa Nui and a comparative study on language ideologies manifest in honorific language.

Chapter Seven Understanding pragmatics: Summary and outlook

The last chapter of this volume first provides a summary in which the three main threads (mentioned above) that run through the six chapters of the volume are picked up again; they will be elaborated on the basis of the insights gained in Chapters One to Six. This summary points out once more that in this volume pragmatics is understood as the transdiscipline that studies context-dependent language and culture-specific forms of language use.

The last chapter ends with a brief outlook on future developments within linguistic pragmatics. In recent years, Sachiko Ide, Yasuhiro Katagiri, William Hanks and other scholars have started a project on what they call 'emancipatory pragmatics' (see Hanks *et al.* 2009b; Hanks *et al.* 2012). They argue for a paradigm shift from 'traditional pragmatics' towards 'emancipatory pragmatics' which no longer solely relies on theories and views of language derived from Euro-American languages and ways of speaking.

NOTES

1   I already reported this in Senft (1995: 217f.).
2   This term was first used by Charles Morris (1938), who – following Charles Sanders Peirce – tried to develop a general science of signs – i.e. semiotics. For the role Peirce plays in and for pragmatics see, e.g. Hookway (1998: 1084–1086). For a survey of the history of the term 'pragmatics' see Levinson (1983: 1ff.) and Gazdar (1979: 1ff.), also Seuren (1998: 406).

Pragmatics and philosophy

What we do when we speak and what we actually mean – speech act theory and the theory of conversational implicature

1.1 INTRODUCTION

One of the central questions of philosophy is how we interpret our world and our lives as being 'meaningful', or, more generally, how we generate meaning in the general sense of 'significance'. One of the most important tools we use to do this is language. And one of the most fascinating fields in linguistics is to study how speakers use their language to generate specific meanings in specific contexts. This is the interface where philosophy meets semantics and pragmatics.

There have been many different approaches by philosophers to answer questions like: *What is the meaning of a word?* and *What does a sentence mean?* At the end of the 1920s and the beginning of the 1930s, a group of philosophers and mathematicians in Vienna and Berlin – among them scholars like Moritz Schlick (1882–1936), Rudolf Carnap (1891–1970), Curt Gödel (1906–1978), Otto Neurath (1882–1945), Carl Hempel (1905–1997) and Hans Reichenbach (1891–1953) – claimed that a sentence is meaningless unless its truth conditions can be tested, that is to say, unless formal logical analyses of this sentence can answer the question under what conditions it is true or false. Sentences must be verifiable in order to be meaningful. This position implied that all texts that were literary, theological or otherwise metaphysical and most of the sentences produced by ordinary speakers in everyday verbal interaction were meaningless! This highly formal and very constrained approach to language – which was called 'logical positivism' – was taken up by a number of other European and American philosophers, like the British philosopher Alfred J. Ayer (1910–1989) who propagated the paradigm of logical positivism and its so-called 'verificationist theory of meaning' in his famous and at the time widely read book *Language, Truth and Logic* (Ayer 1936).

Probably the most important reaction to this approach came from philosophers teaching at Oxford, especially between 1945 and 1970; they formed the so-called school of Ordinary Language Philosophy (Seuren 1998: 367). Influenced by Ludwig Wittgenstein's (1889–1951) teachings at Cambridge during the 1930s and 1940s and his later publications (see Seuren 1998: 419), the scholars who formed this school distrusted the logical paradigm of the formal semantics of their time which was highly influenced by, if not completely based on, the logical positivism approach. They showed that this paradigm could not properly deal with phenomena like anaphora (i.e. roughly speaking, reference to entities mentioned earlier in the discourse), presuppositions (i.e. roughly speaking, information that is taken for granted between interacting speakers)[1] and speech acts realized in ordinary natural language (see Seuren 1998: 367; 2009: Chapter 4). Among these scholars were Gilbert Ryle (1900–1976), Peter Geach (born 1916), Peter Strawson (1919–2006), John Austin (1911–1960), John Searle (born 1932) and H. Paul Grice (1913–1988).

This chapter deals first with the theory of speech acts put forward by John Austin (1962) and John R. Searle (1969). It then presents some of Pieter Seuren's (2009) thoughts on speech acts and their socially binding force and ends with a discussion of H. Paul Grice's theory of implicature and conversational maxims (Grice 1967; 1975; 1978). Both speech act theory and Grice's theory of conversational implicature will be critically assessed from an anthropological-linguistic perspective. This first chapter deals with rather complex theoretical issues and requires careful reading.

1.2 JOHN AUSTIN'S SPEECH ACT THEORY

This section first discusses Austin's differentiation between assertions or statements – to which Austin refers with the term 'constatives' and utterances with which something is done; Austin refers to these utterances with the term 'performatives'. Then the section reveals the two turns in Austin's argument: first he gives up the differentiation between performatives and constatives and then he presents his classification acts which are central for his idea of language as action. He differentiates between *locutions* – that is speech acts which have meaning, *illocutions* – that is speech acts which have a certain force and *perlocutions* – that is speech acts which achieve certain effects. Austin himself is aware of the fact that in his theory he has 'left numerous loose ends' (Austin 1962: 148).

1.2.1 Statements versus utterances that do something: Constatives versus performatives

John Austin's philosophy of language deals with some uses of ordinary language. He was convinced that 'a distinction has to be drawn between the meaning expressed by an utterance and the way in which the utterance is used (i.e. its 'force') and ... that utterances of every kind ... can be considered as acts' (Sbisà 1995: 496). He developed his speech act theory in his 12 William James Lectures which he delivered at Harvard University in 1955 and which were posthumously published in his booklet *How to Do Things with Words* (Austin 1962). Austin's booklet was not intended to present a ready-made theory, so to speak, but as an exposé of his thoughts about language use as they developed.

In his first four lectures he makes a distinction between sentences like (1) and (2) on the one hand and (3) and (4) on the other:

(1)   *I name this ship the Queen Elizabeth* (Austin 1962: 5).

(2)   *I bet you six pence Fury, the black stallion, will win the race.*

and

(3)   *My daughter's name is Frauke and my son is called Sebastian.*

(4)   *We live in a small provincial town in the northwest of Germany.*

He refers to the first two declarative sentences, in which something is *done* in or by *saying* something, as 'performative' sentences; they are characterized by having verbs produced 'in the first person singular present indicative active' (Austin 1962: 5) which make the action performed by the speaker explicit. Thus, these sentences perform an act (like baptizing or betting); they are neither 'true' nor 'false'; 'they are seen … to be … *not* utterances which could be "true" or "false"'. Verbs that can be used performatively are called 'performative verbs'. Sentences like (3) and (4), assertions or statements, are 'constative' sentences in Austin's terminology; in these sentences something is said which can be true or false (Austin 1962: 3, 12).

However, although Austin states that performatives cannot be true or false because, given their specific nature, this question is irrelevant, he points out that nevertheless performatives can go wrong – like announcing the bet in sentence (2) after the race is over. In this situation, the performative utterance is 'in general *unhappy*' (Austin 1962: 14). Thus performatives have to meet at least the following so-called 'felicity conditions':

A.   (i)   There must be a conventional procedure having a conventional effect.
    (ii)   The circumstances and persons must be appropriate, as specified in the procedure.

B.   The procedure must be executed (i) correctly and (ii) completely.

C.   Often (i) the persons must have the requisite thoughts, feelings and intentions, as specified in the procedure, and (ii) if consequent conduct is specified, then the relevant parties must so do.

(Levinson 1983: 229; see Austin 1962: 15)

Austin provides examples for situations in which these conditions are not fulfilled:

A.   (i)   Assume there is a married couple and both are Christians. If the husband says to his wife 'I hereby divorce you' repeating this utterance three times he will not achieve a divorce; however, with a Muslim couple such an action would constitute a divorce.

A.   (ii)   Assume a clergyman baptizing a baby 'Albert' instead of 'Alfred' (see Austin 1962: 27, 35).

B.   (i)   Assume a man says 'my house' when he actually has two (and the context does not make clear which of the two is meant) or 'I bet the race won't be run today' when more than one race was arranged (and the context fails to make clear which race is intended).

B. (ii) A bridegroom's attempt to marry by saying 'I do' is abortive if the bride says 'I do not' (see Austin 1962: 36f.).

Austin calls A and B infelicities 'which are such that the act for the performing of which, and in the performing of which, the verbal formula in question is designed, is not achieved, by the name MISFIRES...' (Austin 1962: 16). Here the actions intended are simply not achieved.

C. (i) Assume somebody is asked for advice and he intentionally gives bad advice.
C. (ii) Assume somebody promises something without any intention whatsoever to keep the promise (see Austin 1962: 42, 45).

C conditions are insincerities and infractions or breaches; Austin's name for those infelicities where the act *is* achieved but insincerely is 'ABUSES' (see Austin 1962: 16, 39).[2]

Austin then points out that constatives are also affected by these felicity conditions. For instance, 'statements which refer to something which does not exist' and he gives the examples (5) to (8) (Austin 1962: 20, 48, 143):

(5)   *The present King of France is bald.*[3]

The utterance given in example (6) violates a felicity condition, namely condition C (i):

(6)   *The cat is on the mat but I do not believe it is.*

A sentence like (7) is neither true nor false, it is simply 'a rough description':

(7)   *France is hexagonal.*

And if someone utters a constative like (8),

(8)   *All Jack's children are bald.*

he or she presupposes that Jack has children; one cannot say *All Jack's children are bald but Jack has no children* or *Jack has no children and all his children are bald* because the presupposition of an utterance like (8), the information that is taken for granted, would be violated. Thus, performatives and constatives are actually affected by phenomena that have something to do with sincerity, commitment and presupposition; thus, they have a 'common underlying structure' (Sbisà 1995: 497). This means that performatives and constatives are not really as distinct from each other as Austin claimed them to be.

1.2.2 Two turns in Austin's argument

To sum up so far, Austin first differentiates between constatives, i.e. utterances that simply say something – and performatives, i.e. utterances that do things, achieving the actions they express because there are conventions that link the utterances to institutionalized procedures. He then shows, however, that this distinction is somewhat artificial. And at the end of the fourth lecture Austin foreshadows a twist in his argument and gradually develops his general conception of speech as action in the next eight lectures. Austin closes his fourth lecture as follows:

> we see that in order to explain what can go wrong with statements we cannot just concentrate on the proposition involved (whatever that is) as has been done traditionally. We must consider the total situation in which the utterance is issued – the total speech-act – if we were to see the parallel between statements and performative utterances, and how each can go wrong. So the total speech act in the total speech situation is emerging from logic piecemeal as important in special cases: and thus we are assimilating the supposed constative utterance to the performative.[4]
>
> (Austin 1962: 52)

Indeed, in the following lectures Austin justifies this assimilation of the constative to the performative, pointing out that there are no absolute grammatical or lexical criteria to justify the distinction he started with. Utterances like (9):

(9)   *It is yours.*

'may be taken as equivalent to either "I give it to you" or "it (already) belongs to you"'. Thus utterances can be used on different occasions as a performative and as a constative. Nevertheless, Austin points out that performatives with verbs in the first person present indicative active deserve special attention. The use of first person present indicative active is 'asymmetrical with respect to other persons and tenses of the indicative mood of the same verb, since these would constitute mere descriptions and reports' (Sbisà 1995: 497). Based on this observation Austin now suggests making a list of explicit performative verbs and claims that all performative utterances which are not in the form 'I x that', 'I x to', or 'I x' can 'be "reduced" to this form' and will then constitute what he calls 'explicit performatives'. These explicit performatives, i.e. performative utterances containing a performative verb, are opposed 'to "primary" performative[s]' (Austin 1962: 69). Primary performatives are performative utterances which are produced without a performative verb. Example (10) is a primary utterance, whereas example (11) is an explicit performative (see Austin 1962: 69):

(10)   *I shall be there.*

(11)   *I (hereby) promise that I shall be there.*

Explicit performatives can be reinforced by adding the adverb 'hereby', although 'it is rather too formal for ordinary purposes' (Austin 1962: 61). Austin claims that the 'explicit performative develops from the primary'; this means that 'every performative could be in principle put into the form of an explicit performative' (Austin 1962: 83, 91).

However, Austin has to point out once more that it is not easy to decide whether an utterance is performative or not. He refers, for example to expressions like 'I approve' and 'I agree' stating that '"I approve" may have the performative force of giving approval or it may have the descriptive meaning: "I favour this"' (Austin 1962: 78). Moreover, performative verbs can also be used descriptively as in sentence (12):

(12)   *I named this ship the Queen Elizabeth.*

In addition, an utterance like 'I state that...' seems to satisfy the requirements of being a performative one, but it clearly is a statement which can be true or false, depending on the included proposition like, for example, 'I state that the Earth is flat'. Here Austin decides that he has to start thinking about the problem from a different perspective (see Austin: 1962: 91).

He now abandons the dichotomy between performatives and constatives. This marks the first turn in Austin's argument: He no longer sees performatives as a 'special class of sentences with peculiar syntactic and pragmatic properties' but points out instead that 'there is a general class of performative utterances that includes ... explicit performatives ... and [primary performatives], the latter including lots of other kinds of utterances, if not all' (Levinson 1983: 231). Moreover, at the end of the seventh lecture at the latest we notice the 'shift from the dichotomy performative/constative to a general theory of illocutionary acts of which the various performatives and constatives are just special sub-cases' (Levinson 1983: 231).[5]

In her seminal article on 'How to read Austin', Marina Sbisà points out that in *How to Do Things with Words* (HTW):

> from the very start the performative/constative distinction plays an instrumental role. The analysis of performative utterances provides a first approach to actions performed in speech, and therefore to the kinds of things that are done by illocutionary acts. Constatives are just a straw man, to be replaced with an analysis of assertion as an illocutionary act ... Confirmation of this reading is scattered throughout initial lectures, in hints that make sense only in the light of the main thesis which will be revealed later in the book, i.e. that all speech should be considered as action.
>
> So, HTW appears as a complex argument in support of the claim that all speech should be considered as action, and, more specifically, that speech can be described as the performing of actions of the same kind as those performed by means of performative utterances. This complex argument has the form of a proof by contradiction. The thesis proposed at the beginning is the opposite of the intended one and its refutation serves as a proof of the intended thesis.
>
> (Sbisà 2007: 462f.)

1.2.3 Utterances which say something, do something and produce effects: Locutionary, illocutionary and perlocutionary acts

Austin now reconsiders 'more generally the senses in which to say something may be to do something, or in saying something we do something...' (Austin 1962: 91) and proposes a framework in terms of which all speech acts, i.e. constatives as well as performatives, can be described. He distinguishes three components in every utterance.

First, he calls the 'act of "saying something" ... a locutionary act, and the study of utterances ... the study of locutions, or of full units of speech' (see Austin 1962: 92ff.). For Austin saying something is:

- to perform a 'phonetic' act (the act of uttering certain noises);

- to perform a 'phatic' act (the act of uttering certain words in a certain grammatical construction);

- to perform a 'rhetic' act (the act of using words with a certain meaning).

Sbisà (1995: 498) points out that when we report a speaker's locutionary act we either focus on the phatic act (e.g. in the utterance: 'He said "The cat is on the mat"') using direct speech or we focus on the rhetic act (e.g. in the utterance: 'He said that the cat was on the mat') using indirect speech which reports the meaning of the utterance but does not quote the words in the form they were uttered.

Austin (1962: 98ff.) then claims that locutionary acts are also and at the same time illocutionary acts, i.e. acts of doing something in saying something like accusing, asking and answering questions, apologizing, blaming, informing, ordering, assuring, warning, announcing an intention, making an appointment, giving a description, promising and stating. Illocutionary acts conform to conventions and have a certain conventional force, the 'illocutionary force' which will cause certain effects.

And Austin finally contrasts locutionary and illocutionary acts with 'perlocutionary' acts, i.e. acts of doing something by saying something like persuading, alerting, convincing, deterring, surprising and getting somebody to do something. Perlocutionary acts produce effects upon the feelings, thoughts or actions of the addressee(s) and thus have psychological and/or behavioural consequences (see Austin 1962: 101f.; also Sbisà 2010: section 3.4).

After this first introduction of locutions, illocutions and perlocutions Austin provides examples like the following (slightly modified) one:

> Locution:
> He said to me 'kiss her!' meaning by 'kiss' kiss and referring by 'her' to *her*.

> Illocution:
> He urged (or advised, ordered, etc.) me to kiss her.

> Perlocution:
> He got me to (or made me, etc.) kiss her.

Thus, a locutionary act (which includes the phonetic, phatic and rhetic acts) just means saying something meaningful in its normal sense. The performance of this locutionary act involves an illocutionary act which has a certain force (like, for example, urging, advising, ordering, forcing, etc.). And the achieved effect of this illocutionary act on the listener (which has consequences for her or him) is the perlocutionary act (see Austin 1962: 121; also Clark 1996a: 146).

Having introduced these acts, Austin concentrates on illocutionary acts and contrasts them with perlocutionary acts.

As already mentioned above, illocutionary acts conform to conventions and have a certain conventional force, the illocutionary force which will cause certain effects. Thus, contrary to a perlocutionary act an illocutionary act produces effects; only if such an effect is achieved, is the illocutionary act performed successfully or happily. He illustrates this with the following example:

> I cannot be said to have warned an audience unless it hears what I say and takes what I say in a certain sense. An effect must be achieved on the audience if the illocutionary act is to be carried out ... So the performance of an illocutionary act involves the securing of *uptake.*
>
> (Austin 1962: 116f.)

'Uptake' is a necessary condition for the successful performance, i.e. the achievement of the core effect of an illocutionary act; and this uptake goes beyond the mere understanding of the illocution. The 'securing of uptake' is the first class of effect of the illocutionary act. It brings about 'the understanding of the meaning and of the force of the locution' (Sbisà 1995: 498; see also 2007: 464).

The second class of effect of the illocutionary act is the production of a conventional effect. Austin (1962: 117f.) describes this as follows: 'The illocutionary act "takes effect" in certain ways, as distinguished from producing consequences in the sense of bringing about states of affairs in the "normal" way, i.e. changes in the natural course of events'. He illustrates this statement with the example of naming a ship (see example (1) above).[6]

And the third class of effect of the illocutionary act is that it invites a response or a sequel; a promise, for example, has to be fulfilled.

Austin summarizes these effects of illocutionary acts and then opposes them to effects which are characteristic of perlocutionary acts:

> So here are three ways, securing uptake, taking effect, and inviting a response, in which illocutionary acts are bound up with effects; and these are all distinct from the producing of effects which is characteristic of the perlocutionary act.
>
> (Austin 1962: 118)

With the perlocutionary act a speaker achieves effects upon the feelings, thoughts or actions of the participant(s) in certain situations and specific circumstances; these effects have psychological and/or behavioural consequences for the participant(s) – be it the audience, the speaker him- or herself, or other persons. Perlocutionary acts are causal. Austin (1962: 119ff.) points out that the response or sequel of perlocutionary acts can also be achieved by non-verbal means: 'thus intimidation may be achieved by waving a stick or pointing a gun'. Contrary to illocutionary acts, perlocutionary acts are not conventional. The effects of the speaker's perlocutionary acts may be intended by the speaker, but they may also be unintended (see Austin 1962: 106f.). However, Sbisà points out that:

> [t]here is agency whenever it is fair to ascribe to an agent responsibility for a certain outcome ... If agents "do" whatever they may be justly ascribed (at least partial) responsibility for, a perlocutionary act is performed whenever the speaker is (at least partially) responsible for some act or state of the listener. And if this holds for the perlocutionary act, the whole locutionary-illocutionary-perlocutionary distinction should ... be read as a distinction ... among the kinds of effects for which speakers may be ascribed responsibility.
>
> (Sbisà 2007: 467)

This is a very interesting way of 'how to read Austin'. However, Austin himself concedes (especially in his tenth lecture) that despite all his efforts to characterize the difference between illocutionary and perlocutionary acts it turns out to be quite difficult to distinguish them clearly.[7]

In his last lecture Austin attempts to come up with a first and quite rudimentary taxonomy of illocutionary verbs, based on their illocutionary force. As mentioned above, Austin is aware of the fact that in his lectures he has 'left numerous loose ends' and that he produced 'a programme, that is, saying what ought to be done rather than doing something' (Austin 1962: 148, 164). Nevertheless, his idea of language as action which he proposed in *How to Do Things with Words* gave rise to 'speech act theory'.

1.3 JOHN SEARLE'S SPEECH ACT THEORY

This section first illustrates what Searle takes a speech act to be. Then it presents his analysis of the illocutionary act of sincere promising and its propositional content conditions. Then it is shown how on the basis of such content conditions he formulates the constitutive rules for illocutionary acts. After the presentation of Searle's classification of illocutionary acts this section ends with a brief discussion of speech act theory from a cross-cultural perspective.

1.3.1 What is a speech act?

It was Austin's student John R. Searle who systematized and somewhat formalized Austin's ideas in his theory of speech acts (see Searle 1965; 1975; 1976; 2006; but especially 1969). Searle points out that 'the basic unit of human linguistic communication is the illocutionary act' in the form of a 'complete sentence' produced under specific conditions (Searle 1976: 1; see also 1965 (1972)[8]: 137; 1969: 25). Illocutionary acts have an 'effect' on the hearer; the hearer understands the speaker's utterance.

For Searle speaking is performing illocutionary acts in a rule-governed form of behaviour. These rules are either regulative and can be paraphrased as imperatives, or they are constitutive and create and define new forms of behaviour. Searle's constitutive rules of speech acts represent Austin's felicity conditions (see Searle 1972: 137ff.; see 1.3.3 below).

Searle's 1965 paper 'What is a speech act' is based on the hypothesis 'that the semantics of a language can be regarded as a series of systems of constitutive rules and that illocutionary acts are acts performed in accordance with these sets of constitutive rules' (Searle 1972: 140). Before Searle illustrates this idea by formulating such a set of constitutive rules for the speech act of 'promising', some further clarifications are necessary. After presenting the following sentences (see Searle 1972: 140f.):

(13)   *Will John leave the room?*

(14)   *John will leave the room.*

(15)   *John, leave the room!*

(16)   *Would that John left the room.*

(17)   *If John will leave the room, I will leave also.*

he first points out that in all these utterances – performances of different illocutionary acts on given occasions – the speaker refers to a particular person, i.e. John and predicates the act of that person leaving the room. Although the illocutionary acts are different, being realized as a question, an assertion about the future, i.e. a prediction, an order, an expression of a wish and a hypothetical expression of intention, the acts of reference and predication are the same because they have a common content. Searle calls this common content a 'proposition'. Thus, when speakers perform an illocutionary act they perform at one and the same time an 'utterance act' (by uttering words) as well as a 'propositional act' (by expressing a proposition in referring to or predicating something). Thus, illocutionary acts not only have a specific illocutionary force, but also a propositional content (see Searle 1969: 31). According to this insight, a sentence has two parts: 'a proposition-indicating element and the function-indicating device' which reveals 'what illocutionary force the utterance is to have' and thus 'what illocutionary act the speaker is performing in the utterance of the sentence'. These devices include – at least for English – 'word order, stress, intonation contour, punctuation, the mood of the verb, and finally a set of so-called performative verbs' (Searle 1972: 142).

Then Searle discusses the questions '...what is it for one to mean something by what one says, and what is it for something to have a meaning?' (Searle 1972: 143). He points out that '[m]eaning is more than a matter of intention, it is also a matter of convention' and emphasizes that:

> one's meaning something when one says something is more than just contingently related to what the sentence means in the language one is speaking. In our analysis of illocutionary acts, we must capture both the intentional and conventional aspects of and especially the relationship between them. In the performance of an illocutionary act the speaker intends to produce a certain effect by means of getting the hearer to recognize his intention to produce this effect, and furthermore, if he is using words literally, he intends this recognition to be achieved in virtue of the fact that the rules for using the expressions he utters associate the expressions with the production of that

effect. It is this *combination* of elements which we shall need to express in our analysis of the illocutionary act.

(Searle 1972: 145f.)

1.3.2 Sincere promising and its propositional content conditions

After these clarifications Searle analyses the illocutionary act of sincere promising.[9] I assume that most people would come up with a rather straightforward answer when they were asked to explain, for example, what it means when they promise their friends with whom they want to go to the cinema to order the tickets. Searle illustrates how complex this speech act is. He starts with describing the situation in which a speaker directs a sentence to a hearer in which he sincerely promises to do something under the following conditions[10]:

1. The utterance is produced in such a way that the hearer understands what the speaker says.

2. The speaker makes the promise by uttering the sentence which is directed towards the hearer. Searle (1972: 148) elaborates on this condition as follows: 'This condition isolates the propositional content from the rest of the speech act and enables us to concentrate on the peculiarities of promising in the rest of the analysis'.

3. The speaker makes a promise. This promise may refer to something he or she may or may not do in the future once or repeatedly, or it may refer to remaining 'in a certain state or condition'. Searle calls conditions (2) and (3) 'the *propositional content conditions*'.

4. The hearer prefers that the speaker does something, and the speaker believes that this is true. Searle elaborates on this condition by pointing out that the utterance must be intended as a promise and not as another speech act, like a threat or a warning. He points out that '"I promise" and "I hereby promise" are among the strongest function indicating devices for commitment provided by the English language'.

5. The speech act to be performed 'must have a point'. Searle elaborates on this condition by pointing out that there is no point in promising something that one will do anyhow. He refers to conditions (4) and (5) as '*preparatory conditions*'.

6. The speaker will keep his or her promise. This is what Searle calls the 'sincerity condition' of the illocutionary act of sincere promising.

7. The speaker who makes the promise feels obliged to keep it. For Searle this is the '*essential condition*' of the illocutionary act of sincere promising.

8. The speaker wants to convince the hearer that the promise made is meant seriously.

9. The promise is produced in a grammatically and semantically adequate way in a situation in which the other eight conditions prevail.

1.3.3 Illocutionary acts and their constitutive rules

Searle points out that conditions (1), (8) and (9) 'apply generally to all kinds of normal illocutionary acts' (Searle 1969: 62). On the basis of the above listed conditions (2) to (7), which are required to make a sincere promise, Searle now extracts the set of rules 'for the use of any function indicating device P for promising':

> Rule 1. [The promise] is to be uttered only in the context of a sentence (or larger stretch of discourse) the utterance of which predicates some future act ... of the Speaker ... I call this the *propositional content rule*. It is derived from the propositional content conditions (2) and (3).
>   Rule 2. [The promise] is to be uttered only if the hearer ... would prefer [the speaker's] doing [the act] to his not doing [the act], and [the speaker] believes [the hearer] would prefer [the speaker's] doing [the act] to his not doing [the act].
>   Rule 3. [The promise] is to be uttered only if it is not obvious to both [the speaker] and [the hearer] that [the speaker] will do [the act] in the normal course of events. I call rules (2) and (3) *preparatory rules*. They are derived from the preparatory conditions (4) and (5).
>   Rule 4. [The promise] is to be uttered only if [the speaker] intends to do [the act]. I call this the *sincerity rule*. It is derived from the sincerity condition (6).
>   Rule 5. The utterance of [the promise] counts as the undertaking of an obligation to do [the act]. I call this the *essential rule*.
>   These rules are ordered: Rules 2–5 apply only if rule 1 is satisifed, and Rule 5 applies only if Rules 2 and 3 are satisfied as well.
>
> (Searle 1969: 63)

Searle's rules are summarized by Sbisà as follows:

- Propositional content rules "specify what kind of propositional content the speech act is to have", i.e. what the speech act is about.
- Preparatory condition rules "specify contextual requirements (especially regarding the speaker's and the hearer's epistemic and volitional states)", i.e. the necessary prerequisites for the speech act.
- Sincerity condition rules specify "which psychological state of the speaker will be expressed by the speech act", i.e. whether the speech act is performed sincerely or not.
- Essential condition rules "say what kind of illocutionary act the utterance is to count as".

(Sbisà 1995: 500)

Searle finishes his paper 'What is a speech act' by pointing out that this analysis of the speech act 'promising' can also be used for the analysis of other speech acts. He provides proposals for the analysis of the speech acts 'giving an order', 'assertion' and 'greeting' (see Searle 1972: 154). In his 1969 book *Speech Acts* he takes up this idea and provides similar analyses for the following types of illocutionary act: request, assert/state (that)/affirm, question, thank (for), advise, warn, greet and congratulate (Searle 1969: 66f.). Table 1.1 illustrates these proposals for the analysis of the speech acts 'request', 'assert' and 'greet' (see Searle 1969: 66f.; 1972: 154) based on their felicity conditions – that is, their constitutive rules.

Table 1.1

Comparison of the analysis of the illocutionary act types 'Request', 'Assert, state (that), affirm' and 'Greet' (based on their felicity conditions, i.e. their constitutive rules)

	Request	Assert, state (that) affirm	Greet
propositional content rule	Future act A of H	Any proposition p	None
preparatory condition rule	1. H is able to do A. S believes H is able to do A. 2. It is not obvious to both S and H that H will do A in the normal course of events of his own accord.	1. S has evidence (reason, etc.) for the truth of p. 2. It is not obvious to both S and H that H knows (does not need to be reminded of, etc.) p.	S has just encountered (or been introduced to, etc.) H.
sincerity condition rule	S wants H to do A.	S believes p.	None
essential condition rule	Counts as an attempt to get H to do A.	Counts as an undertaking to the effect that p represents an actual state of affairs.	Counts as courteous recognition of H by S.

Abbreviations: A = Act, H = Hearer, p = (expression of) proposition, S = Speaker

1.3.4 Searle's classification of illocutionary acts

Searle (1976: 2) claims that there are at least 12 dimensions of variation in which illocutionary acts differ from each other. Among the most important of these dimensions of differences between speech acts are:

- the illocutionary point,

- the direction of fit, and

- the expressed psychological states.

Before the description of these, for Searle, most important dimensions of variation in which speech acts differ from each other, the other nine dimensions he lists in his paper 'A classification of illocutionary acts' will be mentioned. With these dimensions Searle (1976: 5ff.) points at differences:

- *'in the force or strength with which the illocutionary point is presented'* (Searle provides the examples 'I suggest we go to the movies' and 'I insist that we go to the movies' which both have the same illocutionary point but are presented with different strengths);

- *'in the status of position of the speaker and hearer as these bear on the illocutionary force of an utterance'* (Searle refers to a general asking a private to clean up his room – which is a command, and a private asking a general to do the same – which is most probably a suggestion or a proposal, if not an act of insubordination);

- *'in the way the utterance relates to the interest of the speaker and the hearer'* (compare the differences between boasts and laments, congratulations and condolences);

- *'in relations to the rest of the discourse'* (performative expressions like 'I conclude' or adverbs and conjunctions like 'moreover', 'therefore' and 'however' relate an utterance to the rest of the discourse);

- *'in propositional content ... determined by illocutionary-force-indicating devices'* (a report can be about the past or present, a prediction must be about the future);

- *'between those acts that must always be speech acts and those that can be, but need not be performed as speech acts'*;

- *'between those acts that require extra-linguistic institutions for their performance and those that do not'* (in order to bless, christen, pronounce guilty, etc. the speaker must have a position within an extra-linguistic institution; making a statement like 'it is raining' does not require extra-linguistic institutions);

- *'between those acts where the corresponding illocutionary verb has a performative use and those where it does not'* (most illocutionary verbs like 'state', 'promise', 'order' have performative uses, but one cannot perform acts of boasting, for example, by saying 'I hereby boast'); and

- *'in the style of performance of the illocutionary act'* (e.g. the difference between announcing and confiding need not involve a difference in illocutionary point or propositional content, but only in the style of how the illocutionary act is performed).

But back to Searle's most important dimensions of variation in which speech acts differ from each other.

First, '*[d]ifferences in the point (or purpose) of the (type of) act ... affect the attempts to get the hearer to do something*'. Searle points out that the

> point or purpose of a description is that it is a representation (true or false, accurate or inaccurate) of how something is. The point or purpose of a promise is that it is an undertaking of an obligation by the speaker to do something ...

The point or purpose of a type of illocution I shall call its illocutionary point. Illocutionary point is part of but not the same as *illocutionary force*. Thus, e.g., the illocutionary point of request is the same as that of commands: both are attempts to get the hearer to do something. But the illocutionary forces are clearly different.

(Searle 1976: 2f.)

The second most important dimensions of variation in which speech acts differ from each other are '*[d]ifferences in the direction of fit between words and the world*'. Searle (1976: 3) points out that some 'illocutions have as part of their illocutionary point to get the words ... to match the world, others to get the world to match the words. Assertions are in the former category, promises and requests are in the latter'. He illustrates these differences with an example taken from G. E. M. Anscombe (1957). Imagine a man gets a shopping list from his wife with the words 'beans, butter, bacon, and bread' on it and goes to a supermarket. He is followed by a detective who notes down what he takes. When both leave the shop they have two identical lists; however, these lists have different functions. The man who did the shopping is supposed to make his actions fit the list, i.e. to get the world to match the words. The purpose of the detective's list is to make the words match the world, the list has to note the actions of the shopper. If the detective goes home and realizes that the man bought pork chops instead of bacon he can erase the word 'bacon' on his list and write 'pork chops'. The shopper who comes home and is told by his wife that he bought pork chops instead of bacon cannot correct his mistake by erasing 'bacon' from the list and writing 'pork chops' (see Searle 1976: 3).

The third most important dimension of variation in which speech acts differ from each other affects '*[d]ifferences in expressed psychological states*'. Searle illustrates this dimension as follows:

A man who states, explains, asserts or claims that p expresses the belief that p; a man who promises, vows, threatens or pledges to do expresses an intention to do A ... In general, in the performance of any illocutionary act with a propositional content, the speaker expresses some attitude, state, etc., to that propositional content.... The psychological state expressed in the performance of the illocutionary act is the *sincerity condition* of the act... If one tries to do a classification of illocutionary acts based entirely on differently expressed psychological states ... one can get quite a long way...

(Searle 1976: 4)

Searle, however, does not attempt to base his classification of illocutionary acts only on the way psychological states are expressed in performing illocutionary acts. His typology of speech acts is based on the three dimensions 'illocutionary point', 'direction of fit', and 'expressed psychological state'. After a critical survey of Austin's taxonomy for illocutionary verbs presented in his last William James Lecture, Searle presents his own taxonomy, a list of what he regards 'as the basic categories of illocutionary acts' (Searle 1976: 10). This list consists of the following five types:

1. *Representatives*. Like Austin's constatives, representatives have a truth value: They 'commit the speaker to something's being the case, to the truth of the expressed proposition ... The direction of fit is words to the world; the psychological state expressed is Belief (that p)' (Searle 1976: 10f.)[11]. Thus, acts of 'asserting', 'reporting', 'stating', 'concluding', 'deducing', and 'describing' are paradigmatic cases of representatives. Sentence (18) illustrates this type:

(18)   *Barack H. Obama is the forty-fourth President of the United States.*

2. *Directives*. The illocutionary point of directives is that they 'are attempts ... by the speaker to get the hearer to do something ... The direction of fit is world-to-words and the sincerity condition is want (or wish or desire). The propositional content is always that the hearer ... does some future action' (Searle 1976: 11). Acts of 'requesting', 'asking', 'ordering', 'commanding', 'begging', 'pleading', 'praying', 'defying' and 'challenging' are paradigmatic cases of directives. Sentence (19) illustrates this type:

(19)   *Go home.*

3. *Commissives*. They are 'illocutionary acts whose point is to commit the speaker ... to some future course of action ... The direction of fit is world-to-words and the sincerity condition is Intention. The propositional content is always that the speaker ... does some future action ...' (Searle 1976: 11). Acts of 'promising', 'threatening', 'offering' and 'pledging' are paradigmatic cases of commissives. Sentence (20) illustrates this type:

(20)   *I will have written this paper by Friday next week.*

4. *Expressives*. 'The illocutionary point of this class is to express the psychological state specified in the sincerity condition about a state of affairs specified in the propositional contents ... in expressives there is no direction of fit' (Searle 1976: 12). The gist of expressives is that they express the speaker's psychological attitude or state, like joy, grief, sorrow, etc. Acts of 'thanking', 'congratulating', 'apologizing', 'condoling', 'deploring' and 'welcoming' are paradigmatic cases of expressives. Sentence (21) illustrates this type:

(21)   *What a wonderful paper, Mark!*

5. *Declarations*. Searle points out that they 'are a very special category of speech acts'. Declaratives 'bring about some alternation to the status or condition of the referred-to object or objects solely in virtue of the fact that the declaration has been successfully performed'. However, the successful performance of declarations requires the existence of an extra-linguistic institution in which the speaker and the hearer occupy special places. 'The direction of fit is both words-to-world and world-to-words ... there is no sincerity condition' (Searle 1976: 14f.). Paradigmatic cases of declarations are successful acts of 'appointing',

'nominating', 'marrying', 'christening', 'excommunicating', 'declaring war', 'resigning', and 'firing (from employment)'. Example (22) illustrates this type:

(22)   *I now pronounce you Man and Wife.*[12]

1.3.5 Direct and indirect speech acts

Another important distinction Searle makes in his speech act theory is the distinction between direct and indirect speech acts. We all know that we can say one thing that has a specific meaning but that also means something else. A sentence like example (23):

(23)   *Can you pass the salt?*

is at first sight a question. However, we all understand that this question about a specific ability of a hearer is also a request addressed to the hearer that should make him pass the salt to the speaker. In sentences (24) and (25) – the former being a request and the latter being a grammatical imperative – we observe a direct match between the sentence type and its illocutionary force. These sentences illustrate direct speech acts:

(24)   *I request you to pass the salt.*

(25)   *Pass the salt, please.*

In sentence (23), however, we observe that there is 'an ulterior illocutionary point beyond the illocutionary point contained in the meaning of the sentence' (Searle 1975: 74). This sentence illustrates an indirect speech act. Another way of defining indirect speech acts is to define them as utterances 'in which one illocutionary act is performed indirectly by performing another' (Searle 1975: 60). Thus, in indirect speech acts we observe a difference between what is said and what is actually meant by the speaker. Especially with requests we observe that most of them are actually realized as indirect speech acts. Explicit requests and imperatives (as illustrated in sentences (24) and (25)) are rather rarely used in actual conversations. Stephen Levinson (1983: 264f.) points out that speakers of English 'could construct an indefinitely long list of ways of indirectly requesting an addressee' to do something like, e.g. passing the salt or closing the door. He presents the following (non-exhaustive list of) examples:

(26) a.   *I want you to close the door.*
            I'd be much obliged if you'd close the door.
      b.   *Can you close the door?*
            Are you able by any chance to close the door?
      c.   *Would you close the door?*
            Won't you close the door?
      d.   *Would you mind closing the door?*
            Would you be willing closing the door?
      e.   *You ought to close the door.*
            It might help to close the door.

> *Hadn't you better close the door?*
> f.   *May I ask you to close the door?*
>   *Would you mind awfully if I were to ask you to close the door?*
>   *I am sorry to have to tell you to please close the door.*
> g.   *Did you forget the door?*
>   *Do us a favour with the door, love.*
>   *How about a bit less breeze?*
>   *Now Johnny, what do big people do when they come in?*
>   *Okay, Johnny, what am I going to say next?*

Searle explains these speech acts as follows:

> In indirect speech acts the speaker communicates to the hearer more than he actually says by way of relying on their mutually shared background, both linguistic and nonlinguistic, together with the general powers of rationality and inference on the part of the hearer ... [T]he apparatus necessary to explain the indirect part of the indirect speech act includes a theory of speech acts, certain general principles of cooperative conversations ... and mutually shared factual background information of the speaker and the hearer, together with the ability on the part of the hearer to make inferences.
>
> (Searle 1975: 60f.)

The hearer uses the cooperative principle of conversation (which will be discussed in section 1.5 in connection with H. Paul Grice's theory of implicature and conversational maxims) to recognize that there is an ulterior illocutionary point beyond the illocutionary point contained in the meaning of the utterance. The speaker then makes inferences about what this ulterior illocutionary point – the real force of the utterance – is on the basis of his background information about the situation and context in which the indirect speech act is produced and on his general knowledge about the function and felicity conditions of speech acts (see Searle 1975: 74). Thus, in example (23) the hearer would recognize that this sentence 'infringes the felicity condition for the speech act of questioning and queries the preparatory condition for that of requesting' (Huang 2007: 112) and would thus realize that this utterance is an indirect speech act.[13] The hearer then follows the cooperative principle in conversation that operates on both the speaker and the hearer and makes the inference that the speaker wants him to pass the salt. Searle (1975: 61) points out that many indirect speech acts are conventionalized and idiomatically used (see Searle 1975: 69) – mainly because of reasons of politeness: 'Politeness is the most prominent motivation for indirectness in requests, and certain forms naturally tend to become the conventionally polite ways of making indirect requests' (Searle 1975: 76).

The complex domain of politeness cannot be discussed here (see Brown and Levinson 1978), however, it should be noted that it is difficult to clearly differentiate indirect speech acts from Austin's perlocutionary acts. Pieter Seuren comments on this as follows:

A perlocutionary act is defined as a speech act whose communicative function is to be derived by means of sensible social reasoning, as when I say *It's cold in here*, hoping that you will take the hint and turn the heating up or shut the window, as the case may be ...

... Indirect speech acts, including perlocutionary acts, are often subject to social and/ or linguistic convention, which has to be learned in order to participate adequately in a society...

... [The] indirect-speech-act character [of utterances like (23) above, G. S.] is accounted for by an appeal to social, not linguistic, competence. Thus considered, indirect speech acts and perlocutionary acts are of a kind, differing only in the extent to which the intended practical result is reflected in the words used: indirect speech acts are more direct expressions of the result intended than perlocutionary acts.

(Seuren 2009: 143)

1.3.6 Speech act theory from a cross-cultural perspective

As we have already seen in the example Austin (1962: 27) provides to illustrate violations of the felicity condition A (i) of performatives (see subsection 1.2.1 above), speech acts can be highly culture-specific – like speech acts that will constitute a divorce with a Muslim couple, but not with a Christian one. And many sociolinguists and anthropological linguists have confirmed this fact.

Keith Basso (1979), for example, shows in his research on the joking behaviour of Athabaskan Indians how they ridicule compliments made by white North Americans; they feel embarrassed by these, in their minds, excessive expressions of approval (see also Chen 1993; Daikuhara 1986).

John Gumperz (1979) investigated interactions between British-English and Indian-English speakers in England and found that culture-specific differences in expectations of verbal behaviour resulted in miscommunication which made it difficult for interactants to recognize whether a question was asked, an argument was put forward, whether a speaker was polite or rude, etc.

Deborah Tannen (1981) showed that notions like directness and indirectness differ substantially between Greek-Americans and Americans. Even Americans of Greek origin who no longer speak Greek stick to Greek norms for verbal indirectness – even at the risk of being misunderstood by the more 'direct' Americans. And they often interpret directly meant utterances as verbal indirectness. The following example of a brief interaction between a Greek-American husband and his American wife illustrates this point (Tannen 1981: 227):

Husband: Let's go visit my boss tonight.
Wife: Why?
Husband: All right, we don't have to go.

Tannen explains what is going on here as follows:

Both husband and wife agreed that the husband's initial proposal was an indication that he wanted to visit his boss. However, they disagreed on the meaning of the wife's question. "Why?" The wife explained that she meant it as a request for information. Therefore she was confused and frustrated and could not help wondering why she married such an erratic man who suddenly changed his mind only a moment after making a request. The husband, for his part, explained that his wife's question clearly meant that she did not want to go, and he therefore rescinded his request. He was frustrated, however, and resentful of her refusing.

(Tannen 1981: 227)

Shoshona Blum-Kulka and her colleagues (1989) found in their large-scale Cross-Cultural Speech Act Realization Patterns Project great differences with respect to the directness and indirectness of requests and apologies in seven languages.

Harris (1984) notes that the Australian Aboriginal language spoken in north-east Arnhem Land does not contain anything comparable to our speech act of thanking. On the other hand, Hudson (1985) found in the Australian Aboriginal language Walmajari a specific 'speech act of requesting that is based on kinship rights and obligations ... [which] is very difficult to refuse' (Huang 2007: 120f.).

And in 1982 (= 2011) Michelle Rosaldo contrasted in her paper 'The things we do with words' speech acts performed by Ilongots, former headhunters who live on Luzon Island in the Philippines, with Searle's taxonomy of speech acts. Rosaldo (2011: 85) first points out that for the Ilongots 'words are not made to "represent" objective truth, because all truth is relative to the relationships and experiences of those who claim to "know"... For Ilongots ... it's relations, not intentions, that come first'. Then she compares Searle's speech act types with Ilongot names for acts of speech, filing the caveat that 'accounts of verbal action cannot reasonably proceed without attention to the relations between social order, folk ideas about the world, and styles of speaking' (Rosaldo 2011: 88).

In comparison with Searle's assertives the Ilongot are not so much interested in pursuing truths:

> Rather than pursuing truth, Ilongot speakers seem inclined to grant each other privileged claims to things that all, as individuals, may claim to 'know'. And so much less concerned with factual detail than with the question as to who withholds, and who reveals, a knowledge of well-bruited fact – Ilongots use denial and assertion in discourse as a device for the establishment of interactional roles.

(Rosaldo 2011: 89)

As to directives, Rosaldo points out that for the Ilongot commands and other 'directive utterances [are] the very stuff of language: knowing how to speak [is] itself virtually identical to knowing how and when to act' (Rosaldo 2011: 84). Overt performatives are rather rare, though. However, when they are performed they are neither constructed nor perceived as impolite or harsh. The force of directive acts performed is indicated by the use of 'recognized and stereotyped formulae' (Rosaldo 2011: 90).

Rosaldo had difficulties to find commissives in the Ilongot language. She points out that the closest equivalent to the English word 'promise' is the Ilongot word which refers to 'a formulaic oath by salt, wherein participants declare that if their words prove false, their lives, like salt, will be dissolved' (Rosaldo 2011: 94).

Ilongot speech acts that are somehow related to Searle's category of declarations are those 'whose power depends not on a human interlocutor's ear, but the attention of diffuse, yet ever present supernatural forces'.

In her study, Rosaldo (2011: 78) reveals the 'individualistic and relatively asocial biases of [Searle's] essentially intra-cultural account' of speech acts. She closes her article as follows:

> Reflections on Ilongot notions concerning acts of speech should serve then as a reminder that the understanding of linguistic action always, and necessarily, demands much more than an account of what it is that individuals intend to say: because, as Ilongots themselves are well aware, the 'force' of acts of speech depends on things participants expect, and then again, because, as our comparison makes clear, such expectations are themselves the products of particular forms of sociocultural being.
>
> (Rosaldo 2011: 78)

With this impressive refutation of possible claims of the universality of (Searle's and Austin's) speech act theory this section ends.

The next section of this chapter briefly presents some of Pieter Seuren's (2009) thoughts on the socially binding force of speech acts which are based on his conviction that speech acts constitute and create social reality. Austin's and Searle's speech act theory lacks this notion of social reality – and this explains some of the criticisms like those by Rosaldo quoted above.

1.4 PIETER SEUREN ON THE SOCIALLY BINDING FORCE OF SPEECH ACTS

In the fourth chapter of his monograph *Language in Cognition*, the first volume of his two-volume work on *Language from Within*, Pieter A. M. Seuren (2009) points out that both Austin's and Searle's thoughts on speech acts lack a notion of what he calls 'social reality' (Seuren 2011 p.c.). In this chapter on speech acts he devotes 'specific attention to the socially binding force of speech acts' and starts his line of thought by formulating the 'PRINCIPLE OF SOCIAL BINDING' which he considers 'to be axiomatic and defining not only for human language but also for all other systems of human and nonhuman conscious communication' (Seuren 2009: 140). The principle runs:

> Every serious linguistic utterance ... has a FORCE in that it creates a socially binding relation consisting in either a COMMITMENT (of varying strength) on the part of the speaker, or an APPEAL (of varying strength) issued to the listener(s), or the INSTITUTION OF A RULE OF BEHAVIOUR with regard to the proposition expressed in [the utterance], or an APPELATION, as in vocatives ('Hey, you over there!').
>
> The social partners with regard to whom the speech act is valid form the FORCE FIELD of [the utterance].
>
> (Seuren 2009: 140)

For Seuren this principle binds persons who have certain rights and duties, who have responsibilities and personal dignity. These persons are '... accountable and every serious speech act creates an accountability relation, no matter how trivial or insignificant, between speaker and listener' (Seuren 2009: 140). Characterizing the principle of social binding as being 'axiomatic' and 'defining' not only for human language but also for 'any form of communication by means of signs' (see also Seuren 2009: 158) means for this scholar 'that language is primarily an instrument for the creation of accountability relations and not for the transfer of information' (Seuren 2009: 140). He develops these ideas in connection with speech acts and emphasizes that

> all speech acts ... are performative in that they create a socially binding relation or state of affairs ... [T]he primary function of language is not 'communication', in the sense of a transfer of information about the world, but social binding, that is, the creation of specific interpersonal, socially binding relations with regard to the proposition expressed by an utterance or speech act. It will be clear that this kind of social binding is a central element in the social fabric that is a necessary requirement for human communities.
>
> (Seuren 2009: 147).[14]

Seuren argues that the neglect of the socially binding aspect of speech in philosophy and other disciplines has resulted in putting emphasis on the 'intention aspect of speech acts ... and not ... on what is ACTUALLY ACHIEVED when the speaker produces a speech act' (Seuren 2009: 150). According to Seuren, this 'basic blindness to the socially binding aspect ... has given rise to a number of discussions regarding insincere speech acts' (Seuren 2009: 150) and he illustrates this discussion with his critique of Searle's analysis of promises (presented in subsection 1.3.2 [see also 1.3.3] above). This critique cannot be outlined in detail here, but the following quote summarizes the gist of Seuren's arguments:

> The use of sentences like ... Searle's *I promise to do but I do not intend to do [the act]* undermines the implicit social pact upon which all speech acts are based and thus the effectiveness of the speech act in question. In general, speech acts are valid on account of their having been uttered under appropriate conditions. Their validity is part of the semantics of the language in question since it is bound up with the system of the language at type level. Speech acts are effective in virtue of the presumption of the speaker being a properly functioning social being. The effectiveness of a speech act appears to be a matter of PRAGMATICS, as it is bound up with the circumstances in which sentences are uttered. For a speech act to be effective, it must (a) be performed *in a valid way*, that is, uttered under appropriate conditions, and (b) be supported by a *presumption of social competence*. When condition (b) is unfulfilled, the speech act may still be (semantically) valid, but it is (pragmatically) futile and thus not effective.
>
> (Seuren 2009: 153)

With this thought-provoking quote this brief presentation of some of Pieter Seuren's thoughts on speech acts comes to its end. However, it needs to be pointed out that the idea of a *'social contract'* (Rousseau 1762) function of speech will recur in other chapters in this book.

The last section of this chapter comes back to the cooperative principle of conversation Searle referred to in his theory of indirect speech acts. This cooperative principle and its four subcases were formulated by H. Paul Grice, another colleague of Austin's and Searle's, in his theory of conversational implicature.

1.5 MAXIMS THAT GUIDE CONVERSATION: H. PAUL GRICE'S THEORY OF CONVERSATIONAL IMPLICATURE

After a brief introduction to H. Paul Grice's theory, this section presents Grice's Cooperative Principle and its constitutive conversational maxims. It illustrates how these maxims can be violated or 'flouted', and presents the characteristic properties of implicatures. This section ends with a brief look at Grice's theory from an anthropological-linguistic point of view.

1.5.1 Introduction

Like Austin and Searle, Grice was also very much interested in how speakers assign meanings to utterances that are produced in certain contexts. In his William James Lectures delivered at Harvard University in 1967 – excerpts of which were published in two articles in 1975 and 1978 – Grice formulates his theory of 'conversational implicature'. Like the other philosophers who founded the school of Ordinary Language Philosophy, Grice was aware of the tension between logic and ordinary language as pointed out by the very title of his lectures: 'Logic and Conversation'. Like his colleagues he was convinced that (formal) logic is not the only means to decide whether a sentence is meaningful. In the discussion of indirect speech acts in 1.3.5 above, it was pointed out that there is a difference between what is said and what is actually meant – one could also say what is implicated – by the speaker. The hearer has to make certain inferences to recognize and understand this actual meaning which is implicated by the speaker in what he or she said. Levinson (2000: 11) defines the notion of 'a generalized conversational implicature [as] a default inference, one that captures our intuitions about a preferred or normal interpretation' of a sentence, an utterance, a conversation or a text. Thus, if a speaker utters for example a sentence like the following:

(27) *John has three cows.*

a hearer will infer from this sentence that John has only three cows, and no more. And in the following dialogue;

(28) A: *Will you go to Mark's PhD party?*
B: *I have to prepare my inaugural lecture.*

speaker A will understand that speaker B implies with his or her answer (which is an indirect speech act – in Searle's terms) that he or she will not or cannot go to this party.

1.5.2 Grice's cooperation principle and its constitutive conversational maxims

Grice (1975: 45) understands conversational implicatures 'as being essentially connected with certain general features of discourse'. These features include certain expectations, mutually shared by interactants; and knowing – and knowledge about – these expectations enables both speaker and hearer to make inferences about each other's communicative behaviour – which for Grice is always purposive and rational. Thus, as Levinson (2000: 14) points out, 'what is conversationally implicated is not coded but rather inferred on the basis of some basic assumptions about the rational nature of conversational activity'. On the basis of these assumptions interactants engaged in a conversation can rely on the fact that they are generally willing to cooperate and provide information that is relevant for the topic of their conversation. However, on the basis of these assumptions they can also exclude 'possible conversational moves ... as conversationally unsuitable' (Grice 1975: 45; see also Seuren 1998: 406). Grice formulates these 'basic assumptions about the rational nature of conversational activity' in his Cooperative Principle: 'Make your conversational contribution such as is required, at the state at which it occurs, by the accepted purpose or direction of the talk exchange in which you are engaged' (Grice 1975: 45).

This principle is constituted by four maxims which Grice explicitly characterizes as echoing the German philosopher Immanuel Kant (1724–1804). These categories or conversational maxims, claimed to be generally valid, are 'Quantity, Quality, Relation, and Manner'; they are defined as follows:

> The category of QUANTITY relates to the quantity of information to be provided, and under it fall the following maxims:
> 1. Make your contribution as informative as is required (for the current purposes of the exchange).
> 2. Do not make your contribution more informative than is required.

> Under the category of QUALITY falls a supermaxim – 'Try to make your contribution one that is true' – and two more specific maxims:
> 1. Do not say what you believe to be false.
> 2. Do not say that for which you lack adequate evidence.

> Under the category RELATION I place a single maxim, namely, 'Be relevant'.

> Finally, under the category of MANNER, which I understand as relating not (like the previous categories) to what is said but, rather, to HOW what is said is to be said, I include the supermaxim 'Be perspicuous' and various maxims such as:

1. Avoid obscurity of expression.
2. Avoid ambiguity.
3. Be brief (avoid unnecessary prolixity).
4. Be orderly.

(Grice 1975: 45f.)

According to Grice these four conversational maxims serve the basis for figuring out the non-literal meaning of utterances like the one produced by speaker B in example (28) above.

1.5.3 How the conversational maxims can be violated or 'flouted'

Conversational maxims can be violated or 'flouted'. Grice (1975: 51–56) provides examples in which maxims are not violated, and examples in which they are flouted. In what follows we will look at some of them.

In example (29) Grice provides an extract from an imaginary conversation in which no maxim is violated:

(29) A: *Smith doesn't seem to have a girlfriend these days.*
B: *He has been paying a lot of visits to New York lately.*

Grice comments on this as follows: In his reaction to speaker A's utterance speaker B implicates that Smith has, or may have, a girlfriend in New York. That is to say with his utterance speaker B implies that Smith has or may have a girlfriend in New York by referring to Smith's lately recurrent visits to New York – with this reaction he suggests or implies something by saying something else.

In example (30), Grice provides an extract from an imaginary conversation in which a maxim is violated; however, he explains this violation by the supposition of a clash with another maxim:

(30) A: *Where does C live?*
B: *Somewhere in the South of France.*

Grice comments on this example as follows: Speaker A is planning to have a holiday in France, and both speaker A and B know that A wants to see his friend C, who lives in France – if this visit will not be too much of a detour. B's answer to A's question is certainly less informative than required. However, this 'infringement of the first maxim of Quantity can be explained ... by the supposition that B is aware that to be more informative would be to say something that infringed the maxim of Quality, "don't say what you lack adequate evidence for"' (Grice 1975: 51f.). Thus B implicates with his answer that he does not really know where precisely C lives.

The following examples illustrate the flouting and infringements of maxims. Grice presents an imaginary testimonial delivered by a professor about one of his students who applies for a university job as an example to illustrate the flouting of the first maxim of Quantity:

(31)   *Dear Sir,*
Mr. X's command of English is excellent, and his attendance
at tutorials has been regular.
Yours, etc.

He comments on this example as follows: The professor has to be cooperative in this situation, he knows that more information is wanted, but he does not want to say more about the student, although the addressee of the testimonial knows that this person is his student; thus, instead of providing information about the student he is reluctant to write down, he prefers to flout the first maxim of Quantity, implicating that his student is not suited for the vacant job.

An example of a flouting of the second maxim of Quantity (Grice 1975: 52) would be a situation in which speaker A wants to know whether a given proposition is true. Speaker B, who knows whether the proposition is true, not only simply confirms the truth of the proposition, but also volunteers further and uncalled for information on why it is certain that the proposition is true. Now, if it is felt that B does this on purpose, it could implicate that what B claims to be established truth is, in actual fact, controversial.

Grice also illustrates violations of the maxim of Quality in *ironic statements* (as in speaking about a rival as a 'fine friend'), in *metaphors* (like 'You are the cream in my coffee'), and in *understatements* (like speaking about a drunken man who has broken all his furniture as if 'he was a little intoxicated'). Figures of speech like irony, metaphor and understatement are paradigmatic examples of implicatures.

As an example 'in which an implicature is achieved by real, as distinct from apparent, violation of the maxim of Relation' Grice (1975: 54) imagines the following situation illustrated in example (32), meant to occur 'at a genteel tea party':

(32)   A: *Mrs. X is an old bag.*
(silence)
B: *The weather has been quite delightful this summer, hasn't it?*

After the utterance of speaker A there is a moment of embarrassed silence. Then speaker B produces his utterance about the weather, blatantly refusing to make what he or she says relevant to A's preceding remark. With this, speaker B implicates not only that A's remark should be ignored, but also that A has committed a social *faux pas*.

These examples of how conversational maxims can be violated should suffice for the purpose pursued here.

1.5.4 Five properties of implicatures

Grice assumes that the properties implicatures have are easy to predict. Implicatures can be distinguished from other deductive processes (like presuppositions) by five characteristic properties (see Grice 1975: 50, especially 57f.; see also 1978: 116).

First of all, Grice points out that all conversational implicatures are cancellable or defeasible. Levinson (2000: 42) illustrates this property as follows:

    a. *Assertion*: 'John ate some of the cookies.'
    b. *Default implicature*: 'John did not eat all of the cookies.'
    c. *Cancellation of b*: 'John ate some of the cookies. In fact he ate all of them.'

Second, implicatures are non-detachable, which means the implicature attaches to the meaning of the utterance, not to any specific lexical item or sentence form chosen to express the meaning.

    Thus
        John is no rocket scientist.
            not an Einstein.
            not a candidate for the Nobel Prize in physics, etc.
        all implicate 'John is not very smart'.

(Lakoff 1995: 193f.)

Third, implicatures are calculable. That is to say, 'the relation between the implicature-invoking utterance and its maxim-observing equivalent can be ... rigorously and specifically expressed as in the example ... "Boys will be boys"'. In this utterance 'the superficial tautology requires some computation to be understood non-tautologously, i.e. as "boys share certain salient behavioral features"' (Lakoff 1995: 193f.).

Fourth, implicatures are non-conventional. This means that an implicature is 'not part of the "dictionary" meaning of any of the words involved' (Lakoff 1995: 194). To understand the meaning of the sentences Lakoff provides for illustrating the fact that implicatures are non-detachable (John is no rocket scientist, etc.) a dictionary of English need not define 'rocket scientist' as 'a smart person'.

And fifth, implicatures are not fully determinable, that is to say 'there is no one-to-one linkage between the form of an implicature and its intended meaning:

    John is a machine

might mean "John is unemotional", "John is a hard worker", "John is efficient", etc.' (Lakoff 1995: 194).

1.5.5 Grice's theory from an anthropological-linguistic perspective

Elinor (Ochs) Keenan (1976: 67) rightly points out that Grice presented his theory of conversational implicature 'as universal in application'. Keenan was the first scholar who examined Grice's analysis of conversational maxims and implicatures in a non-Indo-European language, namely in Malagasy. She shows that speakers of Malagasy regularly violate Grice's maxim of Quantity ('Be informative') by providing less information than is required by their conversational partners, pointing out that speakers are reluctant to make explicit reference both with respect to past and future events, and she notes that speakers in general do not expect that their interlocutors will satisfy their informational needs. Moreover, Keenan points out that Malagasy speakers are more likely to withhold significant information than not so significant information, especially if imparting a certain information may have unpleasant consequences for the speaker (like information relating to misdeeds of other people). However, if interlocutors are close kinspersons or neighbours, they are inclined to provide more explicit information for each other, and women are more likely to satisfy the informational needs of their partners in conversation than men (Keenan 1976: 70ff.). At the end of her study Keenan points out that 'Grice tantalizes the ethnographer with the possibility of an etic grid for conversation ... The conversational maxims are not presented as working hypotheses but as social facts' (Keenan 1976: 79). Anthropological linguists and linguistic anthropologists agree that every etic grid, i.e. every approach based on Western cultural norms and ideas to ethnolinguistic problems (see subsection 4.4.2 below), is sooner or later doomed to fail to grasp the essential facts in the (non-Western) language and culture investigated. Therefore, an etic grid such as the one provided by the Gricean maxims can only be of secondary importance for linguistic anthropologists. Nevertheless, Keenan sketched a way in which the Gricean framework could be used for anthropological-linguistic research. She states that:

> [w]e can ... take any one maxim and note when it does and does not hold. The motivation for its use or abuse may reveal values and orientations that separate one society from another and that separate social groups ... within a single society

and she evaluates Grice's proposals as providing 'a point of departure for ethnographers who wish to integrate their observations, and to propose stronger hypotheses related to general principles of conversation' (Keenan 1976: 79).

Senft (2008) showed that the Gricean maxims of Quality and Manner do not hold either for Kilivila, especially not for highly ritualized forms of speech and for the so-called '*biga sopa*' variety of Kilivila, the 'joking or lying speech, the indirect speech' which is the Trobriand Islanders' default speech variety. Senft (2008: 144f.) also referred to Haiman's book *Talk is Cheap* in which the author points out that for many linguists and certainly for philosophers of language inspired by Grice the 'bedrock of conversation is plain referential speaking' (Haiman 1998: 99). However, in the postscript of his book Haiman justifies his choice for dealing with un-plain speaking and summarizes the arguments he put forward as follows:

> I concluded with the claim that the ritualization or emancipation process, which transforms sincere spontaneous acts and utterances into autonomous and meaningless formal codes, not only is responsible for apparent excrescences such as sarcasm, formal politeness, phatic communion, ritual speech, and affectation but also is a significant part of human nature and therefore the very essence of culture itself and may have played a necessarily undocumented role in the origin of human language.
>
> (Haiman 1998: 190)

This implies that Gricean maxims are based on a rather uni-dimensional understanding of language and conversation. Of course, there is plain conversation – but how do Gricean maxims deal with all the cases of 'un-plain speaking' which – as Haiman claims – may be much more important for both linguists and philosophers of language in their search for finding 'the essence of language' (Haiman 1998: 191)? If the Gricean maxims can cope neither with forms of ritual communication nor with 'un-plain' forms of speech and communication, they neglect an incredibly broad spectrum of language use. And if they only refer to 'plain referential speaking', then they have to cope with criticisms like that of Kiefer (1979: 57) who criticizes the linguist and philosopher for being 'extremely vague so "that almost anything can be worked out on the basis of almost any meaning" (Sadock 1978: 285). This means that the theory is unfalsifiable, vacuous, and therefore of no explanatory value'.

1.6 CONCLUDING REMARKS

This chapter presented Austin's and Searle's versions of speech act theory and Grice's theory of conversational implicature. All three philosophers and their ideas about language had a strong and important impact on linguistics in general and on pragmatics in particular. Their insights – which are core issues in linguistic pragmatics – can be summarized as follows:

- Speech acts are manifestations of language as action that – driven by intentions of speakers – cause effects and thus have psychological and behavioural consequences in speaker–hearer interactions.

- There is a difference between the way in which an utterance is used and the meaning that is expressed by this utterance in certain contexts.

- Speakers may say one thing that has a specific meaning but that also means something else in certain circumstances because of certain social conventions that are valid within a specific speech community.

Austin, Searle and Grice have certainly co-founded and shaped the discipline and they have initiated important and innovative research within the field – as demonstrated by the brief presentation of Pieter Seuren's recent thoughts on the socially binding force of speech acts. Seuren puts his emphasis on the social reality in which speech acts are performed, pointing out their socially binding force. For him speech acts create accountability relations, they can be seen as a social pact between speaker and hearer which is based on conventions and requires social competence of the interactants.

However, this chapter also revealed that the philosophy of language in which Austin's, Searle's and Grice's theories are rooted is based on West-European and Anglo-American traditions and ways of thinking. This is one of the reasons, if not the most important one, that some of the claims that these philosophers make do not hold for Non-Standard Average European languages and cultures. Nevertheless, as Keenan (1976: 79) rightly points out, speech act theory and the theory of conversational implicature provide an extremely useful 'point of departure' also 'for ethnographers who wish to integrate their observations, and to propose stronger hypotheses related to general principles of conversation'.

What does this chapter tell us about the anecdote which I reported in the introduction to this volume, claiming that my misunderstanding of the Trobriand Islanders question is exemplary for what this book is about? We now know that I misunderstood a complex speech act as a simple request for information. I had to learn that this question in this specific context was inextricably intertwined with a convention that made it not only a form of greeting with an important bonding function but also an effective means of social control for the village community. I had to learn this convention and thus to acquire the social competence necessary to appropriately react to this speech act with the pragmatically effective response. I also had to learn that this response needed to respect the Gricean maxim of Quantity – 'Make your contribution as informative as is required'; otherwise the response would violate the social pact constitutive for the bonding function of this culture-specific speech act.

1.7 EXERCISE/WORK SECTION

- Provide examples for constative and for performative sentences.

- When is a performative utterance 'unhappy/infelicitous'? Provide examples and explain which felicity conditions are not fulfilled by them. Which of these unhappy performative utterances are 'misfires' and which are 'abuses'? Explain why.

- Analyse the illocutionary speech acts Request, Question, Thank (for), Advise, Warn and Congratulate on the basis of their felicity conditions.

- Provide examples for Representatives, Directives, Commissives, Expressives and Declarations.

- Videotape your friends or family having dinner together. Then look for indirect speech acts performed, transcribe them and comment on these acts and on the contexts in which they were produced.

- Imagine a teacher entering a classroom. The pupils have just opened the windows to air the room, but the teacher feels cold. What utterances may the teacher produce to make the pupils close the window?

- Provide and discuss (at least three) examples in which non-native speakers of your mother-tongue have to be familiar with certain culture-specific conventions valid within your speech community to be able to properly react to certain speech acts in specific contexts.

- Discuss (neglected? implied? constitutive?) social aspects of speech acts and of Grice's theory of conversational implicature.

- Provide (at least three) examples (each) of imaginary or real conversation in which Grice's conversational maxims are flouted and briefly discuss them.

1.8 SUGGESTIONS FOR FURTHER READING

Blanco Salgueiro (2010); Castelfranchi and Guerini (2007); Charnock (2009); Clark and Carlson (1982); Davis (1998); Egner (2006); Grice (1981, 1989); Habermas (1984, 1987); Harnish (1994, 2009); Haugh (2002); Holzinger (2004); Horn (2004); Jucker (2009); Kasher (1998); Martínez-Flor and Usó-Juan (2010); Mulamba (2009); Reiss (1985); Sadock (2004); Sbisá (2001); Searle (1968, 1979, 1999); Searle *et al.* (1980, 1992); Smith (2003); Sperber and Wilson (1995); Tsohatzidis (1999, 2007); Warnock (1989).

NOTES

1   The Oxford English Dictionary defines 'presupposition' as a 'fact or condition implied by a sentence and assumed to be understood by the addressee, but not stated explicitly. For example, a statement containing the phrase "my uncle" would imply that the speaker has an uncle' (http://www.oed.com). For a more detailed and sophisticated definition and discussion of this complex concept see, e.g. Levinson (1983: 168) and Seuren (1994).

2   Note that Austin considers an insincere speech act valid but a form of abuse.

3   Note that this example is part of a long-running debate on the possibility of referring to non-existent entities; see Russell (1905) and Strawson (1950).

4   Note that the technical term 'speech act' was first used by Karl Bühler in 1934 (see Bühler 1934: 48; 1990: 57).

5   The next section presents Austin's theory of illocutionary acts and defines them.

6   Sbisà (2007: 464) points out that the 'effect of the naming of a ship consists of a change not in the natural course of events but in norms, that is in something belonging to the realm of social conventions', emphasizing that Austin maintains 'that illocutionary acts have conventional effects' (Sbisà 2007: 464; see also Austin's felicity condition A (i) quoted above).

7   For an interesting attempt to do this see Herbert Clark's (1996a: 147ff.) concept of 'action ladders'.

8   In what follows I quote from the 1972 reprint of the paper which was first published in 1965.

9   See Searle (1969: 57–61); see also Searle (1972: 147–151) and Austin (1961: 97–103). For a recent criticism of this analysis see Seuren (2009: 150ff.), who among other things points out that an insincere promise is still a promise.

10   What follows is a simplified version of Searle 1969: 147–151; direct quotes refer to the pages just mentioned.

11   Note that Searle uses the abbreviation 'p' here to refer to a proposition.

12   For a critical discussion of these types see Levinson (1983: 240ff.).

13   For an excellent study on how listeners understand indirect speech acts and plan responses to them see Clark (1979).

14   For Seuren the 'transfer of information about the world' is only one of many non-primary functions of language (which cannot be ordered hierarchically). Other such functions are 'the speaker's demonstration of rank or status or the expression of the speaker's desire to belong to a particular social group' (Seuren 2009: 148).

Pragmatics and psychology

Deictic reference and gesture

2.1 INTRODUCTION

How do speakers of different languages refer to objects, persons, animals, places, periods of time and even texts or text passages? When speakers make these so-called 'deictic' references, they communicate in certain – linguistic and non-linguistic – contexts, and these contexts influence the shape of our utterances. Natural languages are context-bound – and it is deixis that 'concerns the ways in which languages encode or grammaticalize features of the *context of utterance* or *speech event*, and thus also concerns ways in which the interpretation of utterances depends on the analysis of that context of utterance' (Levinson 1983: 54; see also Senft 2004a: 1). This context-dependence of linguistic reference is known as 'indexicality' and it is taken by philosophers such as Hilary Putnam (1975: 187; see also 193) as a 'constitutive feature of human language' and a general characteristic of language and interaction. Indexicality can broadly be defined as 'the study of expressions relying on the context of use to select items of discourse' (Corazza 2010: 1).

In the first part of this chapter, the phenomenon of deixis is presented and discussed. The historically most influential contribution on the topic of deixis was presented by the German psychologist Karl Bühler (1879–1963) in his by now classic work *Sprachtheorie: Die Darstellungsfunktion der Sprache* (*Theory of Language: The representational function of language* [Bühler 1934; 1990]). Although Bühler's work is still not really known in the USA, despite the fact that a translation of his seminal volume was published in 1990, it is a fact that research on deixis so far has been deeply indebted to Bühler's insights into this topic (see Kendon 2004: 57ff.).

After a general introduction to the topic, a cross-linguistic comparison of language-specific forms of spatial deixis illustrates the broad variety of the means languages offer their speakers for this kind of deictic reference. The first part of this chapter ends with the description of the complex deictic system of Kilivila.

The term 'deixis' is borrowed from the Greek word for 'pointing' or 'indicating' (Bühler 1934: 36f.; 1990: 44f.). We not only 'point' with words, but also with gestures. The second part of this chapter deals with these deictic gestures and with speech accompanying gestures in general. Again it was a German psychologist – Wilhelm Wundt (1832–1920) – whose discussion of gestures and sign languages in the first volume (Wundt 1900) of his seminal work *Völkerpsychologie*[1] (Wundt 1900–1920) set standards for the study of gestures and sign languages. Wundt's groundbreaking insights were taken up by psychologists like Adam Kendon, David McNeill and Susan Goldin-Meadow – who became pioneers of modern gesture research. This part of Chapter Two presents and discusses the various types of gesture and their communicative functions, based on research results published by these pioneers and other specialists in gesture research.

2.2 DEICTIC REFERENCE[2]

Charles Fillmore defines 'deixis' as follows:

> Deixis is the name given to uses of items and categories of lexicon and grammar that are controlled by certain details of the interactional situation in which the utterances are produced. These details include especially the identity of the participants in the communicating situation, their locations and orientation in space, whatever on-going indexing acts the participants may be performing, and the time at which the utterance containing the items is produced.
>
> (Fillmore 1982: 35)

The study of deixis has been an important subfield within (psycho-)linguistics, because, as Levinson (1997: 219) points out, 'most sentences in most natural languages are deictically anchored, that is, they contain linguistic expressions with inbuilt contextual parameters whose interpretation is relative to the context of utterance'. Thus, 'to know what exactly is meant by *She brought this flower for me yesterday* and whether this statement is true, one first needs to know who uttered it, on what day, and where' (Bohnemeyer 2001: 3371); moreover, in this case one may also need a pointing gesture to identify the female referent and the flower that is referred to. Deictic terms or indexicals are expressions whose reference is highly context-dependent and shifts from context to context; they can be defined as follows:

> Deictic terms , such as *here, there, I, you this, that,* derive their interpretation in part from the speaker/listener situation in which the utterance is made. Among these terms only *here, I,* and in some cases *you* are directly referential; given the situation, their reference is unambiguous. The other deictic terms, however, require the speaker to make some form of pointing gesture, for example by nodding the head, visibly directing the gaze, turning the body, or moving arm and hand in the appropriate direction. Without such a paralinguistic gesture, the utterance is incomplete in an essential aspect.
>
> (Levelt *et al.* 1985: 134)[3]

Veronika Ehrich (1992) understands 'deixis' as the general term for Bühler's various *Zeigarten* or 'kinds of pointing' (Bühler 1934: 83; 1990: 97), and *Zeigmodi* or 'modes of pointing' (Bühler 1934: 80; 1990: 94). The following kinds of pointing (Bühler's *'Zeigarten'*) can be differentiated:

- Personal deixis allows distinctions among the speaker ('*I*' = first person), the addressee ('*you*' = second person) and everyone else ('*s/he*', '*they*', '*the spectators*', '*the others*', etc. = third person).

- Social deixis (*'mate'*, *'Sir'*, *'your honour'*, etc.) encodes 'the speaker's social relationship to another party, frequently but not always the addressee, on a dimension of rank' (Levinson 1997: 218).

- Temporal deixis (*'now'*, *'today'*, *'next week'*, *'in 1952'*, etc.) 'allows the speaker to point in time' (Trask 1999: 68).

- Spatial deixis (*'here'*, *'there'*, *'east'*, *'west'*, *'in front of'*, *'behind'*, *'left'*, *'right'*, etc.) allows pointing to spatial locations.

In addition, the following modes of pointing are differentiated by Bühler:

- In the situative modus, situative deictic reference is made to referents within the perceived space of speaker and hearer (i.e. reference *'ad oculos'* [reference in front of the eyes] in Bühler's terms). The following sentence illustrates this modus of pointing:

    (1)　*This is a steam engine.*

- In anaphora we observe the non-deictic usage of expressions[4] that refer to a (mental representation of) a referent or segment mentioned earlier in an utterance, discourse, or text (see Dixon 2003: 111f.). The following little Dutch text illustrates anaphoric reference (with the use of the anaphoric third person singular pronoun 'hij' [he]):

    (2)　*F. C. Donders studeerde geneeskunde en fysiologie. In 1852 werd hij te Utrecht benoemd tot hoogleraar.*
    F. C. Donders studied medicine and physiology. In 1852 he was appointed as a professor in Utrecht.

- In cataphora we also observe the non-deictic usage of expressions that refer to a forthcoming (mental representation of a) referent or segment that will be explicitly introduced in an utterance, discourse or text (see Dixon 2003: 111f.). The following little text illustrates cataphoric reference:

    (3)　*And here he comes, the man who first set foot on the Moon: Neil Armstrong!*

- Imaginative deixis or transposed deixis (Bühler's *'Deixis am Phantasma'*) refers to an imagined situation. This mode of reference is illustrated with the first sentence from Franz Kafka's famous novella *Die Verwandlung* (*The Metamorphosis*) in which the author – writing in German – sketches the situation in which his protagonist finds himself as follows:

    (4)　*Als Gregor Samsa eines Morgens aus unruhigen Träumen erwachte, fand er sich in seinem Bett zu einem ungeheueren Ungeziefer verwandelt.*
    As Gregor Samsa awoke one morning from uneasy dreams he found himself transformed in his bed into a gigantic insect.

The use of spatial deixis in this sentence which points to the place where the protagonist of this work of fiction is situated is an example of imaginative deixis.

Imaginative or transposed deixis characterizes all forms of reference in fictive – imagined – contexts.

Ehrich (1992: 17ff.) refers to anaphora, cataphora and imaginative deixis as 'discourse deixis'. Moreover, with situative deixis she distinguishes between the positional system of reference that localizes areas in space in relation to, and dependent on, the speaker's or the hearer's position – *'here'* and *'there'* in English, *'hier'*, *'da'*, *'dort'* in German – and the dimensional system of reference that defines relations in space dependent on the speaker's or hearer's position and orientation – *'before (in front of)/behind, left/ right, above/below'* in English. There is an important difference between positional and dimensional deixis when used in indirect, reported speech. In reported speech, expressions of positional deixis must be translated from the perspective of the speaker quoted into the perspective of the person who quotes. This observation can be clarified with the following examples: assuming that the person who quotes and the person who is quoted are not at the same place, a speaker's utterance like:

(5a)   *It is beautiful here.*

must be translated in reported speech into:

(5b)   *He said it was beautiful there.*

With expressions of dimensional deixis this translation is not possible. Anderson and Keenan refer to these phenomena with the technical term 'relativized deixis' and emphasize that the 'nature of this process of relativization, and the syntactic and discourse contexts which condition it, are highly complex and poorly understood' (Anderson and Keenan 1985: 301). The next subsection will concentrate on spatial deixis.[5]

2.3 SPATIAL DEIXIS

Languages differ fundamentally in how they refer to space. The Space Project of the Max Planck Institute for Psycholinguistics developed a typology of spatial systems or frames of spatial reference to describe these differences (Haviland 1998; Levinson 2003; Pederson *et al.* 1998; Senft 1997a; 2001; see also subsection 4.3 below). The typology defines three systems that are called 'relative', 'absolute', and 'intrinsic' frames of reference. They differ with respect to how angles are projected from the 'ground' (or *'relatum'*) in order to situate the location of the 'figure' (or 'theme') that is referred to.[6]

Relative systems are viewpoint-dependent: Localizations in space are derived from, and described on the basis of, the position and orientation of the speaker. In these systems sentences like (6) – from English – and (7) – from Ewe, a language spoken in Ghana and belonging to the Kwa family of Niger-Congo (Ameka and Essegbey 2006: 385) – are understood from the speaker's point of view only; the references completely neglect the orientation of the man referred to.

(6)   *The ball is to the right of the man.*

(7) | *E-ke,* | *séfofo-tí-ɛ* | | *vá* | *le* | *emia* |
|---|---|---|---|---|---|
| 3.SG-this | flower-tree-DEF | | come | be.at:PRS | left |
| *me* | | *ye* | *ŋutsu-ɔ* | *le* | *ḍusí* |
| containing_region | | and | man-DEF | be.at:PRS | right |
| *me.* | | | | | |
| containing_region | | | | | |

This one, the flower is on the left and the man is on the right.

Absolute systems operate on absolute concepts of direction. They are based on conventionalized directions or other fixed bearings that can be derived from meteorological, astronomical, or landscape features. In these systems we find sentences like (8) and (9) – from Yukatec Maya (Bohnemeyer and Stolz 2006: 304):

(8)   *The ball is to the west of the man/uphill from the man/seawards to the man.*

(9) | ... *hun-túul* | | *pàal* | *túun* | | *pàakat* | *toh* |
|---|---|---|---|---|---|---|
| one-CLF.AN | | child | PROG:CRA.3 | | look | straight |
| *xaman* | *nohol* | *k-u* | | *p'áat-al* | | *le* | *k'àax* |
| north | south | IMPF:A.3 | | leave\ACAUS-INC | | DEF | bush |
| *ti'-o'* | | | | | | |
| LOC(CRB:3.SG)-DIST2 | | | | | | |

... a child, it is looking straight north, the bush remains south of him.

Intrinsic systems utilize inherent, intrinsic features of an object to derive a projected region or to anchor the spatial reference to an object in these features. In these systems we find sentences like (10) and (11) – from Tamil, a Dravidian language spoken in India (Pederson 2006: 432):

(10)   *The ball is to the man's right.*

(11) | *en* | *viiTTukkupinpakkattil* | *kuTiyirukkiRaan* |
|---|---|---|
| 1SG.OBL | house-Dat+back+side-LOC | reside-PRS-3SG.M |

He is living on my house's backside

Sentence (10) is understood as follows: A man is an object with a front and back, a left and right side assigned to him. In intrinsic systems a sentence like (10) refers to the position of the ball on the basis of the orientation of the man – the ball is at the right side of the man – the orientation of the speaker does not play any role whatsoever and is – within this system – completely irrelevant for the understanding of this sentence. The same argument holds for sentence (11) – houses in the area of India, where Tamil is spoken, are objects with an intrinsic front and back – so the location of the living place of the men referred to is also unequivocal.

However, many speakers who use intrinsic systems for their spatial references also produce in this situation instead of sentence (10), for example, sentence (6) to refer to the same configuration of objects. This shows that languages like English (and German and many others) can be ambiguous with respect to whether they use an intrinsic or a relative perspective in their spatial references (see also Clark 1973: 46). In such a situation the meaning of the sentence can only be disambiguated in the actual situation and context.

All three systems can be found in a given language, and they can be utilized for spatial reference; however, many of the languages that have been studied so far frequently seem to prefer one frame of reference in a particular context (see 2.3.1.4 below).

What kind of means do languages offer their speakers for spatial deictic reference?[7] In many languages the repertoire of elementary linguistic means for spatial deictic reference encompasses:

- prepositions or postpositions (e.g.: *at, on, in* [topological prepositions], *in front of, behind, to the right* [projective prepositions]);

- locatives, i.e. local or place adverbs (e.g.: *here, there*) and local nouns (referring to regions or areas);

- directionals (e.g.: *towards, into, upwards, downwards, upstream*);

- positional and motion verbs or verbal roots (e.g.: *to stand, to come, to go, to bring, to take*);

- presentatives (e.g.: *voici, voilà, ecce, ecco,* here is);

- demonstratives (e.g.: *this, that*).

Moreover, we also find deictic gestures in all speech communities (see subsection 2.4.3 below). The function of all these 'indexicals' is to localize, to inform about, and to identify referents in space. However, we have to keep in mind that with deictic expressions we must differentiate between deictic and non-deictic usages (see subsection 2.2 above). As Levinson (1983: 65–68) illustrates, we must distinguish two kinds of deictic usage, namely gestural and symbolic usage. Within non-deictic usages, we must distinguish anaphoric from non-anaphoric usages. These are Levinson's examples:

(12) '*You, you* but not *you* are dismissed' (deictic, gestural usage).

(13) '*This* city stinks!' (deictic, symbolic usage).

(14) 'I drove the car to the parking lot and left it *there*' (anaphoric usage).

(15) '*There* we go' (non-deictic and non-anaphoric usage).

In the languages of the world we find different systems of demonstrative elements. In their survey on deixis in various languages Anderson and Keenan (1985; for criticism see Hanks 1987) present systems of spatial deictics that consist of two terms (e.g.: English 'this, these/that, those', 'here, there'), three terms (e.g.: Latin '*hic, iste, ille*'), and more than three terms – like Sre (spoken in Vietnam – 4 terms), Daga (spoken in Papua New Guinea – 14 terms), and Alaskan Yup'ik (over 30 terms). Denny (1985: 113, 117–120) mentions even 88 terms in East-Eskimo, an Inuit language spoken in the Western Hudson Bay and on Baffin Island. Anderson and Keenan (1985: 308) draw the conclusion that 'a minimal person/number system and at least a two-term spatial demonstrative system seem to be universal'.

With respect to the development of these systems, Heeschen – in connection with his research on the Mek languages of West Papua – presents the following interesting hypothesis:

> At the origin we have a pure deictic system ... These deictics can be substituted, or accompanied ... by a pointing gesture. The more the ... formations assume discourse functions – i. e., the more they refer not to points in concrete space but to items previously mentioned in the linguistic context – the more they lose their potential for pointing to those things which are truly "up there" or "down there".
>
> (Heeschen 1982: 92)

Denny attempts to explain the differences between deictic systems for spatial reference as follows:

> In a natural environment of non-human spaces one way to relate space to human activity is to use deictic spatial concepts, to center space on the speaker (or other participant). In a man-made environment this is less necessary – non-deictic locatives such as *down the road, through the door* and *around the corner* will relate space to human acts quite directly since the places mentioned are all artifacts designed to aid such acts ... [A]s the degree to which the spatial environment is man-made increases, the size of the spatial deictic system decreases.
>
> (Denny 1978: 80; see also 1985: 123–125)

However, it must be pointed out that this hypothesis is not undisputed.[8]

Of all the various means languages offer their speakers for spatial deictic reference, demonstratives seem to have attracted special attention in linguistics. Green (1995: 15), for example, states that 'for many philosophers and linguists, demonstratives lie at the heart of deictic issues', and Hyslop (1993: 1) claims that 'the best way of studying the expression of spatial deixis in language is via the system of demonstratives'. And this special interest is very well documented in the literature.

I just want to mention here two more studies that deal with the interactional use of demonstratives. In his analyses of Lao demonstratives, Enfield (2003: 108f.) points out that 'speakers frame their linguistic choices under the assumption of a maxim of recipient design' (Sacks & Schegloff 1979). He convincingly shows that:

> speakers tailor their utterance so that addressees are not required to make reference to information that the speaker knows or assumes they do not have access to. In turn, addressees EXPECT speakers' utterances to be tailored so as not to depend on information that is not assumed by speakers to be already shared with addressees ...

… addressee location plays a crucial role in the selection of demonstratives, not only due to addressees' part in affecting the status of shared space …, but also due to their part in determining how speakers' messages are designed.

(Enfield 2003: 108f.)

Some deictic systems also have forms that encode the non-attention of the addressee to the referent. Özyürek (1998) and Özyürek and Kita (2001), for example, redefine the Turkish demonstrative '*su*', traditionally referred to as encoding medial distance in opposition to proximal '*bu*' and distal '*o*', as such a form. In their analyses, it is evident that the referent of '*su*' is 'something you (the addressee) are not attending to now'.

These studies show that 'reference is a collaborative process' (de León 1990: 3) – an aspect that has been neglected in most studies on reference by verbal means in general. The next subsection describes and illustrates the system of spatial deixis in Kilivila.

2.3.1 Spatial deixis in Kilivila[9]

In what follows the Kilivila system of demonstratives (in their function as demonstrative pronouns and as demonstratives used attributively) is discussed first, then locatives and directionals used in spatial deictic reference are presented and finally the use of frames of spatial reference is discussed.

2.3.1.1 *Demonstratives*

Kilivila has a kind of 'general', 'basic' or 'simple' system of demonstrative pronouns (that also take over the function of local or place adverbs) that are obligatorily accompanied by a deictic gesture. The Trobriand Islanders may point at something or someone with their index finger, with their eyes, with a lifted chin or with puckered lips. This basic system is speaker-based and consists of three forms that express proximal, medial and distal distinctions.[10] In these forms the meanings of 'this' and 'here' are conflated:

Besa or *beya* is used to point to a referent close to the speaker and can be glossed as 'this/these' or 'here'.[11] *Besa* is most often used in the question:

(16) *Avaka besa?*
       what this
       What is this?

Here speakers (for example children learning the language) cannot specify the referent more precisely and thus cannot use the more specific demonstrative pronoun that requires a classifier (see below) for its word formation. An answer to such a question (in a given context, of course) may run:

(17) *Besa budubadu gwadina.*
       this many nut
       These are many nuts.

The demonstrative *beyo* is used (together with a deictic gesture) to point to a referent that is further away from the speaker; it can be glossed as 'that/those' or 'there', as illustrated in example:

(18)   *Beyo Dukuboi budubadu kwau.*
        there Dukuboi many shark
        There at Dukuboi point are many sharks.

The demonstrative *beyuuu* is produced with a lengthened final vowel; it points (together with a deictic gesture) to a referent that is far away from the speaker and that even may be invisible in the actual speech situation (see (20) below); it may be glossed as 'that/those over there' or with the archaic expression 'yonder'. The following examples (19) and (20) illustrate the use of this form. The distance between Alotau, the capital of Milne Bay Province, and the Trobriand Islands is more than 200 km.

(19) | *Kumwedona* | *tommota* | *e-kamkwam-si* | | *o* | *baku* |
        |---|---|---|---|---|---|
        | all | people | 3-eat-PL | | LOC | village ground |
        | *Beya* | *mina* | *Tauwema* | *beyo* | *mina* | *Koma* |
        | this | people.from | Tauwema | that | people.from | Koma |
        | *beyuuu* | *mina* | *Simsim.* | | | |
        | yonder | people.from | Simsim | | | |

        All the people eat (together) at the village ground. These are the people from Tauwema, those are the people from Koma, and those over there are the people from Simsim.

(20) | *Tetu* | *e-mwa* | *la-paisewa* | *beyuuu* | *Alotau.* |
        |---|---|---|---|---|
        | year | 3-come.to | 1PAST-work | yonder | Alotau |

        Last year I worked in Alotau over there.

All other demonstrative pronouns consist of a fixed morphological frame, formed by the word-initial morpheme *ma-*, or according to phonological rules, also *m'* or *mi-*, and the word-final morpheme *-na*, and an infixed morpheme, which is a classifier.[12] To distinguish between singular and plural there is also a plural marking morpheme *-si-*, which is infixed between the classifier and the word-final morpheme *-na*. Demonstrative pronouns formed in this way express the concept of 'this/these here'. To express the deictic concept of 'that/those there', the morpheme *-we-* is infixed either in singular forms between the classifier and word-final *-na* or in plural forms between the plural-marker *-si-* and word-final *-na*. To express the kind of deictic concept that comes close to the English demonstrative 'yonder', the Kilivila speaker takes the forms of the demonstrative pronouns expressing the concept of 'that/those there' and changes the final vowel /a/ of the word-final morpheme *-na* to an /e/ that is lengthened and that gets a minor accent. These demonstrative pronouns constitute the second, more complex speaker-based system of demonstratives in Kilivila. The following examples illustrate the rather complex word formation processes of these demonstratives:

(21)	*m-to-na*	*tau*
	DEM-CLF.male-DEM	man
	this man	

	m-to-si-na	*tauwau*
	DEM-CLF.male-PL-DEM	men
	these men	

(22)	*mi-na-we-na*	*vivila*
	DEM-CLF.female-MED-DEM	girl
	that girl	

	mi-na-si-we-na	*vivila*
	DEM-CLF.female-PL-MED-DEM	girl
	those girls	

(23)	*ma-ke-we-neee*	*waga*
	DEM-CLF.wooden-MED-DEM.DIST.	canoe
	the canoe yonder	

	ma-ke-si-we-neee	*waga*
	DEM-CLF.wooden-PL-MED-DEM.DIST	canoe
	those canoes yonder	

Thus, we have two basic sets of demonstratives, one of which obligatorily requires deictic gestures. The system with its proximal, medial, and distal forms is speaker-centred. A specific characteristic of the second set of demonstratives is that they need the incorporation of classifiers in their word formation. These classifiers play an important role for the deictic function of these demonstratives. They provide additional information that contributes to narrow down, and further specify, the search domain for the referent to which these deictic forms point. In what follows I will briefly elaborate on this characteristic feature of Kilivila.

The Kilivila classifiers can be grouped into 20 semantic domains: Person and Body Parts; Animal; Quantity (living beings and things); General classifiers (unmarked forms for inanimates); Measure; Time; Place; Quality; Shape; Tree, Wood, Wooden Things; Utensils; Yam; Part of a Food House, a Canoe, a Creel; Door, Entrance, Window; Fire, Oven; Road, Journey; Text; Ritual Item; Dress, Adornment; Name.

It is obvious that such a categorization of referents in the real world codified by the classifiers heavily supports the deictic functions of the demonstratives that must incorporate these formatives within their word formation. The classifiers are affixed in the morphological frame of the demonstratives (as illustrated in the examples (21) to (23) above). They provide the addressee with information with respect to the quality of the referent the speaker refers to in his or her deictic utterance. These qualities encompass many parameters, like height, state, etc.[13] The following two examples briefly illustrate this point:

(24) *Ku-lilei*   *ma-pwa-si-na*   *tetu*   *olopola* *bwalita.*
      2-throw.away   DEM-CLF.rotten-PL-DEM   yams   into   sea
      Throw these rotten yams into the sea.

This deictic reference is unequivocal for addressees – no matter how big a pile of yams they are confronted with.

(25) *Wei*   *ma-nunu-na*   *bagula*   *va*   *keda*
      look.out   DEM-CLF.garden.corner-DEM   garden   DIR.   path
      bi-la   *Kaduwaga*   *mwata*   *na-veaka*   *e-sisu.*
      3-FUT   Kaduwaga   snake   CLF.animal-big   3-be
      Look out, at this corner of the garden at the path to Kaduwaga there is a big snake!

Here the classifier *-nunu-* within the demonstratives clearly indicates the area in which the speaker saw a snake. This deictic reference is unequivocal for the addressee.

As to the actual usage of the Kilivila demonstratives in 'table-top' space – that is in the space just before the speaker and hearer, within arm's reach – and in the space beyond it we observe the following:

- In general, both sets of demonstratives can be used for spatial deictic reference both in 'table-top' space and in the space beyond it.

- The proximal forms of the demonstratives are semantically unmarked, they are most often used and thus have the widest spatial distribution.

The following sentences and situations illustrate this feature. Sitting with me in my house, one of my consultants is warning me of a mosquito, saying:

(26) *Ku-gisi*   *mi-na-na*   *nim*   *i-gade-m*   *beya.*
      2-look   DEM-CLF.animal-DEM   mosquito 3-bite-you   here
      Look this mosquito is biting you here.

A few minutes later he points into the direction of the fresh water grotto (called *Bugei*), ten minutes walking distance away in the bush and says:

(27) *Beya*   *Bugei*   *sena*   *budubadu*   *nim.*
      here (proximal + gesture)   Bugei   very   many   mosquitoes
      Here at the Bugei (fresh water cave) are many mosquitoes.
      (Note that the appropriate demonstrative for an English speaker for referring to this cave in this situation would be 'there').

Another consultant is sitting with me in my house in Tauwema and explains to a visitor:

(28) *E-sisu*   *beya*   *Germany.*
      3-be   here (proximal + gesture)   Germany
      He lives here in Germany.

(Note that the appropriate demonstrative for an English speaker for referring to Germany in this situation would be '(over) there' or even 'yonder').

Speakers may only use the proximal and medial forms to distinguish between referents that are in medial and distal positions. However, if speakers want to refer to something that is really far away or invisible from their present position, and they want to mark this fact, they use the distal forms. If they want to refer to their own body parts contrastively, they may use the proximal and the medial forms (but not the distal forms). This is illustrated by the following sentences:

(29) *Waga bi-la   beya Bwemwaga igau bi-la   beyo Tuma,*
canoe 3FUT-go   here Bwemwaga then 3FUT-go there Tuma
e   ma-ke-na   waga bi-la   beyuuu   Simsimla.
and   DEM-CLF.wooden-DEM canoe 3FUT-go   yonder   Simsim
The canoe will go here to Bwemwaga and then there to Tuma and this canoe will go over there to Simsim.

(30) *Ma-kwaya-na   tega-la   i-korosim*
DEM-CLF.limb-DEM   ear-his   3-itch
ma-kwaya-we-na   bwena
DEM-CLF.limb-MED-DEM   good
This ear is itching, that (one) is fine.

In their deictic references speakers of Kilivila can take the position of other participants in the speech situation into account. That is to say, speakers can shift their basic reference point, their 'origo' (Bühler 1934: 102 [= 1990: 117]).

This is illustrated by the following utterances elicited with a questionnaire developed by Pederson and Wilkins (1996).[14] Three objects were put on a table in front of a speaker on the sagittal (away) axis. At the right side of the table, from the speaker's point of view, was the addressee, who was facing the table, and opposite the speaker was another person, facing the table and the speaker – as illustrated in Figure 2.1:

Figure 2.1

Speaker   Object1   Object2   Object3   **Other Person**
                              Addressee

To refer to the three objects, speakers produced utterances like the following ones:

Object 1

(31a) *ma-kwe-na   omata-gu*
DEM-CLF.thing-DEM   in.front.of-me
this (one) in front of me

and:

(31b)   *ma-kwe-na*   *o*   *m*   *kivivama*
DEM-CLF.thing-DEM   LOC   your   left
this (one) at your left

Object 2

(31c)   *ma-kwe-na*   *oluvala*
DEM-CLF.thing-DEM   in the middle
this (one) in the middle

Object 3

(31d)   *ma-kwe-na*   *o*   *m*   *kakata*
DEM-CLF.thing-DEM   LOC   your   right
this (one) at your right

and:

(31e)   *ma-kwe-na*   *o*   *mata-la*
DEM-CLF.thing-DEM   LOC   eye-his/her
this (one) in front of him/her

In another situation, three objects were put on a table in front of a speaker on the transverse (across) axis. At the right side of the table, from the speaker's point of view, was the addressee, who was facing the table, and opposite the speaker was another person, facing the table and the speaker – as illustrated in Figure 2.2:

Figure 2.2

	Object 1	
Speaker	Object 2	**Other Person**
	Object 3	
	Addressee	

To refer to the three objects, speakers produced utterances like the following:

Object 1

(32a)   *ma-kwe-na*   *o*   *gu*   *kikivama*
DEM-CLF.thing-DEM   LOC   my   left
this (one) at my left

and:

(32b) *ma-kwe-we-na*   *o*   *la*   *kakata*
DEM-CLF.thing-MED-DEM   LOC   his   right
that (one) at his right

Object 2

(32c) *ma-kwe-na*   *oluvala*
DEM-CLF.thing-DEM   in the middle
this (one) in the middle

and:

(32d) *ma-kwe-na*   *omata-ma*   *yegu*   *mtona*
DEM-CLF.thing-DEM   in.front.of-us (DU.EXCL)   I   him
this (one) in front of us, (in front of) me (and) him

Object 3

(32e) *ma-kwe-na*   *omata-m*
DEM-CLF.thing-DEM   in.front.of-you
this (one) in front of you

Speakers use their distance based systems not only on the 'away' – or sagittal – axis, but also on the across – or left/right – axis.

In the vertical dimension, the Kilivila system is organized around the speaker's torso. The proximal forms are used to refer to referents at a 'chest-belly-head' level, the medial forms refer to referents at the speaker's feet and above his or her head. The distal forms are rather rarely used here; however, when used, they point to referents that are really deep under or high above a speaker.

(33a) *ma-kwe-na*   *o*   *kuku-gu*
DEM-CLF.thing-DEM   LOC   chest-my
this (one) at my chest

(33b) *ma-kwe-na*   *o*   *lopo-gu*
DEM-CLF.thing-DEM   LOC   belly-my
this (one) at my belly

(33c) *ma-kwe-we-na*   *alavigimkoila*   *o*   *kaike-gu*
DEM-CLF.thing-MED-DEM   at the end   LOC   foot-my
that (one) at the end at my foot

(33d) *ma-kwe-we-na*   *o*   *kunu-gu*   *alavigimkoila*
DEM-CLF.thing-MED-DEM   LOC   hair-my   at the end
that (one) at (above) my hair at the end

In space beyond table-top space speakers prefer the use of both sets of demonstratives. The first form used is usually a form belonging to the set of demonstratives that require a classifier for their word formation. This form expresses the 'proximal', 'medial', or 'distal' distinction. The second form then can just be the proximal form of the set of demonstratives that requires accompanying gestures. It seems that this second demonstrative form then has the function to keep the addressee's attention focused on the spatial area marked by the first form. This form of spatial deictic reference is illustrated by the following utterance elicited in a game:

> **(34a)** Menumla (male consultant):
>
> | *Wetana,* | *ku-ne'i* | *yata-la* | | *kaliekwa* | *e-sagisi* |
> |---|---|---|---|---|---|
> | Wetana (name), | 2-find | CLF.flexible-one | | cloth | 3-hang |
> | *kwe-ta* | *kaukweda.* | | | | |
> | CLF.thing-one | veranda | | | | |
>
> Wetana, find a piece of cloth that is hanging at a veranda.

> **(34b)** Wetana (male consultant):
>
> | *Bogwa* | *la-bani* | *mi-ya-we-neee* | | *beya* |
> |---|---|---|---|---|
> | already | 1PAST-find | DEM-CLF.flexible-MED-DEM.DIST | | here |
> | *Topiesi* | *o* | *kaukweda* | *ya-bweyani.* | |
> | Topiesi (name) | LOC | veranda | CLF.flexible-red | |
>
> I already found it, the (one) yonder, here at Topiesi's veranda, the red (one).

2.3.1.2 *Non-spatial uses of the Kilivila demonstratives*

Kilivila demonstrative pronouns that are formed with classifiers are used in discourse deixis for anaphoric reference. With the classifiers incorporated in their word formation, the demonstratives perform the important function of securing coherence in discourse because they also secure semantic concord beyond sentence boundaries. This is illustrated with the following examples:

> **(35)**
>
> | *A-tatai* | *tataba.* | | *Tauwau* | *tabalu* |
> |---|---|---|---|---|
> | 1-carve | tataba-board | | men | Tabalu-subclan |
> | *m-to-si-na* | | *ma-ke-na* | | *si*   *koni.* |
> | DEM-CLF.male-PL-DEM | | DEM-CLF.wooden-DEM | | their sign.of.honour |
>
> I carve a tataba-board. These men belong to the Tabalu-subclan – this is their sign of honour.

With this sentence the speaker refers to a certain board with carved patterns that marks houses, food houses, and canoes as the personal property of men belonging to the Tabalu-subclan. Despite the fact that in the second sentence the nouns to which the demonstratives refer are omitted, the anaphoric reference of the two demonstrative pronouns produced is unequivocal, because in this context the classifier *-to-* can only refer to the noun *tauwau* (men) and the classifier *-ke-* can only refer to the noun *tataba* (tataba-board); the classifiers represent the omitted nouns in a quasi-fragmentary way. As a general rule, once a noun has been introduced, as long as it is not reclassified, e.g.

for stylistic reasons, the following references to this nominal denotatum may consist of the demonstrative pronouns only, that is, the noun itself is then no longer realized; it is omitted in the noun phrases. However, if the noun is reclassified, then it must be realized again as a constituent of the noun phrase to secure unequivocal and unambiguous reference, see example (36).

(36) O   da-valu-si   e-sisu-si   tommota   to-paisewa.
      LOC   1.INCL-village-PL   3-live-PL   people   CLF.human-work
      Vivila   *na-salau,*   *tauwau*   *to-bugubagula.*
      woman   CLF.female-busy   men   CLF.male-work in the garden
      Tommota   *gala*   *to-dubakasala,*   *kena*   *kumwedona*
      people   not   CLF.human-rude   but   all
      e-nukwali-si   *bubune-si*   *bwena.*
      3-know-PL   manners-their   good
      In our village live people taking pleasure in their work. The women are busy, the men are good gardeners. The people are not rude, but all have good manners.

This example illustrates that, in general, reclassification of a noun does not allow its omission. To emphasize the different characterization of men and women on the one hand and all villagers on the other hand, the nouns cannot be omitted. The speaker uses the classifier -*to*- to refer to human beings and to persons of male sex. The classifier -*na*- is used to refer to persons of female sex. If the speaker did not use the noun *tommota* in the last sentence again, then this sentence would refer to persons of male sex only. Cataphoric reference in Kilivila has not been documented so far.

2.3.1.3 *Locatives and directionals*

Kilivila grammaticalizes body part terms into locatives that are used for spatial deictic reference (see Senft 1998). Thus we find expressions like the following ones:

o-daba-la   on, on top (of)
(LOC-*daba*-3.PP.IV[15] – *head, forehead, brain*)

o-kopo'u-la   behind, back, behind him/her
(LOC-*kopo'u*-3.PP.IV – *back*)

o-lopo-la   in, inside (of), in the middle (of)
(LOC-*lopo*-3.PP.IV – *belly, windpipe, innards*)

o-mata-la   in front (of), before, before him/her
(LOC-*mata*-3.PP.IV – *eye*)

o-vado-la   on, on top (of), on the surface (of), at
(LOC-vado-3.PP:IV – *mouth*)   the mouth/opening (of)

We also find the following grammaticalized forms to express the concepts 'left' and 'right':

o-kakata   on the left hand side, on the left
(LOC-*kakata* – left, left hand side)

o-kikivama   on the right hand side, on the right
(LOC-*kikivama* – right, right hand side)

Body part terms like '*mata*-PP.IV' can also be used metaphorically, as illustrated in the following question:

(37)   *Mata-la*   *ma-ke-na*   *kai*   *ambeya,*
       eye-his/her   DEM-CLF.wood/rigid-DEM   stick   where
       e-mwa   *yokwa?*
       3-come.to   you?
       The tip of this stick where (is it), does it come to you?

In this sentence somebody asks for information about a certain direction. To indicate directions and/or locations, Trobriand Islanders have to decide whether they want to specify the goal or location with a personal or place name, or whether they want to specify the goal or location as a specific place, but without a place name or proper name, or whether they want to refer to the goal or location (or to the general direction where this goal or location is) with a general term.

If they want to refer to the goal or location with a place or a proper name, they do not use any locative whatsoever:

(38)   *Ba-la*   *Kaduwaga.*
       1.FUT-go   Kaduwaga (name of a village)
       I will go to Kaduwaga.

If they want to refer to the goal or location with a more specific term or if they want to refer to a specified place at the destination of a motion event, they use the locative *o*; the locative incorporates a feature of definiteness for the governed noun phrase.

(39)   *Ba-la*   *o*   *buyagu.*
       1.FUT-go   to   garden
       I will go to the garden (i.e. my personal, specific garden plot).

If they want to refer to the goal or location with its most general term, if they want to refer to the general direction in which this goal or location is, and/or if they want to refer to an unspecified place at the destination of a motion event, they use the directional *va*:

(40)   *Ba-la*   *va*   *bagula.*
       1.FUT-go   to   garden
       I will go to the garden (general, unspecified expression for 'garden').

The Kilivila system of demonstratives, locatives and directionals allows its speakers to clearly distinguish, and point to, referents in specific spatial relations, at certain locations and in specific directions as idiomatically and unequivocally as possible. Moreover, to do this, positional and sometimes also motion verbs are used together with the respective demonstratives, locatives and directionals. The following examples illustrate such forms of spatial references. A question like:

(41) *Ambe   peni?*
      where   pencil
      Where's the pencil?

can be answered simply with the exophoric demonstrative in (42a) or in a more complex construction illustrated in (42b).

(42a) *Beya!*
       Here!   (+ accompanying gesture to the place where the pencil is).

(42b) *Ma-ke-na*   *peni   odabala   tebeli e-kanukwenu*
       DEM-CLF.wooden.thing-DEM   pencil   on.top.(of) table   3-rest
       mata-la   *e-mikeya-gu.*
       eye-its   3-come.towards-me
       This pencil is lying on top of the table, its tip is pointing towards me.

Moreover, in spatial deictic reference local landmarks and other environmental features are quite often mentioned to make it easier for the addressee to find and identify the object the speaker is pointing at (see sentences [43a and b])[16]:

(43a) *Ku-gisi   ma-ke-we-na*   *mwasawa   b-ima*
       2-see   DEM-CLF.wooden-MED.-DEM   big.canoe   3.FUT-come
       beya va   numia.
       here DIR   stony.reef
       Look at that big canoe sailing towards us there in the direction of the stony reef.

(43b) *Mi-na-we-si-na*   *taninua   galayomala va*
       DEM-CLF.animal-MED-PL-DEM   sardines many   DIR
       dom   e   m-to-si-na   *bi-lo-si   bi-pola-si.*
       muddy.reef   and   DEM-CLF.man-PL-DEM   3.FUT-go-PL 3.FUT-fish-PL
       Those many sardines in the direction of the muddy reef – and these men will go and fish them.

2.3.1.4 *Frames of spatial reference*

Like many other languages, Kilivila allows its speakers to use all three frames of reference presented in subsection 2.3 above. However, as pointed out in Senft (2001: 550) the Trobriand Islanders clearly prefer the intrinsic frame of reference for the location of objects with respect to each other in a given spatial configuration – especially if these objects themselves have intrinsic features. An absolute *ad hoc* landmark frame of reference system (see below) is preferred in referring to the spatial orientation of objects in a given spatial orientation. This is illustrated by the following two descriptions of photographs designed by the Cognitive Anthropology Research Group at the MPI for Psycholinguistics for focused elicitation of verbal references to space in interactional games in the framework of a comparative cross-linguistic and cross-cultural research project on spatial reference (see also subsection 4.3 below):

(44) *Ma-na-na*   *bulumakau o*   *pilakeva e-tota*   *mata-la*
       DEM-CLF.animal-DEM   cow   LOC   topside   3-stand   eye-its
       This cow is standing at the topside, its eye

        e-la   o   *valu*   *poa-la*   *e-seki*   *Tuyabwau*   *e*
        3-go   LOC village back-its 3-be   Tuyabwau.well and
        goes towards the village, its back is towards the Tuyabwau well, and

        ke-ta   *kai*   *ma-na-na*   *bulumakau o*
        CLF.wood-one tree DEM-CLF.animal-DEM   cow   LOC
        kopo'u-la
        behind-it
        a tree, this cow behind it –

        e-tota,   *o*   *tubolo-la*   *bogwa*   *oku-nukwali.* *E*
        3-stand   LOC back-its   already   2-know   And
        it is standing, at its back, you know already. And

        e-mweki ma-na-na osa o kwadeva
        3-come.straight.to DEM-CLF.animal-DEM horse LOC beach
        bogwa
        already
        it comes straight to, this horse, to the beach, already

        makala   *wala,* *mata-la*   *e-la   o*   *laodila* *poa-la*
        like   only   eye-its   3-go LOC bush   back-its
        like (this), well, its eye goes to the bush, its back

        e-seki   *Tuyabwau*   *e*   *kai*   *o*   *kopo'u-la.* *E*
        3-be   Tuyabwau well and   tree LOC behind-it And
        is to the Tuyabwau well, and a tree is behind it. And

        bunukwa *navivila*   *bunukwa* *navivila*   *o*   *mata-si*
        pig   female   pig   female   LOC eyes-their
        a sow, a sow in front of their eyes

e-tota
3-stand.
it is standing (there).

(45) Speaker 1:

Amyaga   buku-vagi   kali
What's.the.name 2.FUT-make   fence
What's the name, you will make a fence

ke-vasi   e-vekeya   o   bwalita e   ma-na-na
CLF.wood-four 3-go to LOC   sea   and DEM-CLF.animal-DEM
(with) four wooden (pieces) it goes (points) to the sea and this

osa   ma-na-na   osa   oluvale-la e-tota   poa-la
horse   DEM-CLF.animal-DEM   horse   inside-it   3-stand   back-it
horse, this horse, it is standing inside (of) it, it stands, its back

e-la   Tuyabwau   mata-la   e-la   o   valu.
3-go   Tuyabwau.well   eye-its   3-go LOC village
goes (to the) Tuyabwau (fresh water well), its eyes go to (the) village.

E   ma-na-na   bulumakau o   kepapa-la   vavagi
and   DEM-CLF.animal-DEM   cow   LOC side-its   thing
And this cow at the side of the thing,

ma-na-kwa   kali   e-tota   poa-la   e-la   o   laodila
DEM-DEM-CLF.thing   fence 3-stand   back-its   3-go LOC bush
this fence it is standing, its back goes to the bush

mata-la   e-mwa   o   kwadeva   e-kululu   e-kamkwam
eye-its   3-come to   LOC   shore   3-look.down   3-eat
its eyes come to the shore, it looks down, it eats,

e-mumum   ala   ti.
3-drink   its   tea
it drinks its tea [this is a joke, of course, G. S.].

Speaker 2:
E   ma-na-na   osa   ambe   e-sisu?
and   DEM-CLF.animal-DEM   horse   where   3-be
And this horse, where is it?

Speaker 1:
Oluvale-la   kali.
inside-its   fence
Inside of its fence.

Speaker 2:

Mata-la	ambe	bi-mwa?
eye-its	where	3.FUT-come.to

And its eye, where will it come to?

Speaker 1:

Bi-la	o	valu.
3.FUT-go	LOC	village.

It will go to the village.

The speakers who describe the photographs rely on the intrinsic frame of reference in order to locate objects in relation to each other. This is illustrated in description (44) above. As pointed out in Senft (2001: 544f.), the expressions *o kopo'ula* (behind it), *o tubolola* (at its back), *o matasi* (in front of their eyes) clearly mark the intrinsic frame of reference the speaker uses for describing the location of the objects in relation to each other. In both descriptions we also immediately notice the use of *ad hoc* landmarks like *laodila* (bush), *kwadeva* (beach), *bwalita* (sea), *valu* (village), *Tuyabwau* (name of a fresh water well), *pilakeva* (topside, landside – versus *pilitinava* = lowland, seaside, beachside) – generally in connection with the locative *o*; thus Kilivila speakers switch to an absolute frame of reference that uses *ad hoc* landmarks to describe the orientation of the objects depicted in the photographs. Among these *ad hoc* landmarks we not only find names of wells, beaches, reefs, rocks, or trees, but also – depending on the context and situation, of course – references to houses and their respective owners and even to people that are sitting in the respective direction. These axes of orientation are indeed created on the spot, very much in an *ad hoc* manner, and they may refer to landmarks both within a big and a small scale environment, like the general environment or marks on the set of the interactional games used for data elicitation. All these axes are used as frequently as the bush–sea or bush–shore axis and therefore no special status is assigned to the latter axis – although this land–sea axis features rather prominently in many other (and not only Austronesian) languages (see Bennardo 2002; Senft 1997a). The examples in (44) and (45) illustrate that Kilivila speakers prefer the use of the intrinsic frame of reference for the location of objects in relation to each other and the use of an *ad hoc* landmark absolute frame of reference for describing the orientation of these objects. The relative-deictic frame of spatial reference is rather rarely used.[17]

2.4 GESTURE

When produced in face-to-face interaction, indexicals are usually accompanied by a pointing gesture. This section deals with gestures in general and with its various forms, including deictic gestures. After a brief introduction to Wilhelm Wundt's groundbreaking ideas on what he called 'the language of gestures', this section provides a survey on gesture research and discusses the relevance of these studies for pragmatics.

2.4.1 Introduction

At the very beginning of this chapter it was pointed out that the term 'deixis' is borrowed from the Greek word for 'pointing' or 'indicating'. Sentences like the following one:

(46) *This bush-knife is sharp, but this one is blunt.*

need an accompanying deictic or 'demonstrative' gesture in order to be understood.

In his pioneering contribution *The language of gestures* Wilhelm Wundt (1973; 1900, first part, Chapter Two) classified such a 'demonstrative gesture' as 'not only the simplest but also the most primary gesture in the effort to communicate' (Wundt 1973: 74). Wundt also pointed out that there are a number of other gesture types besides these demonstrative gestures. In his psychological classification of gestures he differentiated between imitative gestures, connotative gestures, and symbolic gestures and emphasized that there is a syntax of gestural communication. Wundt's classification and his theory about gesture will not be discussed in more detail here. But it should be emphasized that his classification of different forms and functions of gestures and his insight that:

> [n]atural gestural communication, which under similar conditions, develops spontaneously time and again in the same manner, bears its own proof that it is independent from outside coercion and arbitrary invention in its psychological regularity ... [and that] ... this regularity in no way excludes individual influences and artificial inventions which serve to perfect gestural communications in the interest of achieving special purposes.
>
> (Wundt 1973: 145f.)

laid the foundations and set standards for the study of gestures (and sign languages).[18] Among the most influential scholars who took up Wundt's ideas in developing their own theories of gesture are the psychologists Adam Kendon, David McNeill and Susan Goldin-Meadow. Based on the insights of these scholars and of other experts in the field, the next subsection provides a definition of gesture, presents and briefly illustrates the classification of gestures into different types and discusses their functions and the interrelationship with language and mind. Based on Kita (2009), subsection 2.4.3 discusses the pragmatics of gestures and provides a survey of the cross-cultural variation of gestures. And subsection 2.4.4 discusses so-called pragmatic gestures which function as illocutionary and discourse structure markers.

2.4.2 Gesture, language and mind

It is common knowledge that we all produce gestures while we are speaking, that we sometimes produce them instead of speaking and that we sometimes produce them even without the presence of an addressee as, for example, in telephone conversations. And we also know that so far no culture has been found in which gestures are not used as a means of communication. But what are gestures? Gestures were classified for a long time as a means of non-verbal communication (see, e.g. Weitz 1979). However, as early as 1972 Kendon analysed the coordination of speech and body motion in a single speaker and showed that gestures 'are integral parts of the processes of language and its use' (McNeill 2005: 13). Kendon (1980) continued to challenge the view that gestures are forms of non-verbal communication and a few years later McNeill (1985: 1) 'based on the very close temporal, semantic, pragmatic, pathological and developmental parallels between speech and referential and discourse oriented gestures' argued that 'gestures and speech are parts of the same psychological structure'. McNeill's argument put forward in this paper is succinctly summarized by Goldin-Meadow (2006: 337) who points out that 'to ignore the information conveyed in ... these gestures is to ignore parts of the conversation'. McNeill (1992: 1) defined gestures rather straightforwardly as 'movements of the hands and arms that we see when people talk'; however, this definition is rather narrow. In the first issue of the journal *Gesture* its editors Adam Kendon and Cornelia Müller outlined the scope of the new periodical as follows:

> GESTURE is a new journal for the emerging field of 'gesture studies'. The phenomena that this encompasses cannot easily be defined ('gesture' is a concept with fuzzy boundaries), but they include the wide variety of ways in which humans give what is usually regarded as wilful expression to their thoughts and feelings through visible bodily action. Thus, the movement of the body, especially the hands and arms, that are so often integrated with spoken expression, the use of manual actions to convey something without speech, or the manual and facial actions of sign languages, are all recognized as a part of 'gesture', broadly conceived, whereas expressions such as laughing and crying, blushing and the like are less likely to be so considered unless they are feigned or enacted.
>
> (Kendon and Müller 2001: 1)

Despite the caveat that the phenomena which are subsumed under the label 'gesture' are difficult to define, this outline of the scope of the journal implicitly provides an approach to such a definition. In his 2004 monograph Kendon first offers the following definition of gesture:

> 'Gesture' ... is the name for visible action when it is used as an utterance or as a part of an utterance ... [A]n 'utterance' is any unit of activity that is treated by those co-present as a communicative 'move', 'turn' or 'contribution'. Such units of activity may be constructed from speech or from visible bodily action or from the combination of these two modalities ... 'Gesture' is the visible bodily action that has a role in such units of action.
>
> (Kendon 2004: 7)

And then he elaborates on this first definition as follows:

> 'Gesture' ... is a label for actions that have the feature of manifest deliberate expressiveness. They are those actions or those aspects of another's action that, having

these features, tend to be directly perceived as being under the guidance of the observed person's voluntary control and being done for the purpose of expression rather than in the service of some practical aim. Participants in interaction readily recognize such actions and they tend to be accorded the status of actions for which the participants are held responsible.

(Kendon 2004: 15)

There are many different forms of actions that can be subsumed under this definition. On the basis and in honour of Kendon's earlier work McNeill (1992: 37) proposed to order gestures of different kinds along 'Kendon's continuum' in the following way:

Gesticulation → Language-like Gestures → Pantomimes → Emblems → Sign Languages

As we move from left to right: (1) the obligatory presence of speech declines, (2) the presence of language properties increases, and (3) idiosyncratic gestures are replaced by socially regulated signs.

(McNeill 1992: 37)

'Gesticulations' or 'speech framed gestures' or (as McNeill prefers to say) 'gestures' accompany speech spontaneously. McNeill (2006: 60) differentiates them into four subtypes:

- Depictive or representative iconic gestures (i.e. Wundt's symbolic gestures) 'present images of concrete entities and/or actions. For example, appearing to grasp and bend back something while saying "and he bends it way back"'.

- Metaphoric gestures 'picture abstract content, in effect imagining the non-imaginable ... [A]n abstract meaning is presented as if it had form and/or occupied space. For example, a speaker appears to be holding an object, as if presenting it, yet the meaning is not presenting a concrete object but an idea or memory of some other abstract "object"'.

- Deictic gestures point to referents of speech (as already mentioned above).

- Beats are gestures in which 'the hand appears to be beating time ... [they] are mere flicks of the hand(s) up and down or back and forth, zeroing in rhythmically on the prosodic peaks of speech'.

With these gestures Kendon, McNeill and McNeill's former student Sotaro Kita differentiate five gesture phases, the preparation phase, the stroke and the retraction phase as well as a pre- and a post-stroke hold phase. The stroke phase is obligatory because this is the gesture phase with meaning. All other phases are organized around the stroke phase (see, e.g. McNeill 2006: 62).

Language-like gestures are also called 'emblems' or 'quotable gestures'. McNeill (2006: 59) defines them as 'conventionalized signs, such as thumbs up' which are 'culturally specific, have standard forms and significance and ... are meaningful without speech although they also occur with speech'.

Pantomime is defined by McNeill (2006: 59) as 'a gesture or a sequence of gestures conveying a story to tell, produced without speech'.

Sign languages consist of signs that are lexical words. They are linguistic systems in their own rights with own properties.[19]

Kendon as well as McNeill claim that gestures are part of language. In the introduction to his anthology *Language and Gesture* McNeill (2000: 9) states that in this volume 'gestures are regarded as parts of *language itself* – not as embellishments or elaborations, but as integral parts of the processes of language and its use'. Moreover, McNeill (2000: 139) also points out that he and many other colleagues of his understand 'speech-synchronized gestures as windows into the on-line processes of thinking and speaking'. In his contribution to the very same anthology, Kendon answers the question 'Language and gesture: unity or duality?' on the basis of empirical data as follows:

> gestures are organized in relation to the spoken phrases they accompany in such a way that we must say that they are part of the very construction of the utterance itself. Gesture and speech ... are composed together as components of a single overall plan. We have to say that although each expresses somewhat different dimensions of meaning, speech and gesture are co-expressive of a single inclusive ideational complex, and it is this that is the meaning of the utterance ...
>
> If ... we think of 'language' as a complex of instrumentalities which serve in the expression of 'thought' ... then gesture is part of 'language'.
>
> (Kendon 2000: 61f.)

These statements clearly mark the quite extreme position of these two pioneers of gesture research with respect to the relationship between gesture, language and mind. Based on the research of Goldin-Meadow and especially on her 2006 handbook article on the 'hands role in talking and thinking' this relationship with the emphasis on mind will now be discussed in some more detail.

Goldin-Meadow is a specialist in children's use of gesture. Like developmental studies in psycholinguistics, developmental studies on gesture provide insights into children's knowledge and reveal information about their ways of thinking. Goldin-Meadow points out that children start to gesture – without words – at between 8 and 12 months, producing deictic gestures, especially pointing and hold-up gestures as well as conventional gestures like nods and headshakes (to express yes or no) in their culture-specific way. Even children who are born blind or even deaf and blind also start to gesture if and when they acquire language (Goldin-Meadow 2006: 345; Eibl-Eibesfeldt 1973a: 181ff.). Human ethologists take this observation as an indication that gesturing is inborn and can be considered to be a so-called 'fixed action pattern' (Eibl-Eibesfeldt 1973a: 192; see also subsection 3.2.1). Goldin-Meadow (2006: 353) interprets this finding as an indication of the fact that 'gesture seems to be an inevitable part of speaking'.

At the age of about a year (non-handicapped) children start to produce iconic gestures. Metaphoric gestures and beats (i.e. rhythmic beating with a finger, hand or arm), however, are produced much later. With respect to pointing gestures Goldin-Meadow argues that they 'constitute an important early step in symbolic development and pave the way for learning spoken language' (see Goldin-Meadow 2006: 338; also Iverson and Goldin-Meadow 2005). Iconic gestures represent aspects of the referent; therefore they are less context-dependent than pointing gestures, they take on linguistic properties and can function like words. As soon as children learn to produce the word for which they used the gesture, they prefer to produce the word, and when they start to combine words they use fewer gestures and rely more on the verbal expressions. However, before they combine words with words they start to combine words with gestures. Goldin-Meadow (2006: 339) points out that gestures become coordinated and integrated with speech[20] during the one-word period of the language acquisition process in such a way that 'gesture and speech begin to have a *coherent semantic* relationship ... [as well as] ... a *synchronous temporal* relationship'. With this integration the foundation is laid for the production of simple sentences. Just before the two word stage children use the combination of gesture and word for conveying different complementary information. Goldin-Meadow (2006: 341ff.) refers to this phenomenon as 'gesture-speech mismatch' which she and her co-workers (see, e.g. Church and Goldin-Meadow 1986) interpret as an index of knowledge transition to a stage where two ideas are activated at one and the same time. Goldin-Meadow emphasizes that the 'fact that gesture-speech mismatch is a reliable index of a child's transitional status suggests that the two modalities are, in fact, not independent of one another'. These gesture-speech mismatches are found also in older children and in adults; they are an important means for conveying complex information in social interaction. However, at this age, children can understand gestures produced by others and appropriately respond to them. For children in the one-word stage of their language acquisition process it is easier to understand gesture-word combinations than word-word combinations. That three-year-old children can make pragmatic inferences to respond to an adult's indirect speech act 'more likely when they are presented with gesture and speech than with either part alone' (Goldin-Meadow 2006: 343) is illustrated by an experiment reported by Spencer Kelly (2001): In this experiment a child was brought to a room and the door was left open. In a speech only condition the adult in the room said: 'It is going to get cold in here' (see 1.3.5 above). In a gesture only condition the adult just pointed to the door. And in the gesture and speech condition the adult produced the sentence and pointed to the door. Only four-year-olds were able to make the appropriate pragmatic inference from either speech or gesture alone (see Goldin-Meadow 2006: 343ff.). Thus, children get meaning from speech accompanying gestures. It was also found that children 'are significantly more likely to learn a novel word if it is presented with gesture than without it'.

Church and Goldin-Meadow (1986) carried out specific gesture-speech mismatch experiments in which children and adults performed Piagetian conservation tasks. In these experiments the participants were 'asked whether the amount of water changed when it was poured from a tall, skinny container into a short wide container' (Goldin-Meadow 2006: 340f.). And Garber, Alibali and Goldin-Meadow (1998) confronted children with mathematical equivalence problems. The experiments of these scholars show that 'gesture can reflect thoughts that are different from the thoughts a child conveys in speech' (Goldin-Meadow 2006: 350ff.).

Experiments like these reveal that we not only produce co-speech gestures but also co-thought gestures. Co-speech gestures are designed for addressees, be they present or not (as in the case of telephone conversations) and speakers use them (in most cases unconsciously) to communicate. Asli Özyürek (2002: 1) confirms this insight with two experiments that show that:

> speakers change their gestures depending on the location of shared space, that is the intersection of the gesture spaces of the speakers and addressees. Gesture orientations change more frequently when they accompany spatial prepositions such as *into* and *out*, which describe motion that has a beginning and end point rather than *across*, which depicts an unbound path across space. Speakers change their gestures so that they represent the beginning and end point of motion INTO and OUT by moving into and out of the shared space. Thus speakers design their gestures for their addressees and therefore use them to communicate.
>
> (Özyürek 2002: 1; see also 2000)

Speakers use their co-speech gestures primarily for their addressees. Thus co-speech gestures have a strong social component.

Co-thought gestures are 'hand movements produced in silent, noncommunicative, problem-solving situations' (Chu and Kita 2011: 1) by the speaker just for him- or herself. They are rather 'solipsistic'. Chu and Kita – on the basis of three experiments – found the following:

> [W]hen people have difficulty in solving spatial visual problems [in mental rotation tasks or paper folding tasks, G. S.], they spontaneously produce gesture to help them and gestures can indeed improve performance. As they solve more problems, the spatial computation supported by gestures becomes internalized and the gesture frequency decreases. The benefit of gestures persists even in subsequent spatial visualization problems in which gesture is prohibited. Moreover, the beneficial effect of gesturing can be generalized to a different visualization task when two tasks require similar spatial transformation processes.
>
> (Chu and Kita 2011: 1)

These research results seem to confirm the conclusion Goldin-Meadow (2006: 365) drew on the basis of similar problem-solving experiments; she points out that 'gesture does more than just reflect thought' – these results show that gesturing also supports thinking (of gesturers)!

This subsection of Chapter Two has shown that language, gesture and mind are strongly interrelated. Studies on actual language use have largely ignored this insight for a long time. However, future research on forms of actual language use in linguistic pragmatics can hardly neglect the multimodal quality of human face-to-face interaction any more. The next subsection will discuss cross-cultural variation of co-speech gestures and the pragmatics of their use.

2.4.3 Cross-cultural variation of co-speech gestures: The pragmatics of gesture use

As mentioned above, it seems that the occurrence of co-speech gestures is universal, however, the ways gestures are produced vary across cultures. In a paper on this topic Kita (2009) reviews the literature on cross-cultural variation of gestures and identifies four factors that govern it:

- culture specific conventions for form-meaning associations;
- culture specific spatial cognition;
- linguistic differences; and
- culture-specific gestural pragmatics.

(Kita 2009: 145).

To illustrate the variation of gestures that is due to conventions of form-meaning association Kita (2009: 146ff.) uses emblems (or 'quotable' gestures in Kendon's diction) and pointing gestures. The gesture that is made by forming a ring with the thumb and the index finger is certainly a very well-known emblem and means in most European cultures 'OK/good'. However, the dominant meaning of this gesture in France is 'zero' and it is used as an insulting gesture referring to the anus in Greece and Turkey (see also Morris *et al.* 1979). The geographic distribution of emblems can be explained by culture contact – the impact of which can be rather long lasting. Kita points out that 'in Italy the head gesture for negation is a horizontal head shake in the northern part and in Rome, but it is a head toss (i.e. a head jerk up- and backwards) in southern Italy, including Naples and Sicily'. The only other places in Europe where this head toss is used as a gesture for negation are Greece and adjacent areas in Turkey and Bulgaria. About 750 BC the Greeks colonized the south of Italy – Desmond Morris and his colleagues (1979) argue quite plausibly that the head toss spread through the southern parts of Italy because of this early contact with the ancient Greeks.

As already mentioned in subsection 2.3, pointing gestures are important indexicals. People may point to something or someone with their index finger, with their eyes, with puckered lips, etc. Pointing gestures vary from culture to culture. Dixon, for example, notes

> that some languages have different deictic gestures for relating to varying distances and visibility. In the Tucano and Arawak languages of the Vaupés River basin (spanning the border between Brazil and Colombia), for instance, we find (i) pointing with the lips for "visible and near"; (ii) pointing with the lips plus a backwards tilt of the head for "visible and not near"; (iii) pointing with the index finger for "not visible" (if the direction in which the object lies is known).

(Dixon 2003: 87)

Australian Aboriginals speaking Arrernte distinguish six types of pointing gestures that have contrastive functions:

index finger pointing, open hand pointing with the palm down, open hand pointing with the palm vertical, 'horn-hand' pointing (with the thumb, the index finger and the pinkie extended), lip pointing (pointing by protruding lips), and eye-pointing. Open hand pointing with the palm vertical, for example, is used to indicate each straight segment of a complex route. Horn-hand pointing indicates the direction of the end point of a route.

(Wilkins: 2003; Kita 2009: 148)

Enfield discusses lip-pointing by Lao speakers. He observes that these speakers restrict lip-pointing to 'cases in which the location or identity of the referent is in focus in the utterance – these gestures almost exclusively appear as answers to "Where?" or "Which one?" questions' (Enfield 2001: 207). Moreover, he also points out that speakers only seem to produce this kind of pointing when they assume that their interlocutor(s) know the respective referent(s) of this gesture. In addition, this lip-pointing 'is always accompanied by gaze directed towards the referent' – these observations suggest for Enfield 'that the deictic vector is not provided by the action of the lips, but by the *gaze*'. Pointing with the index finger, however, seems to be the default way of the Lao deictic gesture; it is used by Lao speakers in a much broader context.

Kita (2009: 149ff.) illustrates the second type of variation of co-speech gestures that is due to cognitive diversity across cultures referring among other studies to John Haviland's research on pointing gestures made by speakers of the Australian Aboriginal language Guugu Yimidhirr. Haviland showed that this language, besides a rather simple system of four deictics indicating 'here, there, yonder' and 'there, that's the way', has a spatial system which is 'absolute' (see 2.3 above), using a 'four term system of roots' the meanings of which 'correspond roughly to the English compass points' (Haviland 1979: 72ff.). These speakers are always absolutely oriented – and this holds for their gestures as well. The absolute encoding of spatial information is reflected in co-speech gestures. Thus, if these speakers point to a place that is about 80 kilometres away from where they are – and this may be in the middle of the Australian bush – their pointing gestures only have an angular deviation of +/– 14° (Levinson *et al.* 1997: 324; see also Levinson 2003:124ff.). In 1980 Haviland documented one of his consultants telling a story in which his boat capsized and he had to swim more than five kilometres to the shore. In 1982 Levinson filmed the same man again while he was telling the same story. Kita summarizes Haviland's discussion of these two video documents as follows:

> In one telling, [the consultant] was facing west, and in the other, he was facing north. It was found that the gestures consistently depicted motion and location in terms of the absolute frame of reference. For example, the movement from west to east was gesturally depicted as a movement away from the body when facing east, but as a movement from left to right when facing north. Such absolutely anchored gestures were found in both utterances with and without cardinal direction words. Thus, the use of absolute frame of reference in gesture was not simply due to semantic coordination with the concurrent utterance, but it reflects the nature of underlying representations of space.

(Kita 2009: 151ff.)

Kita further points out that spatial metaphors for the concept of time differ across cultures and that these differences are also reflected in gestures. Speakers of English (and of many other languages as well) use the front-back axis for pointing to the future and the past. However, there are also many other languages in which front implies past and back future. The speakers of Aymara, e.g. a language which is spoken in the Andes, base their understanding of past and future 'on a conceptual scheme that what is known (e.g. past) is in front and what is unknown (e.g. future) is behind, which in turn is based on the fact that vision is an important source of information'. Accordingly, speakers of this language point to the front when they talk about events in the past and to the back when they talk about the future (see Núñes and Sweetser 2006). These two examples illustrate that variation in gestures is due to cognitive diversity across cultures.

Variation in co-speech gesture which is due to linguistic diversity is illustrated by Kita (2009: 154ff.) with the results of a study he did in cooperation with Asli Özyürek in 2003. Speakers of Japanese, Turkish and English were shown a cartoon movie and asked to describe the scene to a listener who did not see the film clip. The clip featured an event in which one of the protagonists swung on a rope from a window in one skyscraper to the window of another skyscraper across the street. To refer to such a change of location with an arc trajectory, speakers of English can produce the verb 'to swing'; Japanese and Turkish speakers, however, do not have any equivalent verb or any other easy and straightforward paraphrase that encodes this concept. On the basis of this insight Kita summarizes the results of this study as follows:

> Consequently, Japanese and Turkish speakers' description of the event did not encode the arc trajectory but instead used more generic verbs of motion such as to *go* or to *jump*, while all English speakers used the verb *swing*. The gestural representation of the event showed a parallel cross-linguistic difference. Japanese and Turkish speakers were more likely to produce 'straight gestures', which did not show the arc trajectory than English speakers. English speakers mostly used 'arc gestures' that depicted both the change of location and the arc trajectory. In other words, when the speech does not encode a particular aspect of an event, the accompanying gesture tended not to depict it either.
>
> (Kita 2009: 154f.)

The fact that languages like English encode manner and path of motion in one clause (e.g. *it rolled down the slope*) but languages like Turkish and Japanese do this in two clauses (e.g. *it descended as it rolled*) also influences the production of co-speech gestures. In a number of studies Kita, Özyürek and their colleagues (see e.g. Özyürek and Kita 1999; Özyürek *et al.* 2008) found that:

> Japanese and Turkish speakers were more likely to represent manner and path in two separate gestures, whereas English speakers were more likely to represent manner and path in a single gesture ... In other words, how manner and path were packaged in a clause in a given language is reflected in how the two pieces of information were packaged in gestural representations.
>
> (Kita 2009: 155)

Before Kita illustrates the fourth and last factor – culture-specific gestural pragmatics – that governs variation in co-speech gestures he emphasizes the systematicity of usage of gesture for communication; he refers to this systematicity with the term 'gestural pragmatics' (Kita 2009: 157).

The first example he uses for illustrating variation of co-speech gesture that is due to diversity in gestural pragmatics across cultures reveals that polite and impolite behaviour also extends to gestures. Speakers of Ewe in Ghana respect a gestural taboo; Kita and James Essegbey researched the profound impact of this taboo on the gesture practice of members of this speech community. The two scientists studied pointing gestures during route descriptions that were provided by Ewe speakers. For these speakers pointing by the left hand is considered to be a taboo. Kita and Essegbey (2001: 73) found that there is a convention to place the left hand on the lower back out of politeness while pointing with the right hand. Pointing with the right hand to indicate a leftward direction across the body 'may involve an anatomically straining position': in this case 'right-handed pointing can be "hyper-contra-lateral" ... in the sense that the arm crosses in front of the face or around the neck' (Kita and Essegbey 2001: 83). To point with both hands does not violate the taboo. However, despite the taboo, left-handed pointing is not completely suppressed: 'When the left hand indicates a direction, the gesture is often reduced in size and performed in the periphery. Some gestures are made in such an inconspicuous way ... that they no longer count as gestures for the purpose of taboo' (Kita and Essegbey 2001: 92). With this case study Kita and Essegbey illustrate how the left hand pointing taboo regulates both how to gesture and how not to gesture. The taboo creates 'a complex system of gestural politeness, which gives the Ghanaian gestural practice a distinct flavour' (Kita 2009: 159).

Another obvious difference in co-speech gestures across cultures is the nodding behaviour of Japanese speakers on the one hand and American English speakers (and speakers of many other Indo-European languages) on the other. Maynard (1993) found that Japanese speakers nod three times more often than American English speakers in naturalistic conversations. American English and Japanese speakers usually nod at the end of a proposition; however, in a conversation both Japanese speakers and addressees also systematically nod in the middle of a proposition. Kita and Sachiko Ide (2007) found that the 'major phrase boundaries are all potential locations for the addressee to nod' (Kita 2009: 159). They interpret this finding not only as being responsible for the higher nodding frequency in Japanese conversations, but they also emphasize that these frequent nods establish social bonds between the interactants. Kita elaborates on this important pragmatic function of nods in Japanese as follows – referring to corresponding research by Markus and Kitayama (1991):

> It has been suggested the culture-specific patterns of nodding are due to what is considered to be important in social interaction in the culture. Frequent exchange of nodding in Japanese conversation may stem from Japanese emphasis on cooperation and consideration for others or more generally from socially defined self in Japanese culture ... Japanese tend to see oneself as part of an encompassing social relationship and [recognize] that one's behavior is determined, contingent on, and to a large extent

organized by what the actor perceives to be the thoughts, feelings and actions of others in the relationship.

(Kita 2009: 159f.)

Thus Kita shows that nodding shapes conversations in different ways in different cultures. These differences are due to gestural pragmatics that are based on the respective speakers' culture-specific values with respect to social interaction in general and communication in particular.

2.4.4 Pragmatic gestures

In his notes on pragmatic and social aspects of everyday gestures Lluís Payrató (2004: 107) points out that 'the pragmatic roles and illocutionary values of autonomous gestures have been asserted in many analyses, and were even foreseen by Austin's ... work on speech acts'. And, as Payrató emphasizes, Austin indeed explicitly states:

- that 'many conventional acts, such as betting or conveyance of property, can be performed in non-verbal ways' (Austin 1962: 19);

- that there are 'actions which are non-linguistic but similar to performative utterances in that they are the performance of a conventional action' (Austin 1962: 69);

- that '[w]e may accompany the utterance of the words by gestures (winks, pointings, shruggings, frowns, etc.) or by ceremonial non-verbal actions. These may sometimes serve without the utterance of any words, and their importance is obvious' (Austin 1962: 76); and

- that 'we can for example warn or order or appoint or give or protest or apologize by non-verbal means and these are illocutionary acts' (Austin 1962: 119).

Payrató (2004: 107) also refers to Mary Ritchie Key (1977: 7f.), who lists a number of gestures that have illocutionary force. Most of these gestures are emblems which Kendon (1988a: 136) understands as 'functional equivalents of a complete speech act'. These gestures are conventionalized. There are a number of other gestures that also have a conventionalized form and seem to be standardized with respect to their meanings and functions – like emblems; however, these gestures 'do not display aspects of the propositional content of the verbal utterance, but mark the specific role the verbal element plays in the discourse' (Seyfeddinipur: 2004: 206). Kendon (1995: 247) refers to these gestures as 'pragmatic' gestures. They 'indicate types of speech act or aspects of discourse structure'. Kendon (1995; see also 2000) describes the contexts of use of four such 'pragmatic gestures', two emblems that 'express the illocutionary intent of the spoken utterance associated with them' and two gestures that 'relate to discourse structure', one which 'marks "topic" as distinct from "comment"' and one which 'marks the "focality" of a unit in relation to the theme' (Kendon 1995: 247). These pragmatic gestures were documented during natural conversations made near Salerno in southern Italy.

Kendon describes the use of the two 'illocutionary marker' gestures to which Italian speakers refer as *Mano a borsa* – 'purse hand' and *Mani giunte* – 'joined hands/praying hands'. Kendon describes the *Mano a borsa* as follows:

> In the 'purse hand' ... all the digits of the hand are fully extended, but they are drawn together so that they are in contact with one another at their tips ... The hand, shaped in this fashion is held with the palm facing upwards, although in some cases we see it with the palm facing somewhat toward the body mid-line. It may be moved up and down, by forearm action, usually with movement of relatively short amplitude.
>
> (Kendon 1995: 249)

This gesture indicates that the gesturer is making a request, like 'Come to the point! Explain yourself clearly!', and to accentuate 'the amazed, bored or indifferent tone of the question' (Kendon 1995: 250).[21] Kendon provides a number of contexts in which this gesture is used. In one such situation a speaker is asking an interlocutor whom he can contact to carry out a certain task. 'As he asks the question *"A chi vac' a truva' io mo' a chest?* – Who do I go to find now for this?" he forms the *Mano a borsa* which is maintained throughout the utterance' (Kendon 1995: 251). Kendon states that this gesture can 'serve as the visual equivalent of the grammatical structure and intonation of the speech it accompanies'. However, it can also be continued after the speaker has finished speaking and then serve as the 'visual cue that a question has been asked and an answer is expected' (Kendon 1995: 251f.). According to Kendon the *Mano a borsa* marks that speakers are:

> making a request for some information [when they are] seeking clarification [or] an explanation of justification for something ... [others have] said or done ... The gesture serves ... as a way of making explicit, through visual means, the type of speech act or illocutionary act that the speaker intends or has intended with a given utterance.
>
> (Kendon 1995: 258)

The *Mani giunte* gesture 'is one in which the two hands, each with fingers extended and adducted, are placed in contact, palms facing one another, rather as is done in the gesture commonly employed among Christians as a gesture of religious prayer' (Kendon 1995: 258f.). Kendon describes it as a gesture 'begging for indulgence' and of 'imploring someone insistently' and paraphrases it with the questions 'What can I do? ... And I, what can I do?'. In one of the contexts Kendon provides to illustrate the use of this gesture, somebody is asked to make a phone call. He replies 'But I have a council meeting in a moment! ... [and as] he says this he enacts *Mani giunte* – thus making it clear that he is asking the other person to ... relieve him of the responsibility of making the call'. The gesture 'serves as an appeal to the listener to accept the logical consequences of what the speaker has been saying' (Kendon 1995: 259). Gestures like the *Mano a borsa* and the *Mani giunte* are called illocutionary markers by Kendon because 'they appear to give visible expression to the illocutionary act intended by the speaker' (Kendon 1995: 264).

Other pragmatic gestures mark discourse units. The 'Finger Bunch' – 'a gesture in which the hand is held with fingers drawn together, much as in the *Mano a borsa*, but in which it is moved forward or downward, away from the self' (Kendon 1995: 264) – occurs often when the speaker specifies a topic. When the hand is moved away and downwards and when it opens so that the fingers are extended and spread it then gesturally specifies the comment on the topic gesturally marked before. Kendon points out that this:

> grasping action has been interpreted ... as an action symbolic of seizing something and holding it ... the gesture grasps the topic being specified, holds it up or moves it toward the interlocutor and then, in the terminal finger opening action, the comment made on the topic is presented.
>
> (Kendon 1995: 264)

The 'Ring' – a gesture in which 'the tip of the index finger is brought into contact with that of the thumb' – has several functions. Among other things it:

> occurs in association with a segment of speech that provides precise information, makes a specific reference to something, makes something specific in contrast to other possibilities or in contrast to something more general, or which gives a specific example of something.
>
> (Kendon 1995: 268)

Thus, the 'Ring' also marks discourse units indicating their status within the discourse (see also Neumann 2004).

2.5 CONCLUDING REMARKS

This chapter provided an introduction to another central topic in linguistic pragmatics – namely deixis, the system we use to refer to and communicate about objects, living beings, places, periods of time and even texts or text passages in specific contexts. The study of deixis reveals how languages encode features of the context of the utterance and how they select specific topics and items of their discourse in the various contexts given. After a general characterization of the different kinds and modes of pointing, the characteristic features, the complexities and intricacies of various systems and means of spatial deixis found in the languages of the world were illustrated, emphasizing the context-dependency of the use of these indexicals which shift from context to context. Moreover, it was shown that, like other forms of reference by verbal means, these forms of spatial deictic reference constitute a collaborative task for speaker and hearer.

Deictic gestures and other forms of gesture are also used as indexicals. The second part of this chapter dealt with gestures in general. Discussing the interrelationship between gesture, language and mind, different gesture forms and their communicative and social functions were described; co-speech gestures, which are primarily designed for addressees, were differentiated from co-thought gestures, which are produced by speakers just for themselves; it was pointed out that these co-thought gestures not only reflect thought but support thinking in certain problem-solving situations. It was also pointed out that gesture and speech can be combined to convey different information – that is to say, gestures add information to the speaker's verbal utterance. It was shown that the interrelationship between language, gesture and mind also governs cross-cultural and cross-linguistic variation of gestures. Finally it was illustrated that gestures not only have their own pragmatics, but that there are also pragmatic gestures that serve explicit pragmatic functions.

Both the study of indexicals and co-speech gestures are extremely important for the research of actual language use because they provide direct evidence for the fact that human interaction is multimodal.

What does this chapter tell us about the anecdote which I reported in the introduction to this volume? It illustrates that once I had learned how to appropriately react to the specific form of Trobriand greeting I correctly used indexicals – in the example appropriate motion verbs within a complex serial verb construction – to provide the information wanted. And although I have no video documents of my own behaviour I remember that I pointed to my towel, metaphorically referring to the activity and place related to the use of it, and I am sure that I also pointed to where I thought the fresh water well was located in the bush. This latter gesture was rather vague – the Trobriand Islanders do not have an absolute system of spatial reference that can be compared to that of Australian Aboriginals, so I did not need to learn how to dead-reckon my position with respect to the water cave to be able to produce a correct pointing gesture in such an absolute frame of spatial reference.

2.6 EXERCISE/WORK SECTION

- Take a detective story or any other short story or novel of your choice, check the first five pages for at least two examples of the verbal expressions used by the author for personal, social, temporal and spatial deictic reference and discuss the context-dependence of these indexicals.

- Check a political speech documented in the internet for utterances that document gestural deictic, symbolic deictic, anaphoric and non-anaphoric usage of indexicals.

- Where is '*here*'? Collect about 30 utterances with the word '*here*' – for example from a newspaper or, even better, in documented conversations – and analyse the meaning of '*here*' in the various contexts of its use.

- Collect and video-document route descriptions and describe and analyse what the speakers do, how they do it and how accurate their descriptions are.

- Describe the spatial deictic systems of two languages (not including your mother-tongue) that are documented in the literature, discuss the similarities and differences between these systems and provide reasons for the differences you find.

- Videotape a talk show or a fragment of everyday conversation and describe and analyse what kind of gestures the interactants produce and develop and justify assumptions about the functions these gestures fulfil.

- Describe a few gestures that you take to be culture-specific for your speech community, discuss the contexts of their use and justify your selection.

- Discuss David McNeill's (2000: 139) position that co-speech gestures can be understood as 'windows into the online processes of speaking and thinking'.

- Discuss Adam Kendon's (2000: 61f.) position: 'Gesture is part of language'.

2.7 SUGGESTIONS FOR FURTHER READING

Antonopoulou and Nikiforidou (2002); Baker *et al.* (2003); Basso, E. (2008); Burenhult (2003); Demir *et al.* (2011); Diessel (1999); Duncan *et al.* (2007); Enfield *et al.* (2007), Goldin-Meadow (2003); Grenoble (1998); Guidetti and Colletta (2010); Gullberg and de Bot (2010); Hanks (2009); Haviland (1993, 2000); Holler and Wilkin (2009); Kataoka (2004); Kendon (1988b); Krauss (1998); Liebal *et al.* (2005); Liszkowski (2010); Naruoka (2006); Perniss *et al.* (2007); Stam and Ishino (2011).

NOTES

1 I do not translate this technical term; for critical comments on translations offered for the term *Völkerpsychologie* see Greenwood (2003).

2 This section draws on Senft (2004a: 1–6).

3 For 'unanchored' sentences see Fillmore (1975: 39): 'The worst possible case I can imagine for a totally unanchored occasion-sentence is that of finding afloat in the ocean a bottle with a note which reads, "Meet me here at noon tomorrow with a stick about this big"'.

4 With respect to non-deictic usages of deictic terms Levinson (1983: 67, footnote 6) points out the following: 'One way of thinking about these non-deictic usages is to think of the deictic terms as being relativized to the text instead of to the situation of utterance.' One could argue whether anaphora and cataphora then should be subsumed under what Levinson (1983: 67) and Ehrich (see below) call 'discourse deixis'; given their usage the term 'deixis' is somewhat misleading. See also subsection 2.3 examples (12) to (15) below. Note that '(co-)reference' is a common cover term for discourse-internal use of deictic elements.

5 With respect to the problem of space and time and personal/social deixis see, e.g. Anderson and Keenan (1985); Boroditsky and Gaby (2010); Clark (1973: 48–50); Ehrich (1992); Enfield and Stivers (2007); Fillmore (1975: 28); Lyons (1982: 114f., 121); Weissenborn and Klein (1982).

6 In the sentence '*The socks are in the drawer*' one differentiates between the entity to be situated, the 'theme' or the 'figure', namely *the socks*, and the reference object or the entity in relation to which the theme is situated – which is called the 'relatum' or 'ground' – namely *the drawer*. The spatial relation between 'figure' and 'ground', or 'theme' and 'relatum' in this example is 'being in'.

7 Note that Anderson and Keenan (1985: 277) emphasize that the 'elements most commonly cited as "deictics" are those designating spatial location relative to that of the speech event'.

8 For a modified version of this hypothesis see, e.g. Dixon (2003: 106f., footnote 10). For a rejection of Denny's hypothesis and for a completely different position see Fillmore (1982: 48f.).

9   This subsection is based on the detailed description provided in Senft (2004b).

10 There are other systems of spatial deixis that are not speaker based, like, e.g. the person-oriented system of the Oceanic language Saliba which differentiates on the one hand between a proximal category near the speaker and a proximal category near the addressee; and a general distal category on the other (see Margetts 2004).

11 *Besa* or *beya* are also used as presentatives that can be glossed as 'That's it here!' or as 'There you are'.

12 Kilivila has a numeral classifier system; however, the language uses its classifiers also for the word formation of (all but one) demonstratives and some adjectives. Languages with numeral classifiers have the following characteristic feature: in counting inanimate and animate referents, the numerals (obligatorily) concatenate with a certain morpheme – the so-called 'classifier'. This morpheme classifies and quantifies the respective nominal referent according to semantic criteria (see Senft 1991, 1996a).

13 For details see Senft (1996a).

14 See: http://fieldmanuals.mpi.nl/volumes/1999/1999-demonstrative-questionnaire-this-that/

15 There is a fourfold series of possessive pronouns in Kilivila. The series of pronouns that mark inalienable possession and are suffixed to most of the body part terms are labelled as 'possessive pronouns IV', abbreviated as 'PP.IV'.

16 See also examples 27, 29, 34b, and 38 above.

17 Here is an example: *Tau*   *e-tota*   *omatala*   *kai.*
                            man   3-stand   in.front.of   tree
                            A man is standing in front of a tree.

18 For a survey on the history of Western interest in gesture, see Kendon (2004, Chapters 3 and 4); see also McNeill (1992: 2ff.) and de Jorio (2000); for the discussion of Wundt's role see Kendon (2004: 57ff.); also McNeill (1992: 3).

19 See, e.g. Kendon (2004: 73f.); see also Emmorey (2001); Sandler and Lillo-Martin (2006). Like spoken languages, sign languages are fully formed natural languages in their own right. Therefore, they will not be discussed in more detail here. Note that gestures also co-occur with signing (see, e.g. Liddell [2003]; Duncan [2005]).

20 See also Kelly *et al.* (2010) who confirm the integrated-systems hypothesis and demonstrate that gesture and speech form an integrated system in language comprehension.

21 Some of my Italian colleagues point out that this gesture is also used to express annoyance and even anger and that it is sometimes made with both hands.

3

Pragmatics and human ethology

Biological foundations of communicative behaviour

3.1 INTRODUCTION

Gestures represent only one aspect of the multimodality of speech and verbal interaction. There are a number of other forms of expressive behaviour that accompany speech and are important for verbal interactions. Human ethology is the subdiscipline of biology that deals among other things with the communicative functions of the various forms of expressive behaviour. After a brief discussion of the ethological concepts 'expressive movement' and 'signal', the first part of this chapter discusses the communicatively very important behavioural signals manifest in facial expressions. Ever since Charles Bell (1774–1842), Charles Darwin (1809–1882) and Guillaume Duchenne (1806–1875), facial expressions of emotions and inner feelings have been researched from various angles. The research on emotion by Paul Ekman and his colleagues kept the Darwinian perspective alive. But this research has always been a highly controversial topic. Based on Irenäus Eibl-Eibesfeldt's criticism of Ekman's research on emotions and on his contributions to facial expressions from the perspective of human ethology, the first part of this chapter highlights the form and function of eyebrow raising – a signal that communicates first and foremost a person's openness for social contact.

In 1968 Edward T. Hall showed that people in different cultures utilize different culture-specific distance norms. By means of personal distances we mark individual and group territories – and this has implications for posture behaviour and body motion. The communicative functions of body posture, motion and position will also be discussed in the first part of this chapter.

The second half of this chapter on the influence of human ethology on linguistic pragmatics first discusses the concepts 'ritual' and 'ritual communication' in some more detail and then presents and discusses Eibl-Eibesfeldt's hypothesis regarding universal interaction strategies. He claims that rituals and forms of ritual communication can be understood as the differentiation of what he calls 'basic interaction strategies'. The heuristic value of this assumption is illustrated by rituals of requesting, giving and taking documented in the speech community of the Eipo in West Papua and by complex forms of ritual communication observed and documented during a so-called 'palm fruit festival' celebrated by the Yanomamö of the upper Orinoco in Venezuela. Eibl-Eibesfeldt's hypothesis is then discussed in connection with Stephen Levinson's recent ideas about a 'universal systematics of interaction' and 'building blocks for cultural diversity in social interaction' that are provided by what he calls the 'interaction engine' (Levinson 2006: 61f.).

3.2 EXPRESSIVE MOVEMENTS AND THEIR RITUALIZATION INTO SIGNALS

For human ethologists, that is biologists and behavioural physiologists investigating human behaviour, gestures belong to the class of expressive movements which they define as 'behavior patterns that have undergone distinctive differentiation in the service of signaling' during processes of ritualization (Eibl-Eibesfeldt 1989: 438). They point out that any behavioural pattern can become such a signal either in the course of evolution or because of conventions that are valid within a specific community in which these signals are culturally transmitted and acquired. The prerequisite condition for the development of an expressive movement into a signal is that it has to regularly accompany a specific *arousal condition*. An arousal condition is defined as a psychological and physiological state in humans (and animals) in which an individual is attentive and reactive to perceived stimuli in such a way that others can easily recognize her or his disposition and emotional reaction to these stimuli and her or his intentions for further action. These signals may be physically determined concomitant phenomena of an emotional state, for example blushing or trembling, or they may be behaviour patterns that fulfil a specific function, like forms of friendly bonding behaviour or forms of aggressive behaviour like hitting or just threatening to hit – signals that are immediately understood, even by animals, as being either friendly or dangerous. To emphasize it once more, these expressive movements are performed and perceived as indicators of a person's readiness to act. When behavioural patterns become ritualized and are thus developed into signals, they undergo changes that make the signal more prominent and unequivocal to improve its communicative function. During these ritualization processes the movements are usually simplified and often repeated rhythmically, often getting exaggerated, while they either vary with respect to their intensity or are executed with a typical intensity.

Among these signals we find, for example, aggressive tongue display in sticking out the tongue: here the tongue is protruded or bent downward and held for some time. This is a signal that marks rejection. Human ethologists explain this expressive movement as derived from the refusal to take food in a process of phylogenetic ritualization. However, there is also a friendly form of tongue display, the tongue flicking which is a signal of contact readiness. Here the tongue is either arched upward or simply extended, but for a short period of time. Other such signals are developed in processes of cultural ritualizations, like, for example, the 'measured step of a dignitary' or 'the parade of marching soldiers' (Eibl-Eibesfeldt: 1989: 438ff.).

Facial expressions are a specific form of these signals, because the 'face is one of the most important reference points in interpersonal communication' (Eibl-Eibesfeldt 1989: 443). It is not accidental that we speak of face-to-face interaction and communication. We transmit many signals with our face, be it by moving our eyes, by unconscious changes in the pupillary size[1] or by moving our facial muscles (both consciously and unconsciously). With many of these facial muscle movements we express our emotional states. The next subsection discusses facial expressions.

3.2.1 Facial expressions

Charles Bell (1806), Charles Darwin (1872) and Guillaume Duchenne (1876) were the pioneers in the field of researching the facial expression of emotions. Bell's work and – even more so – Duchenne's studies on facial muscles and emotional expressions in the face played an important role in Darwin's seminal contribution to the field. In Darwin's view, universal emotions and hard-wired facial expressions which reflect them should yield clear universal categories – with predicted agreement across communities in the terminology expressing the corresponding emotions. Duchenne's research question – which facial muscles are used to coordinate facial expressions – was taken up by Carl-Herman Hjortsjö's (1969) study in which he describes 23 facial muscles, lists 24 facial expressions and discusses 'in precise anatomical terms how the contraction of individual muscles influenced the resulting facial expression' (Eibl-Eibesfeldt 1989: 445). His research laid the foundation for Paul Ekman and Wallace Friesen's studies that resulted in their Facial Action Coding System (Ekman and Friesen 1975, 1978). Ekman and his co-workers have played an important role in keeping the Darwinian perspective alive by claiming the existence of a small set of universal basic emotions with universally corresponding expressions reflecting adaptive 'affect programmes' like mating, defence, and flight. Among the basic emotions that are claimed to be recognized from facial expressions by all human beings are (at least) the six emotions 'Happiness, Surprise, Fear, Anger, Disgust' and 'Sadness'. In addition, Ekman (1973: 220) also makes the following rather bold claim: 'Regardless of the language, or whether the culture is ... industrialized or preliterate, facial expressions are labeled with the same emotion terms'. To verify their hypotheses Ekman and his colleagues presented photographs of facial expressions that they themselves had classified as prototypically representing the six emotions claimed to be universal to consultants in various cultures and speech communities.[2]

Research on emotions and their facial expression has a relatively long tradition, but it has always been a highly controversial topic (see, e.g. Eibl-Eibesfeldt 1989: 450ff.; the controversy between Ekman 1994 and Russell 1994; also Izard and Saxton 1988). A rather strong argument against Ekman's approach starts with the observation that emotions are not just displayed by means of facial expressions; on the contrary, the expression of emotions and inner feelings is manifest in complex behaviour patterns which control and regulate not only facial expressions, but also posture and position of the body, muscular tonus, gesture, speech utterances, voice, pitch, personal distance between interactors, eye-contact or its avoidance, skin temperature, pulse rate, etc. Some of the expressive motor patterns that constitute these behaviour patterns are 'fixed action patterns', which are innate – as proven in research on the expressive behaviour of deaf-and-blind-born children, however, many other of these behaviour patterns are ritualized in culture-specific ways. Even if we accept Ekman's claim that there is a set of basic emotions, these basic emotions are expressed not just in the face, but in much more complex interactional behaviour patterns – which may have even evolved into (ritualized) interaction strategies (see Eibl-Eibesfeldt 1973a, 1989: 466, 492, 520f., 546f.). Therefore, photographs of static facial expressions must be taken to be a rather inadequate means to elicit terms for the emotions claimed to be expressed by these 'frozen' facial expressions.

Criticism of Ekman's claims came not only from human ethologists like Eibl-Eibesfeldt and psychologists like Russell, but also from anthropologists. From this tradition of close attention to cultural detail has come severe criticism of Ekman's understanding of basic emotions as universal human traits. Anthropologists noted interesting culture-specific concepts embedded in local 'ethnopsychologies'. Rosaldo (1983), for example, showed that with the Ilongot, an ethnical group living in the Philippines, the concept *liget*, which can be glossed as 'anger', is closely tied to the intense emotions involved in headhunting (for other such examples see the contributions in Levy 1983; see also Kuipers 1998). Pilot studies on the expression of emotions in various languages that were carried out at the MPI for Psycholinguistics also indicate that Ekman's claim that facial expressions are labelled with corresponding emotion terms across languages and cultures is untenable (Senft 2009a, 2012).

There is no space here to discuss Ekman's theories about facial expressions and their universality in more detail. It must be noted, however, that whenever people display emotions and inner feelings through the complex behaviour patterns mentioned above, we are not too bad at recognizing their moods. A plausible explanation for this is that people never express their emotions and inner feelings just by facial expressions – their total behaviour provides us with a number of different cues on which we can base our hypotheses about the mood they are in.

With their Facial Action Coding System, however, Ekman and Friesen (1978) developed a useful tool for describing – but not for interpreting and explaining – facial muscle motions. In what follows I will describe the so-called 'eyebrow flash', the rapid raising of the eyebrows which has been documented on film in various cultures especially by Eibl-Eibesfeldt and his co-workers (see, e.g. Eibl-Eibesfeldt 1989: 117, 452ff.; Grammer *et al.* 1988)[3]. Eibl-Eibesfeldt describes this facial event as follows:

> It follows visual contact and is embedded within a typical sequence of behavioral patterns. Upon establishing visual contact the head is usually lifted a bit and the eyebrows are then raised for approximately 1/3 second, while a smile simultaneously spreads; as a concluding gesture the person often nods the head.
>
> (Eibl-Eibesfeldt 1989: 452f.)

Eibl-Eibesfeldt describes the various expressive functions of eyebrow raising as follows:

> The origin of rapid eyebrow raising is probably a ritualized expression of friendly recognition. It occurs in situations of congenial affection, as in thanking, consenting, flirting, greeting, agreeing, surprise, and encouraging, and thus has a broad spectrum of meanings but always within the context of contact readiness and expressing some kind of assent ... Rapid eyebrow raising is distinguished from a slower raising of the eyebrows, which is an expression of rejection and provocation ... The visual field is expanded by raising the brows and this probably leads to eyebrow raising in contexts of curiosity, surprise, and inquiry ... Finally there is the slow eyebrow raising as an expression of indignation, arrogance, social rejection and factual 'no'.
>
> (Eibl-Eibesfeldt 1989: 453ff.; see also Eibl-Eibesfeldt and Senft 1987: 30)

Eibl-Eibesfeldt notes that he could document this behaviour in mother-child interactions and in situations of friendly contact establishment in all the cultures he studied; however, he concedes that cultural differences exist. Rapid eyebrow raising as an expression of factual 'yes' occurs only in a few cultures (e.g. in Polynesia) while slow eyebrow raising as a factual 'no' is restricted to some Mediterranean people, as is well known. Greeting strangers in a friendly context with the eyebrow flash is observed in many cultures; however, in Japan it would be inappropriate for adults to greet each other in such a way. Eibl-Eibesfeldt conjectures that the origin of the eyebrow flash lies in the functional movement of opening the eyes to see better; he emphasizes, however, that this is just a hypothesis (see Eibl-Eibesfeldt 1989: 455).

Using Ekman's Facial Action Coding System, Karl Grammer and his colleagues analysed 233 events of rapid eyebrow raising in unstaged social interactions that were filmed by Eibl-Eibesfeldt in three cultures – the Eipo of West Papua, the Trobriand Islanders of Papua New Guinea and the Yanomamö Indians of the upper Orinoco in Venezuela. The ethologists observed that the pattern of muscle action was almost identical in the three cultures. Moreover, they found that the time structure of the event is similar in all three cultures:

> The eyebrow movement itself represents a marked change in the behavioural flow: after a pause in all other facial movements it typically starts with a fast onset (80ms), followed by a variable period or standstill, and from where it returns slowly to its starting point (120ms).
>
> (Grammer *et al.* 1988: 297)

Eyebrow raising appears most frequently together with smiling and upward moving of the head. Eibl-Eibesfeldt (1989: 117ff.) takes this result as a confirmation of his interpretation of the eyebrow flash as being first and foremost a form of greeting behaviour that signals 'yes to social contact'. It signals that its sender is ready and willing for interaction and encourages its recipient(s) to initiate interaction. Thus, the eyebrow flash is typically used as a ritualized form of greeting, signalling friendly openness for social contact; it contributes to establishing and maintaining a social bond between interactants. The next subsection shows that we send communicative signals not only with facial expressions, but also with our body motions, postures and positions.

3.2.2 Personal distance and body motion behaviour: Proxemics and kinesics

Ethologists have also shown that humans are both attracted to others and at the same time fear them. They refer to this kind of fear with the technical term 'social fear' and claim that 'it is alleviated with personal acquaintance but remains a principal characteristic of interpersonal behavior'. As a result, 'we maintain various degrees of greater distance between ourselves and others depending on the amount of confidence we have in the other' (Eibl-Eibesfeldt 1989: 335). It is claimed that these individual distances are learned and that they are different in different cultures.

In 1966 Edward T. Hall published his seminal article on human distance maintenance, with which he founded the discipline called 'proxemics'. He defines the discipline as 'the study of man's perception and use of space [that] deals primarily with the out-of-awareness distance-setting' (Hall 1968: 83). His research revealed that people in different cultures differ as to how much berth they give to others when interacting. Hall observed, for example, that

> Americans overseas were confronted with a variety of difficulties because of cultural differences in the handling of space. People stood "too close" during conversations, and when the Americans backed away to a comfortable conversational distance, this was taken to mean that Americans were cold, aloof, withdrawn and disinterested in the people of the country.
>
> (Hall 1968: 84)

He found that 'northern Europeans maintain a greater distance between themselves than Mediterraneans and Arabians do' (Eibl-Eibesfeldt 1989: 335). Moreover, comparing Americans with Arabs, Hall made the following observations:

> The Arab stares; the American does not. The Arab's olfactory sense is actively involved in establishing and maintaining contact. Arabs tend to stay inside the olfactory bubble of their interlocutor, Whereas Americans try to stay outside of it.
>
> (Hall 1968: 94)

He points out that such 'differences in the proxemic behaviour lead to ... "alienation in encounters"' and thus interfere with, or even terminate, verbal interactions between speakers coming from cultures with different needs for personal distance in everyday face-to-face communication. Hall summarizes his observations as follows:

> Physical contact between people, breathing on people or directing one's breath away from people, direct eye contact or averting one's gaze, placing one's face so close to another that visual accommodation is not possible, are all examples of the kind of proxemic behavior that may be perfectly correct in one culture and absolutely taboo in another.
>
> (Hall 1968: 88)

Given these observations he differentiates between 'contact' cultures and 'distance' cultures. On the basis of kinesthesia (e.g. one person has elbow room, just outside of touching distance), thermal receptors, olfaction (e.g. washed skin/hair, breath), and vision he defines for 'Americans of North European heritage' the following four distances – which vary with the relationship and acquaintance of the interactants: intimate distance (0–40cm), personal distance (40–120cm), social distance or normal, social-consultive distance (120–400cm), and public distance (400–800cm), e.g. the distance between a speaker and his audience (see Eibl-Eibesfeldt 1989: 338).

Frederick Erickson (1975: 176) found that 'changes in interpersonal distance during interaction ("proxemic shifts"...) seem to accompany changes in the topic or in the social relationship between speakers'. His analyses of filmed college counselling interviews revealed that:

proxemic shifts occur very frequently at the beginning and ending of segments of interaction that can also be identified by changes of speech content and style, and by changes in the interaction process. This suggests that proxemic shifts may function as indicators of situational shifts and topic changes in an interaction.

(Erickson 1975: 186)

Personal distances are instantiations of human territoriality. We mark personal distance as well as individual and group territories – for example with a 'jacket over a library chair' or a warning sign on one's property like 'No Trespassing', and we respect the space of others (see Eibl-Eibesfeldt 1989: 337).

Human territoriality has also implications for posture behaviour and body motion with which we control the territory that is claimed in, and for (conversational) interaction. Ray Birdwhistell (1970) refers to the study of such forms of communicative body motion behaviour (including gestures) with the term 'Kinesics'. Adam Kendon (1977) and Robert Deutsch (1977) pointed out that participants in conversation (in Europe and in Anglo-Saxon cultures) usually have visual contact and look at each other. Here conversation usually means face-to-face interaction. However, we also observe arrangements in dyadic conversations in which the 'two participants stand so that the frontal surfaces of their bodies fall on the two arms of an L' as well as side-by-side arrangements, 'where they stand close together, both facing the same way' (Kendon 1977: 183). These spatial arrangements may change in association with a change in the topic of the talk (see Kendon 1977: 192ff.). If the participants in a conversation are seated, postural changes indicate such a topic shift.

If two persons talk to each other, a third person who wants to join this dyad cannot simply intrude on such a dyad (nor can a fourth person simply intrude on a triad, etc.) – the interactants have to grant access – and they usually do this by changing their posture and position; they turn away from each other, thus opening the closed dyad and granting access to the new person (Kendon 1977: 202f.; see also Eibl-Eibesfeldt 1989: 488). Similarly, one cannot simply leave such a group; one has to mark with positional changes or with gaze behaviour that one intends to part. Kendon points out that one usually moves away from the position one had in the conversational group, then one steps back, excuses oneself for having to leave and says goodbye. Only then does one walk away, first a few steps in a direction that is different from the direction finally taken. Before one moves towards this final direction one may glance back to the group one is leaving (Kendon 1977: 203). This kind of ritualized form of leaving a group with which one had engaged in conversation is important – at least in Western cultures – 'since an abrupt departure signifies breaking off contact or the threat of such an action. This is avoided in the situation of a friendly farewell' (Eibl-Eibesfeldt 1989: 488 ff.). The reason for this behaviour is to maintain the bond with the members of the group one is leaving and to secure that one is granted access to such a group again when one wants to join it on a possible further occasion.

3.3 RITUALS, RITUAL COMMUNICATION AND INTERACTION STRATEGIES

After some general remarks on ritual and ritual communication, this subsection discusses Eibl-Eibesfeldt's ethological concept of basic interaction strategies. Analyses of little rituals of requesting, giving and taking documented in the speech community of the Eipo of West Papua and of complex forms of ritual communication during a festival celebrated by the Yanomamö illustrate the heuristic value of this paradigm for the pragmatic, anthropological-linguistic analysis of the genres discussed. The section ends with a brief summary of Levinson's ideas about a 'universal systematics of interaction' and 'building blocks for cultural diversity in social interaction' which are provided by what he calls the 'interaction engine'.

3.3.1 Some general remarks on ritual and ritual communication

The expressive movements discussed in the previous subsections are performed and perceived as indicators of a person's readiness to act. In subsection 3.2 it was pointed out that these movements have undergone distinctive differentiation in the service of signalling. In phylogenetic and cultural ritualization processes in which these signals are developed, expressive movements undergo changes that make the signals more prominent and unequivocal to improve their communicative functions: they are usually simplified and often repeated rhythmically, they get exaggerated, and they either vary with respect to their intensity or they are executed with a typical intensity. This makes the behaviour of interactants predictable – at least to a certain degree – and with this increase of the predictability of human behaviour rituals provide security and order in human interaction.

Many discussions of ritual and ritualization, such as Goffman's (1967) essays on face-to-face behaviour (see subsection 5.2 below), emphasize functional criteria. It is pointed out that one of the most important functions of rituals is to create and stabilize social relations. Social rites that serve the functions of bonding and aggression-blocking are central to the interaction of all living beings. Humans, however, do not have to rely on just non-verbal signals to develop rituals; they can also use verbal means to reach this aim.

Thus, with humans we observe not only ritualized forms of non-verbal behaviour that are used as signals in acts of communication – like, for example, the eyebrow flash and proxemic and posture behaviour in social interactions, but also ritualized forms of verbal communication. In the introduction of the anthology *Ritual Communication* the concept is defined as:

> an undertaking or enterprise involving a making of cultural knowledge within locally variant practices of speech-centered human interaction ...
>
> ... [R]itual communication is artful, performed semiosis, predominantly but not only involving speech, that is formulaic and repetitive and therefore anticipated within particular contexts of social interaction. Ritual communication thus has anticipated (but not always achieved) consequences. As performance, it is subject to evaluation by

participants according to standards defined in part by language ideologies, local aesthetics, contexts of use, and, especially, relations of power among participants.

(Basso and Senft 2009: 1)

In Senft (2009b: 81f.) it was also pointed out that anyone who wants successfully to research the role of language in social interaction must know how any society researched constructs its reality (Berger and Luckmann 1966) – one of the essentials of linguistic pragmatics. It is a prerequisite that researchers must be on 'common ground' with the community researched. However, as Goffman (see Chapter Five) notes, this essential precondition is a rather general one: Every speaker of a natural language must learn the rules of communicative behaviour that are valid for her or his speech community. In the course of this learning process, one of the most important objectives is to understand and duplicate the construction of the speech community's common social reality (and this includes discovering norms by making mistakes).

The duplicated social construction of reality must be safeguarded and secured, especially with respect to possible 'sites of fracture' such as cooperation, conflict, and competition within the community. The safeguarding of the duplicated social construction of reality is achieved partly through the ritualization of communication. The ritualization of communication can contribute to relieving tension in critical social situations and to regulating social differences and dissension by increasing the harmonizing functions of speech, by creating and stabilizing social relations, and by distancing emotions, impulses, and intentions. Ritualization of communication can increase the predictability of human behaviour; moreover, it can open up space where behaviour can be tried out without fear of social sanctions.

Therefore, one can characterize ritual communication broadly as a type of strategic action that, among many other things, helps promote social bonding, block aggression, and dispel elements of danger that might affect a community's social harmony. It acts within the verbal domain by enabling people to voice these elements of danger and bring them up for discussion (see also Eibl-Eibesfeldt and Senft 1987: 75ff.).

I will briefly illustrate this with William Labov's work on ritual insults in peer groups of Black adolescents in Harlem, New York (Labov 1972b; see also subsection 6.3 below). These rituals are duels with words. Labov not only analysed the complex structures of this quite sophisticated form of ritual communication, but also emphasized that these verbal duels strengthen solidarity between peer group members by violating American middle class norms. Moreover, they also open up sanctuaries for competition, in which individuals can test out their status with respect to the ranking of other members within the group without too much danger of being sanctioned, because of the overall tacitly understood convention that these insults are ritual ones and thus not meant personally. Possible escalations towards real forms of aggression during sessions of ritual insults can be avoided by emphasizing the non-personal character of the situation as a ritualized language game.[4]

It goes almost without saying, however, that ritual communication does not always successfully fulfil the functions described above. As Ellen Basso (p.c.) has pointed out, the duplication of the social construction of reality or the social truth of a locution does not always accord with either the speaker's or the listener's experiencing of that situation or one alluded to in the locution. However, aggression that might result from this failure is usually suppressed because of the strong general societal requirement to 'be nice', or at least to 'follow the rules', valid for the respective group, even when people do not feel that way. Thus emotions can be calmed, and voicing can be repressed. Especially a society that offers few closed personal spaces to ensure privacy for individuals depends on its members having a strong sense of tact. Houses like those of the Trobriand Islanders that are made out of bush material with leaves as 'walls' provide private space that offers visual but no auditory protection. Therefore, one sometimes has to pretend not to (over)hear and not to note things said and done in the private realm of the inside of the house, and one must learn at an early age that one does not talk about these things. The general requirement of tactful behaviour, the necessity to be nice, and the positive and successful effects of ritual communication contribute to and create social harmony.

3.3.2 The concept of basic interaction strategies

Eibl-Eibesfeldt (1989: 425–547) argues that rituals and forms of ritual communication can be referred back to so-called basic interaction strategies. He claims that all humans have a finite set of these conventionalized strategies at their disposal and assumes that these strategies are universal. Eibl-Eibesfeldt differentiates the following four interaction strategies on the basis of their function and defines and subclassifies them as follows:

1. *Strategies of group maintenance and bonding*
   The function of these strategies is to establish, develop, maintain and repair social relationships, and to maintain group harmony and group unity.
   a.) *Strategies of friendly contact initiation*
   Greeting rituals, strategies of integration
   Strategies of ... sexual approach (contact initiation, flirting)
   Strategies of play solicitation, exploration, and development of commonality
   b.) *Strategies which reinforce bonds*
   Rituals of unification (... mother–child bonding, synchronisation rituals, demonstration of sympathy ..., rituals of group aggression ..., cultivation of common values, indoctrination)
   Rituals of reciprocal care (gift giving rituals, hospitality, "grooming talk")[5]
   c.) *Strategies maintaining group harmony*
   Strategies to maintain group norms (bringing deviants into line by mocking, censure, or aggression to maintain norms)
   Strategies of pacification (mediation, conflict resolution)
   Strategies of support (support, aid)
   Strategies of making amends (reconciliation, excusing oneself, atonement, mediation)
   Strategies to avoid challenges, appeasement (tactful approach, demonstrative respect of the possession norm, rituals of recognition, such as admiration, praise, self deprecation, and other forms of appeasement)

2. *Strategies of social learning and teaching*
    a.) Strategies of social exploration (exploratory aggression, ... imitation)
    b.) Strategies of instruction (encouragement, ... demonstration)
3. *Strategies of rank striving*
    a.) Strategies of self-presentation
    b.) Strategies of rank defense
    c.) Rituals of obedience (discipline reinforcement)
4. *Strategies of fighting*
    a.) Strategies of display and bluffing
    b.) Strategies of challenging
    c.) Strategies of attack and fighting (ritual fights)
    d.) Strategies of defense
    e.) Strategies of withdrawal
    f.) Strategies of reconciliation and peace-making
    g.) Strategies of submission

(Eibl-Eibesfeldt 1989: 520f.)

He assumes that the ways people in different cultures try to acquire status, get a gift from someone, invite someone, or block aggression follow in principle the same basic patterns. On the basis of his own human-ethological field research, Eibl-Eibesfeldt concludes:

> The superficial appearance of human interactive behaviors varies enormously from culture to culture, but with closer examination we can recognize that the various strategies of social interaction share a universal pattern, based upon a universal rule system. Within this regulating system, behaviors of different origins but with similar functions can substitute for each other as functional equivalents ...
>
> ... Those things that children in all cultures express nonverbally in essentially the same way, adults translate into words, but this verbal behavior follows the same rules underlying the corresponding nonverbal interactions.

(Eibl-Eibesfeldt 1989: 522)

Thus – according to Eibl-Eibesfeldt – many rituals and forms of ritual communication can be traced back to, or at least be understood as, the differentiation of this finite set of elemental interaction strategies. Despite their richness of variation, they are just culture-specific expressions of these basic strategies. They constitute a universal system channelling social behaviour.

Rituals and forms of ritual communication can be relatively simple and mundane or highly complex and situation-specific. They can be located on a cline of structural, (con)textual, and sociocultural complexity (see Senft 2009b: 83). In what follows everyday rituals of requesting, giving and taking in the Eipo speech community in West Papua and forms of ritual communication of the Yanomamö of the upper Orinoco in Venezuela will illustrate the heuristic value of Eibl-Eibesfeldt's hypothesis for the anthropological-linguistic – and thus pragmatic[6] – analysis of ritualized types of verbal interaction.

3.3.3 Little rituals: Requesting, giving and taking in the Eipo speech community

In 1974, an interdisciplinary team of German scholars started the project 'People, Culture and Environment in the Central Highlands of West New Guinea' in which they carried out field research with the Eipo, a group of rather martial neolithic horticulturists living in the valley of the Eipomek River in the highlands of West Papua, Indonesia.[7] In 1981, Volker Heeschen, Wulf Schiefenhövel and Irenäus Eibl-Eibesfeldt published a survey on how the Eipo make requests and give and take gifts in everyday interaction and how they behave verbally and non-verbally in doing so. The survey pursues a human-ethological approach combined with anthropological-linguistic aims of inquiry; it is based on the insight that the non-verbal acts – or 'little rituals' (Haviland 2009) – of requesting, giving and taking are 'essential in the bonding processes of a small community' (Heeschen *et al.* 1981: 140). The guiding hypotheses that the authors wanted to verify (or falsify) in this article were

> that nonverbal acts are not only prerequisites, necessary accompaniments, or substitutes of language proper, but that they are means of action in their own right ... [and] ... that for human beings in general it is advantageous to have at their disposal two channels of communication: the verbal and the nonverbal. Thus human beings are enabled to require, beg, approach, and make claims, which can be hostile acts or acts provoking repulsion and aggressivity, on the one channel, while maintaining the bonding process on the other.
>
> (Heeschen *et al.* 1981: 141)

The Eipo understand comments on things they possess as containing a demand to share; therefore, such open comments on something precious must be avoided. People will share voluntarily, according to their own decision. To share is a form of behaviour that is taught to children and they learn it at an early phase in their childhood; sharing behaviour pervades everyday life in the Eipo communities. This is the reason why the Eipo proudly state '*nuun mako niinye gum* – "we are no mean people"' (Heeschen *et al.* 1981: 146).[8] Taking things away, however, is interpreted as an aggressive act; it is immediately punished (see Heeschen *et al.* 1981: 153f.).

The descriptions of the Eipos' little rituals of requesting, giving and taking are based on film documentations. In one such film the researchers make the following observations: In front of a family hut a group of girls is sitting and standing close to each other. One of the girls, 'B', is sitting on a rock, holding a pandanus-fruit that consists of hundreds of nuts. The girl picks the nuts, cracks them with her teeth, eats them or gives them away to some of the girls in the group. 'B' had just given a nut to 'W'. What follows is the minute description of what the researchers observed next:

> [A] little girl, X, of about three years of age is standing on the right side of W, watching B... and W cracking nuts. The distance between the bodies of W and X is only about 10 centimeters, but there is no skin contact. W turns her head and shoulders to the right, very shortly ... glancing at K ..., about 13 years old, who stands at the right end of the row [of girls]. Little X watching W crack the nut so close to her, raises both arms with

the intention of reaching for the nut. The stretching out movement, however, is not completed. With hands and forearms having reached chest level, X draws them back to herself thus derouting the stretching out movement into one of self-embracing. X continues to watch W crack the nut. At the same time B ..., who has just loosened another nut, turns her head and shoulders a little to the right and while cracking the nut between her teeth looks at K. With her head slightly oblique and under continuing eye-contact she offers the just-opened nut to K ... K ... reacts to this offering gesture and stretches her left arm out to reach for the nut. Little X who is now the only one in the group without food turns her head and body towards K ... looking at her with wide-open eyes. At this moment W who has just opened a nut and taken the contents out touches X in the axilla-region. X did not react to her offering the nut some seconds ago. Being touched, X turns back to W and takes the nut out of her hand. At this time all four girls are eating.

(Heeschen *et al.* 1981: 147f.)

The observed acts of requesting, giving and taking documented here were performed non-verbally. The ethologists (Heeschen *et al.* 1981: 149ff.) annotate and interpret these observations as follows: B and W are not close friends, because they do not remain in body contact with each other. Little X performs a derouted begging movement. While she stretches out her arms to beg for a nut, she becomes aware of 'the rule that one should not snatch away things from someone else' (Heeschen *et al.* 1981: 149). She deroutes her begging gesture and transforms it – in a form of displacement activity – into a self-embrace. Self-embracing usually occurs in stressful situations where one cannot seek a hold on the body of another person, a behaviour which 'provides assurance, security and comfort' (Heeschen *et al.* 1981: 149). The older girls do not demand greater shares, and the little girl begged just by 'looking, touching and proxemic shifts' (Heeschen *et al.* 1981: 151). In this way they allow B to either react to their appeals or to overlook them. The authors take these observations as evidence for the fact that '[n]onverbal behavior with its varieties in the sensory channels involved, and the subtle shades of its semantics, constitutes a well-structured system of communication in its own right' (Heeschen *et al.* 1981: 163).

The ethologists then describe an indirect verbal request directed by one man of influence to another man of status who is officially visiting his village. A makes this visit because B hosts and cares for one of A's warriors who was severely wounded during an ambush attack. After A had sat down on the village ground close to B, the two men started a conversation. After a while, B notices that A's bag is decorated with bird of paradise feathers and – while both men have eye-contact with each other – B makes the remark: '*kwelib fotong teleb,* "nice feathers of the bird-of-paradise"' (Heeschen *et al.* 1981: 151). Soon after, A bends down, unties one of the feathers from his net and hands it over to B, who takes it and thanks A with a long smile expressing his satisfaction. B takes the feather and attaches it to his bow – it is only with this bird of paradise feather decoration that the Eipo consider a bow to be complete. The decoration called *yin bata* is highly valued, because birds of paradise are not found in the Eipomek valley. The ethologists interpret this little ritual exchange as follows: The fact that B was a leading man in his village and that he cared for A's wounded warrior put him in the position in which he could make his request for a feather. By giving B the feather A – being a big man himself – not only thanked him for taking responsibility for his wounded warrior but also obliged B to himself (see Heeschen *et al.* 1981: 153).

Gifts can also relieve social tensions when groups of people meet in the Eipomek valley. The ethologists observed that a group of people from another village entered their village of residence, approaching a group of local people. The foreigners were not welcomed by greeting formulae, like *'yanmalam*, "you are coming"' (Heeschen *et al.* 1981: 152). However, they greeted the villagers with eyebrow flashes (see 3.2.1 above); then they halted at a distance from them and avoided any form of eye-contact. Silence and the absence of communicative behaviour can be interpreted as hostility. Tensions between groups that may occur in such encounters can be relieved – either by humorous remarks, or by handing over small gifts, like some tobacco or a piece of sugar cane, to the guests, which helps breaking the silence between the parties. In the case reported here the foreigners responded to this situation simply by going into the men's house. There they started to exchange little gifts with their hosts who joined them after a while. Then the bonding system started on the verbal and on the non-verbal level (see Heeschen *et al.* 1981: 152f.).

Direct requests are interpreted by the Eipo as being close to an aggressive act. They require immediate choice and answer and force the person to whom the request is directed to 'make up his [or her] mind in a minimum of time' (Heeschen *et al.* 1981: 162).

Another form of requesting consists of combining childlike and submissive appeals with verbal requests. These appeals may consist of 'lowering or heightening the voice and in prolonging the final vowel of the request' which can also be produced in a 'whimpering tone'; moreover, the requests 'occur with stretching out of the hand and stroking the chin or beard of the potential giver or with intentions to this gesture' (Heeschen *et al.* 1981: 156). These verbal requests combined with submissive, childlike and smiling behaviour can be repeated – they are generally observed with children and adolescents, but sometimes also with adults.

Indirect requests in everyday interactions (Heeschen *et al.* 1981: 156f.) usually involve a 'slow proxemic shift' of the person who wants to get something towards the potential giver. Children and adolescents prefer to sit down so close to the giver that they have skin contact. The person who wants to get something establishes eye-contact with the giver and may breathe in some air which is then exhaled with the production of the sounds *leklekana*. These sounds are usually made when the Eipo eat hot spices or when they are smoking; they indicate pleasure and delight. Heeschen *et al.* point out that these strategies are ambiguous and do not require a reaction of the person to whom this behaviour is addressed; to clarify that one wants to make a request is to combine these strategies with verbal statements like

> *naiye kwaning teleb*, 'my friend (lit.: father), a good sweet potato', *teleb tong*, 'a good smell', *kwaning fatalonmanil*, 'I have been lacking sweet potatoes', ... *fatan wik*, (I have) a big hunger', or *teleb dibmalam na mune gum se*, 'you are eating well, I am hungry'.
> (Heeschen *et al.* 1981: 157)

These verbal utterances can be made at any time, but they usually follow the non-verbal contact opening behaviour patterns. It is now the addressees' turn to decide whether they will react to these indirect non-verbal and verbal signals and give the desired objects to the addressors. Contrary to direct requests, such indirect requests do not force a decision to give upon their addressees, because 'the illocutionary force' of the utterances in these indirect requests 'is more or less hidden' (Heeschen *et al.* 1981: 157). The authors of this survey point out that these indirect forms of verbal and non-verbal behaviour are the best strategies for making successful requests, because:

> [t]hey all leave some time to the addressee of a request to choose among alternatives and to make up his mind ... the precise moment of handing over the object is up to his decision ... Indirect requests and simple statements give the next speaking turn to the addressee. Thus, while the addressee takes the turn and takes part in structuring the bonding discourse around a topic he has, again, some time to make up his mind.
>
> (Heeschen *et al.* 1981: 163f.)

The most successful strategy for timing indirect requests was some time 'after a conversation had got on its way', because '[o]nce the conversational bonding process has been managed, the equilibrium can hardly be interrupted or disturbed by a request' (Heeschen *et al.* 1981: 158).

The study of the requesting, giving and taking behaviour of the Eipo has shown that 'conversational bonding, and, consequently, the onset of conversation are the best means to guarantee non-antagonizing requesting-giving-taking encounters' (Heeschen *et al.* 1981: 163). With these insights this survey underlines Eibl-Eibesfeldt's claims with respect to the importance of group maintenance and bonding strategies in and for human social interaction.

3.3.4 Forms of ritual communication: The palm fruit festival of the Yanomamö

The Yanomamö (also known as Yanomami, Yanomama or Waika) are a group of indigenous people who live in the Amazon rainforest on the border between Venezuela and Brazil. Their language is called Yanomamö; other names are Yanomami, Yanomame, Guaica, Guaharibo and Guajaribo; the language is split into three dialects: Eastern Yanomami (or Parima), Western Yanomami (or Padamo-Orinoco) and Cobari (or Kobali, Cobariwa). Yanomami is spoken by about 11,000 people. The Yanomamö are hunters and gatherers, fishers and horticulturists who cultivate among other things plantains – a kind of cooking banana – other bananas, manioc and sweet potatoes. They used to live in village communities in what looks like a large round communal house – the *shabono* – that actually consists of a series of individual houses under a single roof with a central plaza; every family occupies a specific sector with its own fireplace within this building that is open towards the village plaza. The Yanomamö are famous because of the picturesque feathers and their body paintings with which they decorate themselves during festivities. Their traditional weapons are bow-and-arrows and they use curare to poison their arrows. Till the end of the last century they were known in anthropological circles as 'the fierce people' (Chagnon 1968) because of the chronic warfare in which they lived with their neighbours and because of the general violence that permeated their everyday life. Given this dominating role of war in their life, smaller villages could only survive if they managed to form alliances with other villages with which they entered into mutual assistance pacts. Such assistance pacts were formed and reconfirmed during festivals in which the guests received presents and were fed and entertained by their hosts. The festivals were usually celebrated when the Pijiguao palm fruit was ripe. In 1969 Eibl-Eibesfeldt documented and analysed such a palm fruit festival of the Yanomamö of the upper Orinoco. What follows is a summary of his report that was published in 1971 (Eibl-Eibesfeldt 1971a; see also Eibl-Eibesfeldt 1973b, 1989: 493 and 497ff.; and Eibl-Eibesfeldt and Senft 1987: 119ff.).

The ethologist accompanied a group of men, women and children on a visit to a neighbouring village. All men carried their arms. Shortly before they entered their hosts' *shabono* the Yanomamö decorated themselves. Men, women and children painted wave-like and circular ornaments on their bodies, some men painted their faces black and put white feathers in their hair. Many men wore bracelets made of black feathers on the upper arm in which they put white and red feathers of parrots to emphasize their strong muscles and broad shoulders. When they finished their decoration, the chief sent one of his warriors into the village to announce the group's arrival. Then the guests entered the *shabono* – one after the other, men first.

Each of the male guests danced a circle on the village plaza with their feet stomping a simple rhythm. The dancers turned left and right, showing themselves from all sides; some of them stuck out their chests and held their heads high, giving them a somewhat arrogant look. While the men danced, they made a few steps straight forward, then they turned around stomping their feet. These powerful movements were accompanied by panting and puffing to emphasize the men's physical strength. The dancers carried either bows and arrows or palm branches, presenting their weapons or their leaves in various ways. Some dancers just carried one or two palm branches, lifting and putting them down again. At times they put them on the ground and danced around them with their hands up in the sky. Some dancers waved with their bow-and-arrow, even occasionally aiming at their hosts, but without bending the bow. These dancers were usually accompanied by children who waved with their palm branches while the warriors danced.

After the men had finished their dance display, a group of women started to dance with the men and finally all the guests danced together around the plaza. Then the guests stopped dancing and visited their friends in the *shabono*, put up their hammocks in their hosts' living quarters and lay down to relax or started gossiping with their hosts.

After a while, a small group of men started to take snuff, blowing a brownish matter called 'yopo' with sticks into each other's nostrils. When the drug showed its effect, the men got up and started to dance, walking up and down and lifting their arms and imploring the help of spirits in their fights with their enemies. Thus intoxicated, the men experienced feelings of high self-esteem. This dance 'unites the warriors in joint aggression' (Eibl-Eibesfeldt 1989: 497).

Late in the afternoon the hosts also decorated themselves and danced for about half an hour in front of their guests, showing them the gifts which they would receive some time later.

In the meantime the hosts had cooked a banana soup which was eaten by all men. After this communal meal, the men started to dance around the plaza but under the roof of the *shabono* – brandishing bushknives, axes and arrows to expel malevolent spirits. After this dance the hosts and the guests came together to bewail their dead with loud cries. Meanwhile, the hosts displayed the calabashes with the ashes of their deceased loved ones. By now night had fallen. After the bewailing of the dead in another demonstration of solidarity and unity, the men gathered in groups of two and started to sing so-called 'contract' songs. During this ceremony which is called '*uayamou*', two men must crouch on the ground, face each other and confront each other with their needs and wishes. After a brief reciprocal speech, the communication develops into a more and more hectic form of ritual verbal recital that becomes increasingly incomprehensible. At the end the singers just shout snatches of conversation at each other. Usually one man is singing sentences or words and the other answers after every utterance with an affirmative grunt or another such expression. The contract songs express requests and intentions of gift giving. A Salesian missionary translated the following excerpts from such a song for the human ethologist (unfortunately Eibl-Eibesfeldt does not provide the original texts in Western Yanomami).[9]

In the song, a guest is interacting with his host. The guest starts and the host answers him after every utterance with an affirmative grunt or another such expression:

... I will speak. We are friends, I speak the truth. We are poor, because we live far away, you are rich, because you live in the vicinity of the foreign mission. Here are the Napeyomas, the Salesian nuns, and ... the lay brother Iglesias. They give you many things. We have nobody whom we could ask for things; but they give you machetes, pots, hammocks, clothes, glass-beads ... (Pause) ...

... To us Patanoueteri came the Pissasaiteri and they attacked us with bows and arrows. They are very bad and evil. They killed one of our men and my wife. I am very sad and very angry about that. You are a friend, get me a machete which you can get from the lay brother and pots which you can get from the nuns.

... I have no dog and I am very angry because of that. You have many dogs. I need one to hunt tapirs. Therefore I make this request. Give me, I pay you, then I can hunt tapirs.

... I do not want to leave this place because you are my friends. I remain in your houses in the bush. Give me a dog, even if it is skinny, I will feed it and hunt tapirs with it. You have many dogs, and you even have bitches who will get puppies, therefore give me a dog.

... (Both men embrace each other and the host responds to his guest as follows:)

I promise to give you a piece of tapir meat, because I have dogs to hunt other ones. Then you can eat platano (bananas) with meat. Moreover, I will give you the dog, so that you later can hunt and eat bananas, meat and Pijiguao (fruits).

(Eibl-Eibesfeldt 1971a: 771)

The host then requests to barter sticks and pieces of bamboo for making arrows. He explains that he needs more arrows because of the many enemies they have. With additional arrows they can unite with all their friends and fight against their enemies.

These contract songs may last up to half an hour; as mentioned above they change their character until just a hectic exchange of words is heard. The men end the contract songs by producing the polite formula 'It was a good talk, it was a beautiful talk'; then they crawl back into their hammocks. Another man can get himself involved into such a song and take it over. However, in general songs are started anew at another place with another partner. This may go on all night long – and this is one of the important ways in which personal relations of friendship are established and maintained.

Next morning a group of men and women comes together to drink the ashes of the deceased members of the *shabono*. Protected by a small number of warriors, the group is crouching around the shaman. The women hold calabashes with the ashes, they cry and sob and bewail the dead, singing songs like the following one: 'Oh my child, why have you gone? Now I have nobody to decorate with colourful feathers'. They look up into the sky and lift their hands in despair. Then they give the calabashes with the ashes to the shaman, who gets up, embraces the calabash and also starts to cry. In a singing manner he calls to the deceased's spirit, however without addressing him or her by name. After a while he pours a portion of the ashes into a calabash full of banana milk and hands it over to a warrior. All warriors receive such a portion of banana milk with the ashes of the dead and drink it.

After this ritualized bewailing of the dead some men gather at the central plaza and have another snuff of *yopo*. Rather abruptly the group starts to move through the *shabono*, waving their weapons in the way they did the day before when they warded off malevolent spirits. Then the men meet in dyadic groups again and continue to sing contract songs and embracing each other.

In the meantime, the women have put banana leaves on the ground of the plaza on which they had put baskets full of Pijiguao fruits, smoked monkeys, birds, armadillos and other such foodstuffs as presents for the guests. After the distribution of these gifts the hosts request countergifts and receive pieces of cloth, pots and machetes. With these gift distributions the palm fruit festival comes to its end.

From an ethological point of view these complex forms of ritual communication are analysed as follows: Feasts and festivals have an important group bonding function: 'As a binding rite the festival established and enforced friendly relations between hosts and guests' (Eibl-Eibesfeldt 1971a: 777). Individuals and even village groups made friends with each other, existing relationships were confirmed and maintained. The interacting groups and individuals emphasized their peaceful intentions. However, when the male guests danced into their host's *shabono* introducing themselves, they performed aggressive display behaviour which can easily provoke aggression. But this behaviour was appeased by appeals by children and adults who did not wear arms but green palm branches (a symbol of peace in many cultures). Appeasing appeals with regard to children are also found in other cultures – children obviously manifest signals to which adults react in a friendly way – thus they are perfect agents of peacemaking and bonding. One wonders, however, why the Yanomamö warriors show this aggressive display, given the fact that they are aware of the fact that what is needed is appeasement. It seems to be a general feature of contact situations that the parties involved boast and show off. During official state visits, politicians are greeted with salutes and with rows of soldiers presenting their weapons. This form of self-presentation is probably intended to show one's fitness to fight and to point out that one is – or could be – a valuable ally in conflicts. Even handshakes contain such a component of boasting physical strength.

Communal meals constitute another important bonding ritual – offering food is a friendly gesture in contact situations and helps to establish good relationships with others; it has appeasing functions, too. The meals shared by both hosts and guests are an important ritual that enhances the bonding function of the social encounters during the palm fruit festival. The same holds for a number of other rituals, like the exchange of gifts, the joint expelling of malevolent spirits, which demonstrates the readiness of both hosts and guests to join each other in fighting a common enemy, and the common mourning rituals, in which the mourners demonstrate that they are willing to share each other's joys and sorrows in life. All these forms of behaviour reinforce the bond between visitors and hosts.

The conversations of the Yanomamö that are ritualized into antiphonies are of special interest. The principle 'you give me something, I give you something' is constitutive for these contract songs. In the example mentioned above the guest starts his song by pointing out how poor his life is in comparison to that of his host who can rely on support by the mission. The guest then informs his host about his recent calamities and his sorrow caused by attacking enemies who killed his wife. With this sad news he elicits sympathy in the host. The guest is seeking pity and compassion to check whether he is synchronized with his host. If this is the case, the interactants have established a general feeling of harmony between each other which constitutes the basis for a successful contract song. On this common basis, created during these first moments of an encounter, interactants realize that they are willing to understand each other in the conversation to follow. The developing conversation is gradually ritualized into antiphonies that provide a special frame for making requests which may otherwise be too direct, impolite and embarrassing and it offers the receiver of these requests a forum in which he can show his generosity and his willingness to keep up his friendship with his partner in the contract song. The fact that at the end of these contract songs the antiphonies change into unintelligible but coordinately alternating fragmentary verbal utterances indicates that this specific form of communication at this phase of the interaction no longer conveys any information of whatever kind; it now just signals harmony, synchrony and a strong friendly bond between the singers. The success of the song presented above is demonstrated by the partners' embrace, by the hosts' gifts and by the guests' readiness to engage with them in barter. Thus, the contract songs during the palm fruit festival constitute an important bonding ritual that is existential for the survival of smaller village groups in a general atmosphere of violence and aggression created by the chronic warfare in which they lived with their neighbours.

This festival – like many other rituals of friendly encounter (like, for example, complex greeting rituals) – is structured in the following way (see also Eibl-Eibesfeldt 1989: 498):

First there is an opening phase with a strong greeting component. In this phase, which constitutes the opening of friendly contact without components of submission, we observe rituals of self-presentation, of bonding and of appeasement as well as aggressive display behaviour combined with appeasing appeals that function as signals of peacemaking and bonding.

Then there is a phase of reinforcing bonding which serves as a basis for factual contracts. In this phase we observe avowals of mutual sympathy and harmony in verbal interactions and solidarity expressed in communal actions, joint meals and dances as well as communal mourning and staged fighting behaviour.

Finally, there is a phase of bidding farewell which contributes to securing the established and reinforced bonds. In this phase we observe the exchange of gifts, good wishes for the future and the affirmation of mutual trust, consent, agreement and continuing solidarity.

This analysis of the complex forms of ritual communication that are enacted during the palm fruit festival of the Yanomamö illustrates the explanatory power of human-ethological concepts and insight with regard to pragmatic analyses of verbal and non-verbal behaviour in forms of ritual communication in social interactions.

3.3.5 The human 'interaction engine'

In 2006 Stephen Levinson presented his human 'interaction engine' hypothesis; he claimed that:

> the roots of human sociality lie in a special capacity for social interaction, which itself holds the key to human evolution, the evolution of language, the nature of much of our daily concerns, the building blocks of social systems, and even the limitations of our political systems.
>
> (Levinson 2006: 39)

He supported this claim of the (at least partial) independence of human interactional abilities from language and culture by pointing out:

- that we can interact without language simply by using 'mime and gesture' even in first contact situations (see Connolly and Anderson 1987),
- that infants interact with each other 'long before they speak',
- that interaction does not disappear when language is lost,
- that there 'is some evidence for a distinct "social intelligence" ... from inherited deficits and neurological case studies',
- that speakers can switch languages 'midstream in interaction ... leaving the interactional framework undisturbed',
- that ethnographic research reveals a 'cultural shaping of all the modalities of interaction',
- that cross-linguistic and cross-cultural research on the structure of conversations indicate that there is a 'shared universal framework for verbal interaction', and
- that contrary to other primates humans invest a large 'amount of time and effort ... in interaction'.

> (see Levinson 2006: 40ff.)

On the basis of these observations Levinson put forward

> the proposal that, from an ethological point of view, humans have a distinctive, pan-specific pattern of interaction with conspecifics, marked by (1) intensity and duration, (2) specific structural properties, and (3) those properties separable from the language with which it is normally conducted.
>
> (Levinson 2006: 42)

For Levinson – who explicitly takes an ethological point of view at the start of his developing argument – interaction has absolute priority over language (which is only later integrated into the interaction engine in language- and culture-specific ways). He argues that 'humans did not evolve language, then get involved in a special kind of social life ... [L]anguage must have evolved *for* something for which there was already a need – that is, for communication in interaction' (Levinson 2006: 42; see also 53f.).

By excluding the observed diversity of languages and cultures, Levinson joins the human ethologists' universalist position in claiming that 'there has to be some powerful meaning-making machinery that we all share'. With this position he comes close to Eibl-Eibesfeldt's claim quoted above that despite the huge variety of human forms of interactive behaviours they can all be reduced to a limited number of universal and elementary human social interaction strategies (see Eibl-Eibesfeldt 1989: 522). Levinson's discussion of cultural variation in forms of human interaction seems to mirror this ethological claim:

> This idea – that the local, cultural specialization is a variation of a universal theme – is potentially powerful, because as we learn more about conversational organization we see that there are relatively few, crucial organization principles.
>
> (Levinson 2006: 61)

However, Levinson also combines ethological claims and insights with findings in anthropology, in linguistics, especially in Conversation Analysis (see subsection 5.4 below), and in other cognitive sciences when he presents his idea 'in a nutshell':

> [H]umans are natively endowed with a set of cognitive abilities and behavioral dispositions that synergistically work together to endow human face-to-face interaction with certain special qualities. I call these elements collectively the human *interaction engine* (which is meant to suggest both dedicated mental machinery and motive power, i.e., both "savvy" and "oomph") ... What I am entertaining is that there are underlying universal properties of human interaction that can be thought of as having a cognitive-and-ethological foundation.
>
> (Levinson 2006: 44)

This 'interaction engine' makes it possible to interpret and even predict the behaviour of others and thus allows interactants to attribute intentions to their respective interlocutors. It allows 'us to simulate the other simulating us', and to recognize and understand intentions (Levinson 2006: 54). This is one of the crucial prerequisites for cooperative interaction (see Clark 1996a: 191ff.). However, Levinson (2006: 56) emphasizes that 'the interaction engine is not to be understood as an invariant, a fixed machine with fixed output, but as a set of principles that can interdigitate with local principles, to generate different local flavors'.

Thus, this set of basic organizing principles 'provides the building blocks for cultural diversity in social interaction ... it provides the parameters for variation with default values that account for the surprising commonalities in the patterns of informal interchange across cultures'.

Put differently, the enormous variety of human interaction observed in different cultures can be attributed to and explained by a few organizing principles. Levinson's idea that a 'core interaction engine [drives] human social life' (Levinson 2006: 62) is certainly a daring, but also an extremely interesting and fascinating hypothesis with important consequences for linguistic pragmatics (and semantics). However, like Eibl-Eibesfeldt's claim for universal human interaction strategies, Levinson's interaction engine hypothesis requires a vast amount of empirical and comparative research to be verified – or falsified (see Senft 2009b: 99). Nevertheless, both these hypotheses highlight the fact that the study of language use is a transdisciplinary enterprise that must be guided by the insight that language use is just a part – although a very important one – of human interaction which is fundamentally multimodal in nature.

3.4 CONCLUDING REMARKS

This chapter introduced the human-ethological concept of expressive movements that are differentiated in such a way that they function as communicative signals. These signals are very important for social interaction because they allow one to make predictions about an individual's disposition and her or his intentions and actions. A special form of these signals are facial expressions which have been researched ever since Darwin and his contemporaries. The claim of Ekman and his colleagues, who argue – in Darwin's tradition – that there are universal facial expressions of emotions that are recognized in every culture and expressed with the same emotional terms in all languages was rejected on ethological, anthropological and linguistic grounds. However, Ekman's research has resulted in the development of a tool for describing facial muscle motions and has turned out to be extremely useful for researching facial expressions like the eyebrow flash. After a description of the various functions of this eyebrow raising it was shown that its form was almost identical in different cultures; moreover, in these cultures this signal communicates first and foremost a person's openness for social contact. Besides facial expressions we also send communicative and interactional signals with our territorial behaviour which is expressed in personal distances and forms of positional behaviour. Being aware of the fact that facial expressions are important signals in face-to-face communication, that there are culture-specific needs to maintain distance in interactions and that interactants signal their readiness (or unwillingness) to open their group to a third party are important aspects for understanding communicative behaviour and culturally appropriate forms of language use. Realizing the importance of these ritualized and culture-specific forms of expressive behaviour that frame the situative context of verbal interactions is necessary to be able to adequately engage and participate in such interactions. Familiarity with these forms of ritualized behaviour patterns is the prerequisite for getting access to a group of interlocutors engaged in conversation and for establishing and maintaining a bond that guarantees the possibility of further interaction with members of this speech community. After a general discussion of ritual and the process of ritualization in which expressive movements are developed into communicative interactional signals, the concept of 'ritual communication' was defined as 'artful, performed semiosis, predominantly but not only involving speech, that is formulaic and repetitive and therefore anticipated within particular contexts of social interaction' (Basso and Senft 2009: 1). It was pointed out that human ethologists like Eibl-Eibesfeldt trace rituals and ritual communication back to a finite set of universal interaction strategies. Interaction strategies in ritual communication were illustrated with the results of a study of the 'little' rituals constituted by the requesting, giving and taking behaviour of the Eipo and with an analysis of the complex palm fruit festival of the Yanomamö; it was shown that the previously introduced human-ethological concept of interaction strategies provides additional strength to pragmatic analyses of verbal – and non-verbal – behaviour in social interactions. The chapter ended with a brief sketch of Levinson's idea of a human 'interaction engine' that consists of a set of basic principles which organize human interaction and drive social life. Levinson argues that the enormous variety of forms of human interaction in different cultures can be attributed to and explained by a few of these principles. The hypothesis about the existence of universal interaction strategies as well as the interaction engine hypothesis are extremely interesting and fascinating, however, much research is needed to verify or falsify them. Nevertheless, these hypotheses emphasize that the study of language use is a transdisciplinary enterprise guided by the insight that human interaction is fundamentally multimodal.

What does this chapter tell us about the anecdote reported in the introduction to this volume? It reveals that I was unable to read the Trobriand Islanders' body language which signalled that more was at issue when they greeted me with the question 'Where do you go'? Their greeting was always accompanied by an eyebrow flash, a greeting which I returned (the eyebrow flash as a form of greeting is ubiquitous on the Trobriands), but – being unaware of the complexity of this greeting ritual as a socially important bonding and bond-reinforcing form of ritual communication I did not properly respond to this offer for a brief verbal interaction in which I was meant to answer the question in a proper way. I just naively and in a rather ethnocentric way interpreted this culture-specific form of greeting as being equivalent to a casual Western form of greeting like 'Hello' or 'Hi'.

3.5 EXERCISE/WORK SECTION

- Discuss and explain the function of (at least six) expressive movements in your culture that have developed into signals in processes of phylogenetic and cultural ritualization.

- What are your assumptions about which complex behaviour patterns are involved in expressing the emotions 'fear', 'anger', 'happiness' and 'sadness' and what is the communicative function of these expressive patterns?

- Let one of your friends videotape you at a party or a meeting in which you do not respect the norms of personal distance that are valid in your culture. Report on the verbal and non-verbal reactions of your interlocutors and the influence of too far away and too close personal distances in your dyadic conversations.

- Observe the verbal and non-verbal behaviour of people when they enter a lift, when they go up and down with it and when they leave it. Explain why these forms of behaviour can be interpreted as signals.

- Videotape groups of people at a party. Describe how individuals try to join an ongoing conversation and how the interactants in this conversation react verbally and non-verbally – especially with their posture and position – to this attempt.

- Use a documentation of a TV talk show on the internet and describe the coordination of the interactants' forms of verbal and non-verbal behaviour. Explain which of these forms of interaction are forms of ritual communication.

- Participate as an observant in a funeral ceremony/a church service/a festive occasion and describe which verbal and non-verbal forms of ritual communication you notice. Explain your observations on the basis of their interactive communicative functions and elaborate on the interactional strategies that may underlie these forms of ritual communication.

- Observe your personal forms of greeting behaviour and those of your friends, colleagues and acquaintances and explain observed differences from a linguistic, sociological and ethological point of view.

3.6 SUGGESTIONS FOR FURTHER READING

Baron-Cohen (2003); Batic (2011); Eibl-Eibesfeldt (1979, 1996); Harré (1988); Hassall (1999); Levinson and Jaisson (2006); Lorenz (1977); Russell and Fernández-Dols (1997); Sauter *et al.* (2010, 2011); Scheflen (1964); Schmitt *et al.* (1997); von Cranach *et al.* (1979); Wilce (2009).

NOTES

1   Pupils briefly dilate when something stimulates our interest and they contract when we perceive something we reject (see Eibl-Eibesfeldt 1989: 444).

2   For the photographs that depict these emotions see Ekman and Friesen (1975: 175–201). To mention just one piece of counterevidence to the claim that these photos depict universally recognizable emotions: Stephen Levinson (p.c.) reports that the photograph for 'disgust' which depicts a pronounced nose-wrinkling is understood by the Rossel Islanders of Papua New Guinea as expressing either 'conventional surprise' or 'not-wanting'.

3   Ekman (1979: 187) categorizes the eyebrow flash as a 'conversational signal', which he differentiates from emotional signals.

4   See also Dundes *et al.* (1972); Goffman (1961: 58f.). For a survey and reinterpretation of ritualized verbal duels across the world, see Pagliai (2009).

5   See also subsection 4.2 below.

6   William Foley (1997: 29) states that 'the boundary between pragmatics and anthropological linguistics or sociolinguistics is impossible to draw at present'.

7   For a review of the project and its results, see Ploeg (2004). The community studied consisted of about 400 speakers.

8   The language of the Eipo is also called Eipo. It belongs to the Mek language family which is integrated into the Trans New Guinea family of Papuan languages. The Mek languages are spoken by about 3,000 speakers. See Heeschen (1998).

9   The translation from German to English is mine (G. S.).

4

Pragmatics and ethnology

The interface of language, culture and cognition

4.1 INTRODUCTION

In his textbook on *Anthropological Linguistics*, published in 1997, William Foley explicitly states that 'the boundary between pragmatics and anthropological linguistics or sociolinguistics is impossible to draw at present' (Foley 1997: 29). A look at the history of anthropological linguistics from the days of Johann Gottfried Herder (1744–1803) and Wilhelm von Humboldt (1767–1835) to the present reveals that these disciplines have always been very close to each other (see Senft 2009c). This chapter deals with the interrelationship of language, culture and cognition.

One of the anthropologists whose linguistic insights became extremely influential in pragmatics was Bronislaw Malinowski (1884–1942). The first part of this chapter presents his ideas about context and meaning and his concept of 'phatic communion' which he developed during his field research on the Trobriand Islands in Papua New Guinea. Malinowski's concept of phatic communion is critically assessed and illustrated with phatic expressions in Korean.

Then – in connection with Edward Sapir's (1884–1939) and Benjamin Lee Whorf's (1897–1941) linguistic relativity hypothesis – the interrelationship of language, culture and cognition will be further discussed and illustrated with cross-cultural research on conceptions of space and frames of spatial reference in various languages.

The third part of this chapter on the influence of ethnology on pragmatics presents a discussion of Dell Hymes's (1927–2009) and John Gumperz's (1922–2013) ethnography of speaking paradigm with illustrations from Joel Sherzer's research on the *Kuna Ways of Speaking.*

4.2 PHATIC COMMUNION

Bronislaw Malinowski is generally recognized as one of the founders of social anthropology, transforming nineteenth century speculative anthropology into a field-oriented science that is based on empirical research. Malinowski is principally associated with his field research on the Trobriand Islanders' culture. However, he must also be mentioned as one of the apologists, pioneers and founding fathers of anthropological linguistics as a discipline in its own right.[1] As early as 1920 he made the claim that 'linguistics without ethnography would fare as badly as ethnography without the light thrown in it by language' (Malinowski 1920: 78).[2]

Malinowski became interested in linguistics when he found that he could not realize his project of writing a grammar of Kilivila because he had no linguistic training and because he was convinced that the grammatical categories offered by the linguistic theories of his time did not fit for the description of a language like Kilivila (Malinowski 1920: 74). In 1920 he explicitly stated the following:

> there is an urgent need for an Ethno-linguistic theory, a theory for the guidance of linguistic research to be done among natives and in connexion with ethnographic study... A theory which, moreover, aims not at hypothetical constructions – 'origins', 'historical developments', 'cultural transferences', and similar speculations – but a theory concerned with the intrinsic relation of facts. A theory which in linguistics would show us what is essential in language and what therefore must remain the same throughout the whole range of linguistic varieties; how linguistic forms are influenced by physiological, mental, social, and other cultural elements; what is the real nature of Meaning and Form, and how they correspond; a theory which, in fine, would give us a set of well-founded plastic definitions of grammatical concepts.
>
> (Malinowski 1920: 69)

Malinowski's linguistic interests 'centered on language as a mode of behavior and on problems of culturally determined meaning' (Métraux 1968: 524). He developed his ethnographic theory of language mainly in connection with his attempts to translate the Trobriand Islanders' magical formulae. Malinowski realized that the Trobriand Islanders believed in the power of the words in the magical formulae: they used these formulae to reach certain aims with the firm conviction that they could thus influence and control nature and the course of, and events in, their lives. Thus, in the domain of magic language is doing something, it has certain effects, it has power and force. Malinowski (1922: 432) summarized this observation as follows: 'Magic is ... an instrument serving special purposes, intended for the exercise of man's specific power over things, and *its meaning* ... can be understood only in correlation to this aim'. For him 'it is the use of words which invoke, state, or command the desired aim' (Malinowski 1974: 74). Thus, Malinowski explicitly equates meaning with pragmatic function. He characterized his – pragmatic – theory of meaning as a theory that insists on the

> linking up of ethnographic descriptions with linguistic analysis which provides language with its cultural context and culture with its linguistic interpretation. Within this latter ... [I have] ... continually striven to link up grammar with the context of situation and with the context of culture.
>
> (Malinowski 1935: 73)

For Malinowski (as well as for Wittgenstein, by the way) the meaning of a word lies in its use. Thus, to study meaning one cannot examine isolated words but one must consider sentences or utterances in their situative context: 'the real understanding of words is always ultimately derived from active experience of those aspects of reality to which the words belong' (Malinowski 1935: 58). For Malinowski 'the real linguistic fact is the full utterance within its context of situation' (Malinowski 1935: 11). Thus, meaning is function within context.[3] This 'context theory' of meaning is based on a rather broad definition of the concept of context: Malinowski points out

> that it is very profitable in linguistics to widen the concept of context so that it embraces not only spoken words but facial expression, gesture, bodily activities, the whole group of people present during an exchange of utterances and the part of the environment in which these people are engaged.
>
> (Malinowski 1935 vol. II: 22; see also pp. 26, 30, 40)

Malinowski (1936: 296, 309ff.) illustrates how the meaning of utterances can be determined in what he calls 'the essential primitive uses of speech: speech in action, ritual handling of words, the narrative, "phatic communion" (speech in social intercourse)'.[4] The last of these four types of language use which are fundamental for Malinowski needs some brief comments. Discussing language used in what he calls 'free, aimless social intercourse', like greeting formulae, passing inquiries about someone's health, comments on the weather, and comments on what is obvious Malinowski points out the following:

> to a natural man another man's silence is not a reassuring factor, but on the contrary, something alarming and dangerous ... The breaking of silence, the communion of words is the first act to establish links of fellowship, which is consummated only by the breaking of bread and the communion of food. The modern English expression, 'Nice day to-day' or the Melanesian phrase 'Whence comest thou?' are needed to get over the strange unpleasant tension which men feel when facing each other in silence.
>
> After the first formula, there comes a flow of language, purpose-less expressions of preference or aversion, accounts of irrelevant happenings, comments on what is perfectly obvious ...
>
> There can be no doubt that we have a new type of linguistic use – *phatic communion* I am tempted to call it ... – a type of speech in which ties of union are created by a mere exchange of words. ... Are words in Phatic Communion used primarily to convey meaning, the meaning which is symbolically theirs? Certainly not! They fulfil a social function and that is their principal aim, they are neither the result of intellectual reflection, nor do they necessarily arouse reflection in the listener. ... Each utterance is an act serving the direct aim of binding hearer to speaker by a tie of some social sentiment or other. Once more, language appears to us in this function not as an instrument of reflection but as a mode of action ...
>
> ... 'phatic communion' serves to establish bonds of personal union between people brought together by the mere need of companionship and does not serve any purpose of communicating ideas.
>
> (Malinowski 1936: 313ff.)

After this definition of the concept 'phatic communion' he emphasizes again his main position with respect to language:

[L]anguage in its primitive function and original form has an essentially pragmatic character; ... it is a mode of behaviour, an indispensable element of concerted human action ... to regard it as a means for the embodiment or expression of thought is to take a one-sided view of one of its most derivate and specialized functions.

(Malinowski 1936: 316)[5]

Malinowski's concept of 'phatic (from Greek *phatos*, 'spoken') communion' highlights the 'bonding function' of language. Konrad Ehlich (1993: 317) interprets Malinowski's use of the word 'communion' with its religious connotation as a means for emphasizing the intensity of this type of speech. Malinowski's concept was borrowed and slightly modified by Roman Jakobson (1960) in his expansion of Karl Bühler's (1934) organon model of language to refer 'to that function of language which is channel-oriented in that it contributes to the establishment and maintenance of communicative contact' (Lyons 1977: 53f.). It is quite likely that, because of Jakobson's influential article, most linguists and anthropologists nowadays refer to Malinowski's concept with the technical term 'phatic communication'. However, the term 'phatic communication' is not synonymous with the term 'phatic communion'. As Adam Kendon (p.c.) points out, the term 'phatic communication' is probably used because people tend to forget the more general meaning of the term 'communion'; it is precisely that achievement of 'rapport' through the use of speech – a kind of communion, indeed – that Malinowski emphasized, and this is different from what is often thought to be the meaning of 'communication'.

To summarize, the term phatic communion is generally used to refer to utterances that are said to have exclusively social bonding functions like establishing and maintaining a friendly and harmonious atmosphere in interpersonal relations, especially during the opening and closing stages of social encounters.

Desmond Morris (1978: 82) described phatic communion as 'grooming talk' (see also subsection 3.3.2); this grooming-like function of phatic communion is central to Robin Dunbar's theory on the origin of language. Dunbar proposes that

> language evolved to service social bonds in a more generic sense by providing a substitute for social grooming, the main mechanism that our fellow primates use for bonding social relationships ... For humans, as with all primates, effectively bonded social groups are essential for successful survival and reproduction, and since grooming has a natural limit on the size of group that can be bonded by it, language was necessary to break through this glass ceiling and allow larger groups to evolve.
>
> (Dunbar 2009: 14; see also 1993)

It is obvious that Malinowski heavily emphasizes the bonding function of phatic communion. In his definition of the concept he explicitly mentioned 'the Melanesian phrase "Whence comest thou?"' (Malinowski: 1936: 314) as a prototypical example for phatic communion. The anecdote reported at the very beginning of this volume topicalizes exactly this greeting behaviour of the Trobriand Islanders. However, it shows that this Melanesian phrase conveys more than just the social function of creating a bond between speaker and addressee; as a binding ritual it certainly signals security within the whole social network of the community in which this greeting formula is used, but it may also initiate exchanges that can be rather rich in information.

There is thus often more behind an utterance which is said to serve only a phatic function. This observation also holds for a number of studies that explicitly deal with the concept of phatic communion. Thus, in his anthology *Conversational Routine* we find a contribution by Florian Coulmas on Japanese in which he emphasizes that although 'most apologies observed in everyday interaction' seem to be 'desubstantialized routines with no semantic content, merely functioning as means of "phatic communion"' the situation is more complex: 'the functionally similar employment of apology and gratitude expressions must be seen as a significant reflection of social values and attitudes prevailing in Japanese culture' (Coulmas 1981: 87).

In the same volume, John Laver points out that the 'linguistic behavior of conversational routines, including greetings and partings, as well as please, thanks, excuses, apologies and small talk, is part of the linguistic repertoire of politeness' (Laver 1981: 290). Discussing utterances of phatic communion, he finds that besides the two social functions already mentioned by Malinowski – that is to 'defuse the potential hostility of silence' and to allow participants in a social verbal encounter 'to cooperate in getting the interaction comfortably under way' – these linguistic routines also have a third and probably more important function in the initial phase of conversation: 'phatic communion ... allows the participants to feel their way towards the working consensus of their interaction ... partly revealing their perception and their relative social status' (Laver 1981: 301).

In an earlier, and most important paper for the discussion of Malinowski's concept, Laver (1975: 217) elaborates on all 'communicative functions of phatic communion' in detail – based on data from English-speaking cultures. In this paper, he first points out that 'the fundamental function of the ... communicative behavior that accompanies and includes phatic communion is the detailed management of interpersonal relationships during the psychologically crucial margins of interactions'. This communicative behaviour includes 'posture, body orientations, gesture, facial expression and eye contacts' and is more than 'a mere exchange of words' as Malinowski described it (Laver 1975: 232). Laver then describes and analyses the functions of utterances and other communicative forms of behaviour that are claimed to represent phatic communion in the opening and closing phases of interaction, especially with respect to the transition phases from 'noninteraction to full interaction' – in which phatic communion establishes contact between the interactants – and from 'interaction back to noninteraction' – in which phatic communion achieves a cooperative parting and helps secure the established bonds between the interactants (Laver 1975: 232).[6] In the opening phase of an interaction Laver (1975: 223) differentiates three different 'tokens' with which phatic communion is initiated: neutral tokens, like a description ('Terrible night last night') or talking about the weather ('Nice day'), self-oriented tokens usually in the form of declarative statements ('Hot work this') and other-oriented tokens usually presented as questions ('Do you come here often?'). In the opening phase of an interaction, phatic communion has the function 'to lubricate the transition from noninteraction to interaction, and to ease the potentially awkward tension of the early moments of the encounter, "breaking the ice", so to speak' (Laver

1975: 218). Laver claims that the choice of the tokens used 'establish and consolidate the interpersonal relationship between ... participants' in terms of status and solidarity (Laver 1975: 236). In the closing phase of an interaction, Laver (1975: 230) argues, phatic communion has the function of 'assuaging the noninitiating participant' ('I'm sorry, I have to go') and to consolidate 'the relationship between the ... interactants' ('Take care, now').

Laver points out that '[s]kill in managing the behavioral resources of phatic communion ... [is] ... a very basic skill essential to a major part of the psychosocial transactions that make up daily life' (Laver 1975: 233). He summarizes his discussion of phatic communion as follows:

> [P]hatic communion is a complex part of a ritual, highly skilled mosaic of communicative behavior whose function is to facilitate the management of interpersonal relationships. The information exchanged between the participants in this communicative process is not primarily referential information, but rather is indexical information about aspects of the participants' social identity relevant to structuring the interactional consensus of the present and future encounters. The function of phatic communion thus goes beyond the creation, in Malinowski's phrase, of 'ties of union': it certainly does serve to establish such broad ties in that the tokens of phatic communion are tokens exchanged in the ritual transactions of psychosocial acceptance, but it also provides the participants with a subtle tool for use in staking indexical claims which shape and constrain their detailed relationship in the crucial marginal phases of encounters when their psychological comfort is most at risk.
>
> (Laver 1975: 236)

In what follows the concept of phatic communion is further illustrated with examples from Korean.

Duk-Soo Park (2006: 156–162) presents the phatic expressions quoted below which are used in opening and closing phases of Korean conversations. He differentiates between greetings used in the conversation opening phase, flattering, humble and neutral expressions used in the opening or in the medial phase of conversation and expressions used in the closing phase of a conversation. Park's examples (1) and (2) are Korean greetings:

(1) *Yoyŭm saŏb-ŭn chal toe-sijiyo?*
'Is your business doing well these days?'
Ne, tŏkpun-e (chal toe-mnida).
'Yes (it is), thanks to you.'

Greetings like this elicit positive responses; Park points out that the worst response one could get after greeting people by inquiring after their or their family's well-being or after their business will be *kŭjŏ kŭraeyo* 'so-so'.

(2) *Ŏdi ka-seyo?*
lit., 'Are you going somewhere?'

Ne, ŏdi ka-yo. Ŏdi ka-seyo?
lit., 'Yes, I am. Are you going somewhere?'

This form of greeting is similar to the Trobriand Islanders' greeting '*Ambe?*', however, the Korean question has a completely different function than the Melanesian phrase 'Whence comest thou?'. Park points out that the greeting

> *ŏdi ka-seyo?* 'Hi!' (*lit.*, Are you going somewhere?) often creates a great deal of confusion for foreigners. Since *ŏdi* can be 'where' as well as 'somewhere', it can be interpreted as 'Where are you going?' I personally have encountered many foreigners, who had been in Korea for a considerable length of time, wondering why Koreans are so keen to know other people's destinations when they meet on the street. Obviously, it is a misunderstanding of the utterance: Koreans do not ask for your destination by saying 'Hi!' and even if we are allowed to interpret the utterance literally, it is a yes-or-no question, not a WH-question. What you have to say in response is *ne, ŏdi ka-yo* 'Yes, I am going somewhere', *ne, ŏdi ka-seyo* 'Yes (I am), are you going somewhere?' or even *ne, annyŏngha-seyo?* 'Yes, I am, how are you?'
>
> (Park 2006: 157)

Park's example (3) presents 'a fixed, foolproof ritual of phatic communion ... strangers should follow ... in a formal business setting':

(3) A: *Ch'ŏŭm poep-kessŭmnida. Chŏ-nŭn KBS-ŭi A i-mnida.*
         'Nice to meet you. (*lit.*, I see you for the first time). I am A from KBS.'
     B: *Ne, ch'ŏŭm poep-kessŭmnida. MBC-ŭi B i-mnida.*
         'Nice to meet you. I am B from MBC.'
     A: *Chal put'ak tŭri-mnida.*
         'I request your guidance.'
     B: *Wŏn pyŏl malssŭm-ŭl (ta ha-simnida). Che-ga put'ak tŭry-ŏyajo.*
         'You shouldn't have said that. I am the one who should ask for your guidance.'

Park points out that the verbal frame of this ritualized phatic formula is more or less meaningless, what matters in such an encounter are the names of the persons and the names of the companies represented by the interactants.

Park's example (4) presents a flattering expression which makes use of 'elevated other-oriented tokens such as the listeners themselves, or their children, property or food'. These compliments are made when people visit each other.

(4) *Chŏgŏdo sim-nyŏn-ŭn chŏlm-ŏ poi-simnida.*
     'You look at least ten years younger.'

Park's example (5) illustrates the ritual a Korean speaker follows when one gives and receives a gift:

(5) A: *Igŏ pyŏlgŏ ani-jiman pad-a chu-seyo.*
         'This is nothing special, but please accept it from me.'

B: *Wŏn pyŏl kŏ-l ta kajy-ŏ o-syŏssŭmnida. Kŭrŏm, yŏmch'i ŏp-chiman pat-kessŭmnida.*
'You shouldn't have brought this. (*lit.*, You even brought something special) Then, although it is shameless of me, I will accept it.'

A presents the gift with the 'humble self-oriented token' – 'nothing special' – while B finally accepts the gift; the reference to this 'shameless behaviour' represents 'a humble self-oriented token'. Park points out that Koreans do not thank for being praised or being offered a gift immediately after they hear the praise or get the gift. It is considered impolite to accept compliments and offers right away. In these cases Koreans say 'not at all' instead of 'thank you' (*komap-sŭmnida*). Similarly, 'when they are invited for a party, they would say 'You don't have to do that, since you must be busy ...'. This is illustrated in Park's examples (6) and (7):

(6)   A: *Chib-i ch'am k'ŭ-go cho-ssŭmnida.*
'Your house is very big and nice.'
B: *Wŏn pyŏl malssŭm-ŭl ta ha-simnida.*
'Not at all.' (You said something extraordinary.)

(7)   A: *Ibŏn t'oyoir-e uri chib-esŏ chŏnyŏg-ina kach'i ha-psida.*
'This Saturday, let's have dinner together at my place.'
B: *Pappŭ-sil t'ende, kŭrŏ-siji anha-do toe-nŭndeyo ...*
'As you must be busy, you don't have to do that ...'

Park's example (8) provides a neutral, trivial token with which one can start a conversation. Park points out that such a '"weather chat" is a real ice-breaker':

(8)   *Tar-i ch'am pal-chiyo?*
'The moon is very bright, isn't it?'

Park's examples (9) and (10) illustrate 'typical closing expressions' which use 'other oriented tokens (e.g. mentioning time) or self-oriented ones (e.g. another appointment ...)':

(9)   *Ani pŏlssŏ yŏl-han si-ga twae-nne.*
'Oh, it's already 11 o'clock.'

(10)   *Chŏ-nŭn iman tarŭn yaksog-i iss-ŏsŏyo ...*
'Now, since I have another appointment ...'

An indirect speech act like the one illustrated in example (11) can also signal a speaker's intention to end the conversation:

(11)   *Sigan-ŭl nŏmu mani ppaeas-ŏsŏ choesongha-mnida.*
'I am sorry for having taken up so much of your time'.

Finally, referring to meetings in the future is another way to close interactions. Park points out that even invitations that are made in this situation – like the one illustrated in example (12) – are 'just meaningless closings remarks':

(12) *Ŏnje uri chib-e han pŏn wa-ya ha-nŭnde.*
'You should come to my place sometime.'

Park (2006: 162) includes the caveat that 'the recipient of these kinds of remarks should not pursue or confirm further details about the next meeting ... s/he may casually repeat what s/he has heard or could use another meaningless expression like *Ne, kŭrŏ-psida* 'Let's do that'.

With these Korean phatic expressions Park prominently illustrates the 'ice-breaking' function of phatic communion in the opening phase of a conversation; he points out the ritualized use of phatic expressions in specific settings in which interlocutors interact and he illustrates how phatic expressions are used to assuage non-initiating participants in conversation closing phases. His claim, however, that propositions that are made in acts of phatic communion – like the one in example (12) – are meaningless (Park 2006: 162) only refers to the fact that this utterance must not be understood literally. The situative context and the interactants' common cultural knowledge provide the necessary information for understanding such a phatic expression as a means to consolidate the relationship between the interactants. Thus, even if what is said is not to be taken literally or seriously, it has some meaning for the relationship of the interlocutors engaged in this phatic communion.

With his concept of 'phatic communion' Malinowski emphasized that language can be used without any purpose of communicating ideas; however, as pointed out above, this is only one aspect of his linguistic thinking. As one of the founding fathers of anthropological linguistics as a discipline in its own right, he pleaded for a linguistic theory that 'would show us what is essential in language and what therefore must remain the same throughout the whole range of linguistic varieties [and] how linguistic forms are influenced by physiological, mental, social, and other cultural elements' (Malinowski: 1920: 69). Thus, he was interested both in universal features of language and in the interrelationship between language, culture and cognition that is expressed in culture-specific features and phenomena of languages.

Malinowski's contemporary Franz Boas (1858–1942), one of the founders of both American anthropology and descriptive-structural linguistics, also understood language as an unalterable prerequisite for his research (see Senft 2009c: 8). As Michael Agar (1994: 49) points out, 'language was then ... a part of anthropological fieldwork, and the point of fieldwork was to get to culture. Culture was the destination; language was the path; grammar and dictionary marked the trail'. Regna Darnell notes that Boas saw language as a symbolic form through which culture becomes accessible to study. Like Wilhelm von Humboldt – who strongly influenced him – Boas was convinced that languages have an inner form, that they deserve to be described in their own terms. Darnell emphasizes that:

> Boas argued that each language stood as an independent packaging of what Sapir's student Benjamin Lee Whorf would later see as an amalgam of 'language, thought and reality.' The so-called Sapir-Whorf hypothesis of the relationship between habitual thought to linguistic categories has its roots in this Boasian insistence on the unique perceptual patterning of each language and the equal value and expressive capacity of

every natural language. Cultural relativism ... began with Boas' recognition that Indo-European categories distorted languages on which they were imposed.

(Darnell 2009: 46)

The next subsection will discuss Edward Sapir's and especially Benjamin Lee Whorf's hypotheses about linguistic relativity.

4.3 LINGUISTIC RELATIVITY: THE SAPIR-WHORF HYPOTHESIS

Edward Sapir, one of Boas's students, was very much interested in the relationship between language, culture and cognition. He took up Boas' rather cautiously formulated idea that 'it may be well to discuss the relation between language and thought. It has been claimed that the conciseness and clearness of thought of people depend to a great extent upon their language' (Boas 1911: 60)[7] and then summarized his own ideas about the topic in the following provocative statements:

> Language is a guide to 'social reality'. Though language is not ordinarily thought of as of essential interest to the students of social science, it powerfully conditions all our thinking around social problems and processes. Human beings do not live in the objective world alone, nor alone in the world of social activity as ordinarily understood, but are very much at the mercy of the particular language which has become the medium of expression for their society. It is quite an illusion to imagine that one adjusts to reality essentially without the use of language and that language is merely an incidental means of solving specific problems of communication or reflection. The fact of the matter is that the 'real world' is to a large extent unconsciously built up on the language habits of the group. No two languages are ever sufficiently similar to be considered as representing the same social reality. The worlds in which different societies live are distinct worlds, not merely the same world with different labels.

(Sapir 1929: 210)

A few years later he even speaks of 'the tyrannical hold that linguistic form has upon our orientation in the world' (Sapir 1931: 578). However, it was Sapir's student Benjamin Lee Whorf who finally came up with the formulation of the concept of linguistic relativity, namely in two papers that were published in 1940 (and reprinted in 1956)[8]. There Whorf states the following:

> We dissect nature along lines laid down by our native languages. The categories and types that we isolate from the world of phenomena we do not find there because they stare every observer in the face; on the contrary, the world is presented in a kaleidoscopic flux of impressions which has to be organized by our minds – and this means largely by the linguistic systems of our minds.

(Whorf 1956: 213 [1940a])

This is the weak formulation of the Sapir-Whorf (or rather the Whorf) hypothesis,[9] because of 'the escape hatch built into the thesis by means of the word "largely"' (Seuren 2013: 41). The strong version reads as follows:

> The phenomena of language are background phenomena of which the talkers are unaware or, at most, dimly aware ... These automatic, involuntary patterns of language are not the same for all men but are specific for each language and constitute the formalized side of the language, or its "grammar" ... From this fact proceeds what I have called the "linguistic relativity principle", which means, in informal terms, that users of markedly different grammars are pointed by their grammars toward different types of observations and different evaluations of externally similar acts of observation, and hence are not equivalent as observers, but must arrive at somewhat different views of the world.
>
> (Whorf 1956: 221 [1940b])

Whorf did not present these claims as a hypothesis but as established fact – he was convinced that languages control the cognitive processes of their speakers – and this direction of causality – from language to thought – is crucial for his argument.

Since the late 1950s this hypothesis – especially its strong version which claims that language determines thought – has been discussed quite controversially in linguistic, anthropological and sociological circles. However, many cognitive scientists, including linguists and anthropologists, have been fascinated by the challenge presented in the weaker version of the hypothesis – which claims that language influences thought. Is there a way to empirically test this claim?

In the 1990s a number of linguists and anthropologists attempted to test the weak version of the Sapir-Whorf hypothesis. They tried to study the relationship between language, culture and cognition by conducting fieldwork on issues of common interest to anthropology, psychology, and linguistics (see Levinson 2003). This research aimed to contribute to the development of more sophisticated theories about the relationship between learned and native abilities, about the contribution of culture to cognition, and about the nature and transmission of culture itself and its relation to social structures and processes. The discussion of research questions like these has a rather long tradition, of course, in which philosophers and scientists like Herder, Humboldt, and especially Boas, Sapir, and Whorf played a prominent role. A group of researchers at the Max Planck Institute for Psycholinguistics have been trying to empirically investigate some of these questions on possible interdependencies between language, culture and cognition via the following stratagem, summarized by Penelope Brown and Stephen Levinson:

> (a) first, pick a conceptual domain; (b) second, find two or more languages which contrast in the semantic treatment of that domain (i.e., where very different semantic parameters are employed); (c) third, develop non-linguistic tasks which will behaviourally reveal the conceptual parameters utilized to solve them; (d) compare the linguistic and non-linguistic representation systems as revealed by (b) and (c), and assess whether there is any correlation between linguistic and non-linguistic codings in the same domain.
>
> (Brown and Levinson 1993: 1)

The first conceptual domain that was 'picked' by these researchers was the domain of 'space' with the major goal to investigate the conceptualization of space and spatial reference in a cross-cultural/cross-linguistic perspective (see Pederson *et al.* 1998; Senft 2001). To achieve this aim, the researchers developed specific methods to build a comparative database through parallel field research in different languages and cultures. Inspired by research done by Herbert Clark and Deanna Wilkes-Gibbs (1986) these methods of data elicitation make use of various sets of interactive 'games' which are used to elicit task-oriented verbal descriptions in native speakers of the language being studied. Most of these tasks involve the recognition or the construction of spatial arrays from systematic sets of two- or three-dimensional stimuli. All interactional games for focused linguistic elicitation involve a 'director' consultant who is allowed to see a certain stimulus, and a 'matcher' who is not. The players are sitting side by side with a screen separating them so that they cannot see each other's stimuli. The orientation of the players is taken note of, and the field researcher instructs the players what to do in their own language – all instructions are standardized. Moreover, the field researcher encourages the players to interact verbally, especially if they think they have difficulties understanding each other. On the basis of the verbal descriptions given by the 'director' in the game, the 'matcher' is asked in some games to reproduce three-dimensional configurations of familiar objects with intrinsic orientations, like a human statuette in various body poses and mini-landscapes inhabited by toy animals, as well as unfamiliar and abstract objects. Other games also involve the matching of photographs on the basis of verbal descriptions; these photographs systematically cover certain spatial oppositions. With these methods, large corpora of contextually anchored yet complex interactive texts that incorporate many examples of spatial language were elicited.[10] The overall corpus includes data from 12 languages.

The analyses of the verbal data collected for the languages Longgu and Kilivila (Austronesian; Oceanic), Kgalagadi (Bantu), Dutch (Indo-European), Japanese, Hai//om (Khoisan),[11] Tzeltal and Mopan (Maya), Mparntwe Arrernte (Pama-Nyungan), Tamil (Tamil), Belhara (Tibeto-Burman) and Totonac (Totonac) revealed fundamental differences in how speakers of these languages refer to space. For describing these differences, the typology of spatial systems or frames of spatial reference illustrated in Chapter Two (subsections 2.3 and 2.3.1.4) was used. The typology defines a 'relative', an 'absolute', and an 'intrinsic' frame of reference. The systems differ with respect to how angles are projected from the 'ground' (or 'relatum') in order to situate the location of the focal object, the 'figure' (or 'theme') that is referred to.[12] As mentioned in Chapter Two, all three systems can be found in a given language, and they can be utilized for spatial reference; however, most of the languages seem to prefer one frame of reference in a particular context. On the basis of these observations, the researchers came up with the following hypothesis:

> If speakers of a language preferentially use one reference system in a particular spatial domain, then these speakers will rely on a comparable coding system for memorizing spatial configurations and making inferences with respect to these spatial configurations in non-verbal problem solving.

(Senft 2001: 527)

To falsify or verify this hypothesis, experiments to test the interrelationship between space and cognition were developed.

The experiments are based on the cognitive implications of the three systems of verbal spatial reference. Relative (R), absolute (A), and intrinsic (I) systems differ with respect to their dependence (+) or independence (–)

> – with respect to the speaker's location and orientation,
> R + A – I –
> – with respect to the rotation of the spatial configuration,
> R + A + I –
> and
> – with respect to the rotation of the ground
> R – A – I+.

The experiments for the investigation of non-verbal spatial cognition explore the nature of the spatial coding for (recall and recognition) memory and (transitive) inference, and make it possible to determine whether this non-verbal coding has certain specific properties. These properties were compared to the verbal codings elicited with the interactional games to see whether there was a correlation between the verbal and the non-verbal systems of spatial coding. The tasks developed serve to investigate the opposition between the relative and intrinsic frames of reference that use expressions like 'left/right/front/back' for spatial references on the one hand and the absolute system that uses expressions like 'north/south/east/west, uphill/ downhill, seawards/landwards, upriver/downriver', etc., for spatial references on the other.[13]

All tasks have the same fundamental design. The consultants are shown a stimulus on one table (Table 1) and are instructed to memorize what they have seen. After a short delay they are rotated 180° and led across to another table (Table 2) at a certain distance which faces in the opposite direction from Table 1. The consultants are now asked to reconstruct the same array, or to select the same array from a set provided. The stimulus arrays are so designed that they have either a left/right or a front/back asymmetry when viewed on Table 1. Figure 4.1 illustrates the design of these tasks (see Brown and Levinson 1993: 8; Senft 1994: 421). Suppose the consultants see an arrow on Table 1 that is pointing from their point of view to the right. After a short pause and after having been turned 180° they are led to Table 2. There they find two arrows; again, from their point of view one arrow is pointing to the right and the other arrow is pointing to the left. The consultants are asked now to choose the arrow that resembles the one they just saw half a minute ago on Table 1. Consultants who memorized the orientation of the arrow on Table 1 on the basis of a relative system of spatial coding will select at Table 2 the arrow that – from their point of view – is also pointing to the right – here the fact that standing in front of Table 2 the consultants have turned 180° is of crucial importance. Consultants, however, that use an absolute system of spatial coding, memorize the fact that the arrow on Table 1 pointed, e.g. towards north – they will then select the arrow which is also pointing towards this direction on Table 2, regardless of the fact that they have turned 180° (see Senft 2001: 528ff.).

Figure 4.1
Design of the experiments for the non-verbal solving of spatial problems

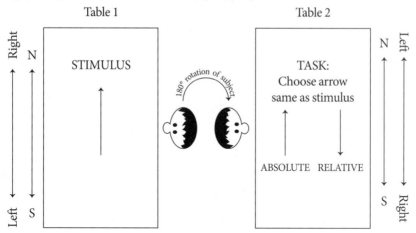

The analyses of the elicited verbal data revealed which systems of spatial reference were to be found in the languages researched and which systems were preferentially used by the speakers of these languages. Based on these results and with the general hypothesis in mind, the researchers made predictions with respect to which results could be expected in the non-verbal cognitive tasks for the various speech communities. Table 4.1 summarizes these predictions and presents the results actually observed in analysing the subjects' behaviour in the non-verbal tasks.

Table 4.1
Verbal and non-verbal codification of spatial configurations

language	preferred system(s) of verbal codification	system(s) non-verbal codification	
		predicted	found
Arrernte	A	A	most A
Hai//om	A, (I)	A	most A
Tzeltal	A	A	A
Longgu	A	A	A, also R
Dutch	R	R	R
Japanese	R	R	R, also A
Kilivila	I, A (R)	I, A	I, A
Belhara	A	A	most A
Tamil (rural)	A	A	A
Tamil (city)	R	R	R
Kgalagadi	R (A, I)	R	R, also A
Mopan	I	*ad hoc*	R, A
Totonac	I	*ad hoc*	R, A

A = absolute frame of reference
R = relative frame of reference
I = intrinsic frame of reference

This table shows that the researchers' hypothesis with respect to the interrelationship between verbal and non-verbal coding of spatial configurations is verified (for all languages except Mopan and Totonac; see Levinson 2003: 81ff., 93 and 188f. for an explanation). Thus it seems that languages indeed allow inferences to be made about the choice and the kind of conceptual parameters their speakers will use to solve certain non-verbal problems within the domain 'space', about how they memorize certain spatial configurations and about how they represent them in their long-term memory. Thus, these results support the hypothesis that languages contribute in shaping thinking for non-verbal problem solving instances.

However, even with results of studies like the one presented here, it remains somewhat problematic to argue that it is only language that influences thought in general. Although the research results show that speakers of specific languages have clear preferences for frames of spatial reference in their verbal behaviour and that these preferences allow for predictions with respect to the speakers' behaviour in non-verbal problem solving tasks in the spatial domain, it should be taken into account that all the speakers who prefer the absolute system can easily switch to forms of behaviour that are based on a relative system of spatial reference if necessary, for example when driving a car and respecting right of way traffic rules. However, speakers that prefer a relative or an intrinsic frame of spatial reference have severe difficulties in switching to an absolute system without using devices like a compass or a GPI system. It is interesting to connect these observations with Dan Slobin's insight that

> the expression of experience in linguistic terms constitutes **thinking for speaking** – a special form of thought that is mobilized for communication. Whatever effects grammar may or may not have outside of the act of speaking, the sort of mental activity that goes on while formulating utterances is not trivial or obvious, and deserves our attention. We encounter the contents of the mind in a special way when they are being accessed for use. That is, the activity of thinking takes on a particular quality when it is employed in the activity of speaking. In the evanescent time frame of constructing utterances in discourse, one fits one's thoughts into available linguistic frames. "Thinking for speaking" involves picking those characteristics of objects and events that (a) fit some conceptualization of the event, and (b) are readily encodable in the language ...
>
> (Slobin 1996: 76)

Slobin also points out that the

> languages we learn in childhood are not neutral coding systems of an objective reality. Rather, each one is a subjective orientation to the world of human experience, and this orientation **affects the ways in which we think while we are speaking**.
>
> (Slobin 1996: 91; see also 1991: 23).

A similar idea to Slobin's concept of 'thinking for speaking' seems to be the basis for Steven Pinker's criticism of Whorf. Pinker states that

Whorf was surely wrong when he said that one's language determines how one conceptualizes reality in general. But he was probably correct in a much weaker sense: one's language does determine how one must conceptualize reality when one has to talk about it.

(Pinker 1989: 360)

And Herbert Clark comments on Whorf's hypotheses in his article 'Communities, Commonalities and Communication' as follows:

Whorf seemed to take for granted that language is primarily an instrument of thought. Yet, this premise is false. Language is first and foremost an instrument of communication – the '*exchange* of thoughts' – as one dictionary puts it – and it is only derivatively an instrument of thought. If language has an influence on thought, as Whorf believed, that influence must be mediated by the way language is used for communication. The alliteration[14] in my title is not accidental, for communication, as its Latin root suggests, is itself built on commonalities of thought between people, especially those taken for granted in the communities in which each language is used. Once this is made explicit, I suggest, we will find it difficult to distinguish many potential influences of language on thought from the influences of other commonalities of mental life, especially the beliefs, practices, and norms of the communities to which we belong.

(Clark 1996b: 325)

By pointing out that language is not primarily an instrument of thought and just one part of many 'other commonalities of mental life' Clark reduces the impact of even the weak version of the Whorf hypothesis to a piece, albeit an important one, within the complex mosaic of the interrelationship between language, culture and cognition. Consequently, Clark defines his position with respect to Whorf's doctrines as follows: 'There can be no [human, G. S.] communication without commonalities of thought. But there can be commonalities of thought, without communication' (Clark 1996b: 353).

It should be evident by now that researching the relationship between language, culture and cognition is a challenging but rewarding enterprise. Malinowski, Boas and Sapir insisted that the use of language must be studied in its social context. As pointed out in subsection 3.3.1 above and elsewhere (Senft 2010a: 279), whoever wants to investigate the role of language, culture and cognition in social interaction must know how the researched society constructs its reality. Researchers need to be on 'common ground' with the researched communities, and this common ground knowledge is the prerequisite for any successful research within this domain. To achieve this aim the 'ethnography of speaking' approach provides a useful framework, because – as Joel Sherzer pointed out –

[l]ike ethnoscience and cognitive anthropology as well as symbolic anthropology, the ethnography of speaking is concerned with the community members' conceptions and representations of their culture and with their formalized frames for communicative action and interpretation.

(Sherzer 1983: 16)

The next subsection of this chapter sketches out the characteristic features of this paradigm, its accomplishments and the criticism it has been facing since its introduction to the field of linguistic pragmatics.

4.4 THE ETHNOGRAPHY OF SPEAKING[15]

The ethnography of speaking paradigm goes back to Dell Hymes' programmatic paper first published in 1962 (and republished in 1978). In the tradition of researchers like Malinowski, Jakobson, Boas, Sapir and Whorf, he pointed out the fact that the study of speech is of 'crucial importance to a science of man' (Hymes [1962] 1978: 99; see also 1974: 446). Therefore he called for "ethological' studies of speaking in context' and advocated 'a science of behavior' which he called the 'ethnography of speaking' (Hymes [1962] 1978: 130ff.). As Sherzer has succinctly summarized, Hymes argued

> that language and speech have a patterning of their own, as do social organization, politics, religion, economics and law, and that therefore they merit attention by anthropologists – they cannot be taken for granted as somehow given or everywhere the same. This patterning is not identical to the grammar of a language in the traditional sense and yet is linguistic as well as cultural in organization.
>
> (Sherzer 1983: 11)

Hymes introduced the notions of 'speech style' and 'speech or communicative event' and argued that the meaning of an utterance can only be understood in relation to the speech event in which it is embedded.[16] Analyses of these styles or events require the minute study of, and the interrelationship between, what he called 'components'. He grouped these components into the following eight main entries that could be remembered with the acronym SPEAKING (Hymes 1972a; see also Duranti 1988: 218):

> S (situation: setting and scene); P (participants: speaker/sender, addressor, hearer/ receiver/audience, addressee); E (ends: outcome, goals); A (act sequence: message form and message content); K (key [i.e., tone and manner in which something is said, G. S.]); I (instrumentalities: channel, forms of speech); N (norms: norms of interaction and interpretation); and G (genres).

As Fitch and Philipsen (1995: 264) point out, these components were not 'a checklist of things to describe' but rather 'an initial set of questions and descriptive possibilities in the study of ways of speaking in particular communities'. Research within this paradigm results in descriptions that capture 'each society's unique cultural organization of language and speech' (Sherzer 1977: 44). This organization cannot be grasped by a traditional grammar. Agreeing with Newman (1964: 448) that a grammar of a language tells us 'what a language can do but not what it considers worthwhile doing', Hymes emphasizes that a learner of a language need not only acquire the grammatical algorithm of this language, but also the rules that guide the communicative behaviour of members of the speech community that speak this language. Hymes argues as follows:

We have ... to account for the fact that a normal child acquires knowledge of sentences, not only as grammatical, but also as appropriate. He or she acquires competence as to when to speak, when not, and as to what to talk about with whom, when, where, in what manner. In short, a child becomes able to accomplish a repertoire of speech acts, to take part in speech events, and to evaluate their accomplishments by others. This competence, moreover, is integral with attitudes, values, and motivations concerning language, its features and uses, and integral with competence for, and attitudes toward, the interrelation of language, with the other codes of communicative conduct.

(Hymes 1972b: 277f.; see also [1962] 1978: 101).

This 'communicative competence' is expressed and therefore analysable 'in terms of determinate ways of speaking' (Hymes 1972a: 58). Hymes differentiates between the label 'ethnography of speaking' as a name for the approach and an ethnography of speaking which studies how a specific speech community 'X' actually is speaking. For these latter studies he prefers the label 'X's ways of speaking'. He justifies this as follows:

First, terms derived from 'speak' and 'speech' in English suffer from a history of association with something marginal or redundant ... 'speech' should indicate use in a positive sense ... My second reason for favoring *ways of speaking* is that it has analogy with 'ways of life', on the one hand, and Whorf's term 'fashions of speaking' on the other. The first analogy helps remind anthropologists that the ways of mankind do include ways of speaking, and helps remind linguists that speaking does come in ways, that is, shows cultural patterning. And since Whorf was the first in American linguistic and anthropological tradition, so far as I know, to name a mode of organization of linguistic means cutting across the compartments of grammar, it is good to honor his precedence, while letting the difference in terms reflect the difference in scope of reference.

(Hymes 1974: 445f.)

'Ways of speaking' or 'speech styles' are formally marked and therefore can be recognized. Hymes further differentiates between 'varieties', which are defined as 'major speech styles [which are] associated with social groups', 'registers', which are defined as 'major speech styles associated with recurrent types of situations', and '*personal, situational,* and *genre* styles' (Hymes 1974: 440). As a 'good ethnographic technique' to classify speech events, speech styles, and ways of speaking, Hymes proposed to start looking at the metalinguistic labels the speech community under research uses to refer to them.

All the fine-grained differentiations Hymes proposes for doing research within the ethnography of speaking paradigm allow for minute studies of various forms of language use within specific speech communities. These studies are based on ethnographic methods that are supplemented by other techniques for data gathering and analyses developed within related disciplines like, for example, sociolinguistics, discourse and conversation analysis, pragmatics, and anthropological linguistics/ linguistic anthropology. The paradigm understands 'linguistic performance as the locus of the relationship between language and the sociocultural order' and studies 'what is accomplished through speaking and how speech is related to and is constructed by particular aspects of social organization and speakers' assumptions, values, and beliefs about the world' (Duranti 1988: 210).

It is obvious that the goal of the ethnography of speaking paradigm was from its very beginning extremely ambitious. In the 1960s and 1970s, a number of scholars, like those who contributed to the volumes edited by Gumperz and Hymes (1964, 1972) and by Bauman and Sherzer (1974) contributed to establish and to develop the field. Yet the paradigm's high scientific standards and its more or less implicit aim to emphasize the complex diversity of speech rather than reduce it to abstract principles and generalizations has given rise to critical comments.

In his review of Bauman's and Sherzer's (1974) anthology, one of the by now classic publications in the ethnography of speaking paradigm, Maurice Bloch first points out that:

> to document the range of linguistic styles available to speakers in specific situations and then understand the use of these styles for social action ... means a really high level of linguistic ability ... [W]hat is required is the hypersensitivity which comes from a total control of the finest subtleties of language and social situations ... The fieldworker must also have an extremely thorough knowledge of the social organisation, the kinship system, the political system, the economic system, the trends towards change at work in the society concerned ... In other words, the task of the ethnographer of speaking ... is of almost insurmountable difficulty.
>
> (Bloch 1976: 231ff.)

Then he points out that despite the fact that one of the main concerns of the ethnography of speaking paradigm is the analysis of 'mundane ordinary speech intercourse' (Bloch 1976: 233), the volume is dominated by studies that either deal with forms of ritual and artistic performance or with folk classifications concerning speech and communication.

Bloch's third point of criticism concerns the claim of the paradigm to include all aspects of speech events in its descriptions. For him this aim is illusory because 'there is no end to reality and the description of ever smaller events, ever more carefully, gets us no nearer' (Bloch 1976: 234).

His last point of criticism concerns the fact that studies in the paradigm result in 'a mass of items from around the globe, all very valuable in themselves but not forming together an attempt to solve common problems and to move forward to ever more documented and incisive generalizations' (Bloch 1976: 234; see also 4.4.2 below).

Sherzer – responding to Bloch's criticism in 1977 – agreed that the paradigm so far does not offer a *tertium comparationis*[17] which could serve as a basis for comparing studies which are carried out in various speech communities by different researchers within the framework of the ethnography of speaking paradigm. He also pointed out the need for filtering generalizations out of the vast number of different insights gained by these studies. Moreover, Sherzer agreed that future studies within the paradigm should put at least as much emphasis on the study of everyday forms of speech as on the study of formalized speech genres used in ritualized and ceremonial contexts and situations (see Sherzer 1977: 50). Six years later Sherzer took up the challenge of Bloch's criticism and provided, with his book '*Kuna Ways of Speaking*', an exemplary contribution to the paradigm.

4.4.1 Kuna ways of speaking

The Kuna are native Americans living in Panama and Colombia. They are agriculturalists who cultivate the jungle using the slash and burn technique. The Kuna language to which they refer with the term *tule kaya* belongs to the Chibchan family; it is spoken by more than 50,000 people. With his monograph *Kuna Ways of Speaking*, Sherzer provides an ethnography of speaking for the Kuna who live in the region of San Blas on the Caribbean coast of Panama (see Sherzer 1983: 3).

The Kuna metalinguistically mark the differentiation between their own language – *tule kaya* – the Kuna language (note that *tule* translates as 'person') and other languages like, for example the Spanish language – *waka kaya*, the English language – *merki kaya*, the neighbouring Choco language – *sokko kaya*, and so on. The *tule kaya* is differentiated into the *tule kaya* proper and its ritual varieties *sakla kaya* – the chiefs' language or the gathering house language, the *suar nuchu kaya* – the stick doll language – this label refers to carved wooden stick dolls that represent spirits and serve as addressees for chants during curing rituals and as mediators between curers and evil spirits – and the *kantule kaya* – the language used by the director of girls' puberty rites (the *kantule*) to address the spirit who is believed to be involved in these rituals (see Sherzer 1983: 22). These varieties of the Kuna language are phonologically, morpho-syntactically and lexico-semantically so different from each other that they have to be learned separately (see Sherzer 1983: 35). To give just a few examples for lexical differentiation (see Sherzer 1983: 26ff.), the word for 'foreigner' in *tule kaya* – in everyday Kuna – is *waka*, but in the chief language, *sakla kaya*, the word used to refer to such a person is *tulepiitti*. The word for 'woman' in the *tule kaya* is *ome* but in the *suar nuchu kaya* variety it is *walepunkwa* and in the *kantule kaya* variety it is *yai*. In addition there are so-called play names or nicknames for animals that can serve as synonyms for the everyday Kuna word that refers to this animal. Thus, the word for 'deer' in everyday Kuna is *koe*, but the nickname of this animal is *upsan saya* which translates as 'cotton ass'. Although the four varieties of Kuna have the same phonemic inventory, the three ritual varieties use longer word forms than the variety used in everyday interaction. The longer forms are characteristic of the slower formal speech of the ritual varieties of Kuna. In the *tule kaya* variety of Kuna, speech is rapid and informal, final vowels and even syllables are often deleted and consonants are assimilated so that the deleted word form agrees with Kuna phonological rules and syllable structures. To briefly illustrate this phenomenon: the English gloss 'to go to help' translates both the long Kuna word form *penetakkenae* and the short form *pentaynae*, the English gloss 'in the hammock' translates the long form *kachikine* and the short form *kaski* and the English gloss 'he is mentioning me' translates the long word form *aninukapipiemaiye* as well as the short form *annuypimai* (see Sherzer 1983: 36f.).

Sherzer illustrates the everyday variety and the three other varieties of the Kuna language which pervade the areas of politics, curing and magic as well as puberty rites in Kuna ritual life with a number of examples.[18] Unfortunately, he does not discuss ordinary everyday conversation as detailed as the verbal art genres.

In what follows, Kuna ways of speaking will be illustrated by Kuna forms of greeting and leave-taking, by excerpts from curing and magical *ikarkana* formulae and from the *kantule ikar* – the way of the *kantule* – which is shouted during the Kuna girls' puberty rites.

4.4.1.1 *Kuna ways of greeting and leave-taking*

Kuna ways of greeting and leave-taking depend on the social relationship of the individuals involved, on the time of the day and on the period of time which has elapsed since friends and family members last saw each other. In general, greetings are not obligatory (see Sherzer 1983: 159ff.). However, a greeting is usually initiated by saying *tekitte* – which Sherzer glosses as 'well, then, hello'. The response to this formula is *anna, na* – which Sherzer glosses as 'utterances with no translatable meaning'. In the mainland jungle, however, greetings are obligatory and the simple exchange of greetings just illustrated is usually expanded with an exchange of questions about the other person's planned or performed activities. However, when people leave their villages for work in the morning and when they return again in the afternoon they may expand their greetings with questions like *Pia pe nae*? – 'Where are you going?' and *Pia pe tanikki*? – 'Where are you coming from?' (Sherzer 1983: 160).[19]

Longer greeting rituals are only performed by members of the same community or friends or kin-persons who have not seen each other for some time, by members of different communities visiting each other, or by two chiefs during an official visit when the greeting is public. In the latter case greetings are chanted by the chiefs in the gathering house of the visited village. The chants consist of questions and answers about each other's health, activities and travel experiences. This form of greeting is called *arkan kae* – which literally means 'handshake'. It is the only form of greeting which is metalinguistically labelled. Real handshakes also occur, however, only between men with official positions within a village who have not seen each other for some time. If close friends and family members have been separated for a long time, they pretend not to see each other and avoid one another when they meet for the first time. They do not greet each other verbally, despite the fact that they are clearly aware of each other's presence. Although the individuals involved are aware of the fact that the person who stayed at home stopped his or her usual everyday activities to be at the place where the returning friend or relative is expected to arrive, there is no interaction between the two people involved until much later when they have arrived at home and relax. Then they will greet each other 'asking and replying to a series of questions about travels, activities and health, a pattern very much like the *arkan kae* performed by "chiefs"' (Sherzer 1983: 160). Sherzer explains this marked form of avoidance behaviour as follows:

> [T]his seeming avoidance – actually mutually acknowledged copresence – should be viewed not as the absence of greeting but as a slowing down and stretching out of the total greeting process, in which the initial portion is nonverbal. This slowing and stretching requires interactional work and is a reflection of a more general rule, namely, the more special and significant the social relationship between individuals, the greater

the amount of interaction necessary to mark and restore this relationship in greetings. Thus close friends and family members prolong the greeting process by combining public nonverbal, mutually acknowledged copresence with later private questioning and answering. And two 'chiefs', the political and ritual leaders of two distinct communities, prolong the greeting process by chanting a lengthy and public ritual greeting in an esoteric language.

(Sherzer 1983: 161)

The ways of leave-taking are parallel to the greetings, however, they are not as elaborate. Even so, Sherzer points out the following:

In a daily manifestation of the mutually acknowledged copresence greeting and leave-taking pattern, Kuna wives accompany their husbands to their canoes as they leave for work in the morning and meet them as they return, often without exchanging words.

(Sherzer 1983: 161)

Sherzer's observations reveal that these rituals of greeting and leave-taking fulfil functions of securing and re-establishing bonds between individuals in the Kuna communities.

4.4.1.2 *Curing and magical* ikarkana *formulae*

The Kuna – like the Trobriand Islanders – believe in the power of magic. They use magical formulae to reach certain aims with the conviction that expert magicians can control spirits of good and evil by addressing them with them. The formulae are called *ikarkana* (which Sherzer glosses as 'ways, texts') and the magicians are referred to as *ikar wismalat* – *ikar* knowers (see Sherzer 1983: 110ff.). The formulae are believed to activate the powers of the good spirits and to neutralize the influence of the evil spirits. They constitute a specific genre which is produced in curing rituals and other forms of magic. Sherzer summarizes the characteristic features of this text type as follows:

Curing and magical *ikarkana* consist of a series of themes, topics, and episodes which are strung together. While a primary characteristic of these *ikarkana* is that they are putatively fixed or unchangeable in form, and thus must be learned by rote memorization, there is some variation. Depending on the particular origins of the disease or on the particular object of several possible objects to be controlled, choices are made in the selection of topics or themes. ... *Ikarkana* can also be made longer or shorter, according to the selection of appropriate episodes or themes. Once the selection has been made, however, the '*ikar* knower' proceeds according to a line-by-line fixed text.

(Sherzer 1983: 127)

A typical feature of the *ikarkana* is parallelism – 'the patterned repetition of sounds, forms, and meanings' (Sherzer 1983: 128). The following excerpt of a curing *ikarkana* illustrates the specifics of this Kuna way of speaking magical formulae.

Sherzer (1983: 129f.) provides only English glosses for a curing formula called 'the way of the cooling off':

> Our child has a feverish spirit.
> We must cool off his spirit for him.
> We must really cool off his spirit.

This basic form of the formula is repeated five more times, with the words for 'blood', 'skin', 'body', 'head' and 'hair' replacing the word for 'spirit'.

This curing formula confirms the definition of ritual communication quoted in Chapter Three (subsection 3.3.1), which points out that 'ritual communication is artful, performed semiosis, predominantly ... involving speech, that is formulaic and repetitive and therefore anticipated within particular contexts of social interaction' (Basso and Senft 2009: 1). The form, structure and function of the Kuna formulae Sherzer presents in his monograph show many parallels with magical formulae documented in other languages and cultures (see, e.g. Endicott 1991; Malinowski 1935, Vol. II; Senft 2010a: 40ff.; Skeat 1984).

4.4.1.3 *Excerpts from the* kantule ikar *shouted during the girls' puberty rites*

When a Kuna girl reaches puberty, the Kuna celebrate this rite of passage with puberty rites and festivities – the *inna* rites – that include cutting the girls' hair as short as is appropriate for adult women as well as communal meals and drinking of alcoholic beverages by all members of the girl's village community (see Sherzer 1983: 139ff.).[20] The central part of these rites is the shouting of a text (*ikar*) by the director (*the kantule*) of these rites and rituals and his apprentices in an especially constructed *inna* house. The *kantule* and his apprentices stand, sit or lie in their hammocks in this enclosure and 'two at a time shout the very long *kantule ikar* (the way of the *kantule*), shaking rattles and blowing on the long flute (*kammu*) as they shout' (Sherzer 1983: 144). The *kantule ikar* addresses the spirit of the *kammu* flute. The *inna* may last for two or more days. As mentioned above, the language of the *kantule ikar* is a highly ritualized variety of the Kuna language called *kantule kaya* that is completely different from everyday colloquial Kuna, especially with regard to vocabulary and thus extremely difficult to understand for non-experts. Like curing and magical formulae, the *kantule ikar* describe in detail in a kind of verse structure every part of the puberty rite and the activities that accompany it – from the preparation of the participants in the rite to the cutting of the initiates' hair to the communal eating and drinking. The long text represents 'the most immutable of all Kuna ritual discourse. It is repeated identically, including every single phoneme and morpheme, each time it is performed' (Sherzer 1983: 144). The following excerpts of the *kantule ikar* describe women participating in the rite:

> *yaikana uuparpa imakte.*
> The women's underwear makes noise.
> *yaikana uuparpa pukki nite.*
> The women's underwear can be heard far away.

yaikana kala tere imakte.
The women's coin necklaces make noise.
yaikana kala tere pukki nite,
The women's coin necklaces can be heard far away.
yaikana kala purwa imakte.
The women's bead necklaces make noise.
yaikana kala purwa pukki nite.
The women's bead necklaces can be heard far away.

(Sherzer 1983: 145f.)

Sherzer (1983: 147) points out that this text has 'a clearly defined poetic line structure. In this passage every line begins with the noun *yaikana* (women) and ends with the tense-aspect and also line-final marker *te* (then)'.

Like the curing and magical formulae the *kantule ikar* constitutes a specific form of ritual communication as defined in Chapter Three.

With his monograph, Sherzer attempted to present a more or less exhaustive typology of a specific speech community's ways of speaking that are expressed in specific metalinguistically differentiated varieties and which are manifest in a number of genres or text categories.[21] Besides the different Kuna ways of speaking and the three genres illustrated here, Sherzer also provides and analyses examples of commanding and requesting, narratives, gossip, humour, forms of speech play and verbal art, co-speech gestures, and chants and thus documents (almost) all the major forms of social interactions and speech situations of the Kuna (with the exception of ordinary conversation). In addition, he also discusses 'the relationship between musical structure and Kuna discourse structure' (Sherzer 1983: 12f.). Sherzer points out that 'all Kuna speaking can be viewed as highly adaptive and strategic, finely attuned to contexts of usage and able to change in order to meet challenges from both within and without Kuna society' (Sherzer 1983: 13). To achieve linguistic and cultural competence in the Kuna speech community requires the understanding of how it structures, patterns and regulates its ways of speaking (see also Senft 2010a: 286). Sherzer also points out that his close analysis of the Kuna ways of speaking also contributes to more general theoretical issues, like, for example, 'the role of language and speech among American Indians, the relationship between ritual and everyday speech and the nature of verbal art and verbal performance in nonliterate societies' (Sherzer 1983: 14). In what follows the ethnography of speech paradigm will be assessed.

4.4.2 The ethnography of speaking paradigm: a critical assessment

In his presentation of the paradigm, Alessandro Duranti (1988: 219) points out that the 'grid' of Hymes' SPEAKING model 'has always maintained an *etic* status and was never accomplished by a (general) theory of the possible relationships among the various components' (see Senft 2010a: 284). The emic/etic distinction (from phonemic versus phonetic) made here goes back to Kenneth Pike (1954). Gustav Jahoda (1995: 129) quotes French who defines the two approaches as follows:

Pike identifies the emic approach as a structural one. The investigator assumes that human behaviour is patterned, even though the members of the society being studied may not be aware of many units of the structuring. In Pike's view, the goal of the emic approach is to discover and describe the behavioural system in its own terms, identifying not only the structural units but also the structural classes to which they belong.

In contrast, an etic approach can be characterized as an external one. Items of behaviour are examined not in the light of the systems in which they occur, but rather in that of criteria brought to bear on them by the observer. The observer classifies all comparable data into a system which he is creating, using criteria which were in existence before the classification began.

(French 1963: 398)

Duranti also notes that many studies within the ethnography of speaking paradigm try to show that the relationship among the components of the model is 'meaningful within a particular society' but that this is done in emic descriptions; thus, the majority of these studies 'do not ... exemplify any universal principle of the relation between speech and context in *societies* in general' (Duranti 1988: 219). He explains this theoretical deficit as a possible 'reflection of the cultural relativism that [the ethnography of speaking paradigm] shares with most of modern anthropology' and points out that 'the care for specific *emic* accounts and the reluctance to posit universal principles ... is strongly related to the fundamental anti-Universalism that characterizes [the ethnography of speaking paradigm] as originally defined by Hymes' (Duranti 1988: 219). Fitch and Philipsen (1995: 264) also emphasize that 'comparison across case studies is one of the central theoretical moves of the ethnography of speaking, abstraction from the complexities of particular cases into universal, independent principles is not'; they also state, even more emphatically, that 'the thrust of the ethnography of speaking has been to map the cultural and linguistic relativity of language use, universal features or aspects of language use have been a secondary (or more commonly, nonexistent) concern' (Fitch and Philipsen 1995: 267). Indeed, the fact that most publications within the paradigm have been restricted to one or two of its foci makes it extremely difficult, if not impossible, to compare these studies in order to extract possible theoretical generalizations.

However, ever since the publication of the anthologies edited by Gumperz and Hymes (1964, 1972) and by Bauman and Sherzer (1974), a large body of field work has been conducted under the auspices of the paradigm. In the 1970s and 1980s a large number of dissertations, books and articles were published, such as, for example, E. Basso (1985), K. H. Basso (1979), Feld (1982), and Gossen (1974). It is true that most researchers focused their studies on specialized topics within the paradigm, such as intercultural communication (Gumperz 1982), verbal art (Sherzer and Urban 1986), or the acquisition of communicative competence (Schieffelin and Ochs 1986). Nevertheless, the impact the paradigm had on anthropological linguistics and linguistic anthropology is impressively mirrored in Foley (1997), who dedicates one of the six parts of his introduction to anthropological linguistics to the ethnography of speaking framework (Foley 1997: 249–378). Moreover, almost all the characteristic features of the paradigm surface in the titles of the contributions to the anthology edited by Duranti (2004). Researchers working in the ethnography of speaking paradigm have shown how important this framework with its components is for the research of speech in interaction and for the understanding of language use.[22]

4.5 CONCLUDING REMARKS

This chapter first introduced Malinowski's theory about meaning and language. It was pointed out that he saw language as a mode of behaviour, a mode of action in which the meaning of a word or an utterance is constituted by its function within situative, cultural and social contexts. Meaning is also determined by essential uses of language. One of these essential forms of language use is realized in what Malinowski calls phatic communion, a type of speech that is used at the beginning and at the end of social interactions to establish and secure personal bonds between the interactants. He points out that phatic communion does not serve any purpose of communicating ideas and emphasizes that the expression of thoughts in speech is the most derivative and specialized use of language. However, it was shown that the function of phatic communion goes beyond the creation of ties of union: as a binding ritual it establishes and maintains a harmonious atmosphere and solidarity in interpersonal relations during the opening and closing phases of social interactions. It also has indexical functions with respect to the interactants' status and social identity and it initiates routine exchanges that can be rather rich in information. Although Malinowski pointed out that language can be used without any purpose of communicating ideas, he nevertheless was very much interested in the interrelationship between language, culture and cognition.

This interest was shared by Malinowski's contemporary Boas and his younger colleagues Sapir and Whorf. Contrary to Malinowski, Sapir and especially Whorf saw language primarily as an instrument of thought. Sapir and especially Whorf argued that language determines, or at least influences, thought. This idea became known as the Sapir-Whorf hypothesis. The second part of this chapter presented the hypothesis in the light of a research project on spatial reference and the conceptualization of space in different languages and cultures. The results of this project support the hypothesis that language contributes to shaping thinking for non-verbal problem solving. However, it was pointed out that it still remains problematic to argue that it is only language that influences thought in general. Slobin's concept of 'thinking for speaking' as a special form of thought and Clark's comments on the Sapir-Whorf hypothesis in which he emphasizes the fact that language is just one part of many other commonalities of mental life, that there is no speaking without mental activity but that there is mental activity without speaking, reveal that further research is necessary to really understand the complex interface of language, culture and thought.

Malinowski, Boas and Sapir pointed out that speech must be studied in its social context. One of the prerequisites for studying the relationship between language, culture and cognition is to know how the researched speech communities construct their social and cultural realities. Researchers have to be on common ground with the communities they study and they have to acquire linguistic and cultural competence within these communities to understand how they structure, pattern and regulate their ways of speaking. The ethnography of speaking paradigm founded by Dell Hymes offers an excellent, though complex, framework for pursuing these ambitious aims. The last part of this chapter provided a brief introduction to the ethnography of speaking framework which seeks to study the influence of situations, participants, ends, act sequences, keys, instrumentalities, norms and genres of speech styles and speech events. This approach to understanding language use was illustrated with examples from Joel Sherzer's seminal study of the Kuna ways of speaking. When one assesses the ethnography of speaking approach one must concede that the vast majority of research results gained so far are case studies that make it extremely difficult to come up with generalizations. However, this research has proved that the study of speech in interaction needs to be rooted in such complex frameworks like the one provided by the ethnography of speaking paradigm.

What does this chapter tell us about the anecdote reported in the introduction to this volume? It reveals once more that I misunderstood the Trobriand Islanders' greeting ritual as just phatic communion in Malinowski's sense. The question of the greeting was actually meant to elicit information – which I provided in complex serial verb constructions once I had learned how to adequately respond to this greeting formula. This insight into the Trobriand Islanders' ways of greeting was one of many steps towards getting on common ground with the community I wanted to study and thus towards acquiring the communicative competence necessary to achieve this aim (see Senft 2010a). By contrast, the greeting question 'Are you going somewhere?', provided as one of the examples from Korean to illustrate the concept of phatic communion, is not meant to elicit information. Thus, my first reactions towards the Trobrianders' greeting question would have been culturally appropriate in social interactions with speakers of Korean.

4.6 EXERCISE/WORK SECTION

- Discuss Malinowski's position that 'to regard language as a means for the expression of thought is to take a one-sided view of its most derivative and specialized functions'.

- Carry out an experiment in which you video-document an encounter between at least three dyads of friends, co-students or other acquaintances of yours (one dyad consisting of males and one of females only, the third dyad consisting of a male and a female participant). One of the interactants should be sitting on a chair in a room while the camera (which is in sight of the participants) is running. You ask the other interactant to enter the room and sit down on the chair close to the other person. After ten minutes you enter the room and tell the participants that you have to stop the experiment now – but you let the camera run until the participants in your experiment have left the room. Describe and analyse how the participants in this experiment open and close their interaction and look for what kind of forms or tokens of phatic communion you observe and if they differ with respect to gender. Feel free to come up with other designs of such an experiment on the use of tokens of phatic communion at the beginning and at the end of an encounter between two or more people (who may or may not know each other) in more natural locations and situations.

- Look at film scenes that depict first encounters of two interactants and describe whether you can observe tokens of phatic communion and if so, what kinds of tokens of phatic communion are used in these dialogues. If you cannot observe any forms of phatic communion during such first encounter scenes, try to explain why.

- Discuss whether or not the strong form of the Sapir-Whorf hypothesis which claims that language determines thought is a tenable hypothesis.

- Think of one other domain than space in which one could find effects that may support at least the weak form of the Sapir-Whorf hypothesis, explain why you chose this domain and elaborate on ways to test your hypothesis.

- Compare the ways of speaking you understand as being typical for your mother-tongue with the ways of speaking you or others take as being typical of another language community.

4.7 SUGGESTIONS FOR FURTHER READING

Auer and di Luzio (1992); Basso, K. H. (1979); Bazzanella (1990); Boroditsky (2001); Coupland (2000); Dumont (1977); Dunbar (1996, 2007); Eibl-Eibesfeldt (1968, 1971b); Frake (1980); Hunt and Agnoli (1991); Gentner and Goldin-Meadow (2003); Lucy (1997); Malotki (1983); Muhawi (1999); Niemeier and Dirven (2000); Pederson (2007); Pullum (1991); Saville-Troike (2003); Sherzer (1990); Smith (2010); Stenström and Jörgensen (2008); Werner (1998).

NOTES

1   For more information about Malinowski see Young (2004) and Senft (1997b, 2005, 2006, 2009d). For phatic communion see Senft (1996b, 2009e).
2   This statement is echoed by Hockett (1973: 675) who points out that '[l]inguistics without anthropology is sterile; anthropology without linguistics is blind'.
3   Compare Richard Bauman (1992: 147) who also emphasizes that 'meaning resides in the pragmatic function of an utterance'.
4   Note that 'phatic communion' must not be confused with Austin's 'phatic act'. See subsection 1.2.3 of Chapter One.
5   John Laver (1975: 221) refers to David Abercrombie who points out that '[t]he actual sense of the words used in phatic communion matters little' (Abercrombie 1956). Abercrombie then 'goes on to recount the story of Dorothy Parker [an American poet and short story writer. G. S.], alone and rather bored at a party, [who was] asked "How are you? What have you been doing?" by a succession of distant acquaintances. To each she replied "I've just

killed my husband with an axe, and I feel fine." Her intonation and expression were appropriate to party-talk, and with a smile and a nod each acquaintance, unastonished, drifted on'. See also Parker's short story 'Here we are' in Parker (1944).

6 But note that Duk-Soo Park (2006: 156) refers to Cheepen (1988: 20f.) who points out that 'phatic communion is not confined to the opening and closing phases, but also occurs as short words or phrases (e.g. "well", or "you know") among other, non-phatic speech, and it can also (and often does) extend over a whole encounter (such as a chat), which may last for several hours'.

7 Boas himself never pursued this idea – which he may have taken from Wilhelm von Humboldt.

8 But see also Whorf (1956: 134–159 [1941]). For a survey of the origins and the influence of the Sapir-Whorf hypothesis see Koerner (2000) and Lee (1996, 2010).

9 I agree with Pieter Seuren (2013) that it is more appropriate to speak of the 'Whorf hypothesis'; however, given the fact that the term 'Sapir-Whorf hypothesis' by now has a certain tradition in linguistics, I use this label to refer to Whorf's claims about the relationship between language, culture and cognition.

10 For a description and a critical assessment of these methods see Senft (2001) and especially (2007).

11 The // in the name of the language Hai//om is the symbol for a non-pulmonic consonant, the voiceless alveolar lateral click.

12 In the sentence '*The socks are in the drawer*' one differentiates between the entity to be situated, the 'theme' or the 'figure', namely *the socks*, and the reference object or the entity in relation to which the theme is situated – which is called the 'relatum' or 'ground' – namely *the drawer*. The spatial relation between 'figure' and 'ground', or 'theme' and 'relatum' in this example is 'being in'.

13 The design of these experiments enables one to distinguish between absolute and other frames of references, though not between intrinsic and relative frames. Speakers of languages which prefer the intrinsic system for verbal spatial references will behave in these experiments like speakers of languages which prefer the relative frame of spatial reference.

14 That is, all nouns in the title of Clark's paper start with a 'c'.

15 The first part of this subsection draws on Senft (2010a: 280ff.).

16 Note Malinowski's influence with respect to the role of context for meaning.

17 A *tertium comparationis* (the third in comparison) is the element that remains constant when different things, features, etc. are compared.

18 It has to be noted, though, that he does not always provide the original Kuna transcription; moreover, he does not present morpheme-interlinearized transcriptions either.

19 This is reminiscent of the Trobriand Islanders' greeting behaviour; however, Sherzer does not provide any information about the degree of truth expected by the Kuna in the answers to these questions.

20 There are no puberty rites for Kuna boys (see Sherzer 1983: 140).

21 For another such attempt see Senft (2010a).

22 The debate about diversity versus universality and/or specificity versus generalization seems to be a recurrent pattern in theoretical discussions within the humanities. Compare, for example, the critical discussion of the ethnography of speaking paradigm presented here with the reaction of the linguistic peer group to Evan's and Levinson's (2009a and b) papers on 'The myth of language universals' in Volume 32(5) of the journal *Brain and Behavioral Sciences* and in Volume 120(12) of the journal *Lingua* (see Levinson and Evans 2010) or with the discussion about generalizations and other claims about human psychology and behaviour that are based on experiments with WEIRD (i.e. western, educated, industrialized, rich and democratic) subjects, initiated by Henrich *et al.* (2010a and b).

Pragmatics and sociology

Everyday social interaction

5.1 INTRODUCTION

In the 1960s and 1970s the research of three North American sociologists had a strong impact on the understanding of human everyday face-to-face interaction in general and on the understanding of communicative behaviour and language use in particular – especially in conversation.

The first part of this chapter features Erving Goffman's (1922–1982) insights in, and ideas about, social interaction.

The second part of this chapter deals with Harold Garfinkel's (1917–2011) ethnomethodological studies on social order, his understanding of everyday 'common sense' knowledge and his ideas about how we make sense of our social world.

Influenced by Garfinkel, but also by Goffman, Harvey Sacks (1935–1975) developed the field of 'Conversation Analysis' (CA) to research how conversation is ordered and structurally organized. The third part of this chapter presents central aspects and research results of the CA approach and recent developments within this field.

5.2 ERVING GOFFMAN'S INTERACTION ORDER

Erving Goffman's research focused on social interaction that is guided and regulated by normative rights and obligations. He understood the study of face-to-face interactions as a subdiscipline of sociology. In his 1983 (undelivered) presidential address to the American Sociological Association Goffman proposed to call this subarea of his discipline 'the interaction order'. Kendon notes that American sociologists before Goffman had studied interaction as 'a means to an end':

> [Their] approaches took the view that the phenomena of usual concern to sociology and social psychology – leadership, social stratification, organization of authority, and the like – must be grounded in the patterning of specific acts of interaction between society's members. Such acts were to form the basic data upon which the investigation of such phenomena was to be based. However, the acts of interaction were not themselves studied. Only an aspect of them was seized upon as a means toward studying something else. Goffman recognized this and made it clear that what he was concerned with was different: it was to raise the question as how interaction is possible in the first place.
>
> (Kendon 1988c: 19)

Goffman (1967: 2) made it clear that for him 'the proper study of interaction is not the individual and his psychology, but rather the syntactical relations among the acts of different persons mutually present to one another'.[1] Based on the Aristotelian insight that human beings are social animals who spend most of their daily life 'in the immediate presence of others', he pointed out that all their 'doings are likely to be ... *socially situated*' (Goffman 1983a: 2). Face-to-face interactions occur in social situations in which persons are 'co-present with one another' and where 'they must sense that they are close enough to be perceived in whatever they are doing, including their experiencing of others and close enough to be perceived in this sensing of being perceived' (Goffman 1963: 17). This concept of the social situation is central for Goffman's research. He refers to a social situation in which 'people effectively agree to sustain for a time a single focus of cognitive and visual attention, as in a conversation', as a 'focused gathering' or an 'encounter'; and he differentiates such an encounter from 'unfocused interaction' which 'consists of those interpersonal communications that result solely by virtue of persons being in one another's presence', like, for example people walking along in a city or town street (Goffman 1961: 8). In Goffman's interaction order:

> the engrossment and involvement of the participants – if only their attention – is critical ... Emotion, mood, cognition, bodily orientation, and muscular effort are intrinsically involved, introducing an inevitable psychobiological element. Ease and uneasiness, unselfconsciousness and wariness are central.
>
> (Goffman 1983a: 3)

Thus, even in unfocused forms of interaction like walking in a street, people mutually coordinate their behaviour. Goffman describes this behaviour as a minimal interactive ritual which he calls 'civil inattention'. In this situation people who pass each other may 'glance at one another but mutually agree not to let their eyes meet, and do so in a way that lets each know that the other is not scared, hostile or that he regards the other as an automaton' (Kendon 1988c: 25). Focused gatherings, however, are much more complex. Goffman points out that:

> [o]nce individuals – for whatever reason – come into one another's immediate presence, a fundamental condition of social life becomes enormously pronounced, namely its promissory, evidential character. It is not only that our appearance and manner provide evidence of our statuses and relationships. It is also that the line of our visual regard, the intensity of our involvement, and the shape of our initial actions, allow others to glean our immediate intent and purpose, and all this whether or not we are engaged in talk with them at the time. Correspondingly, we are constantly in a position to facilitate this revealment, or block it, or even misdirect our viewers. The gleaned character of these observations is itself facilitated and complicated by a general process yet to be systematically studied – social ritualization – that is, the standardization of bodily and vocal behavior through socialization, affording such behavior – such gestures, if you will – a specialized communicative function in the stream of behavior.
>
> (Goffman 1983a: 3)

In these encounters, participants 'provide information in two ways: they *give* it, and they *give it off*' (Kendon 1988c: 22). This holds when people talk with each other as well, of course. Besides the information provided through the verbal channel, additional information is provided by the interactants; however, it is for the respective participant in the interaction to decide whether this information is given voluntarily or involuntarily by his or her co-participant. Kendon emphasizes that Goffman's observation is extremely important for the study of all forms of social interaction, including conversations:

> In any situation of interaction ... participants treat only some aspects of each other's behaviour as if it is deliberately intended to convey something. In conversations it is usually the something called 'content of talk' that is treated in this way, not the manner of talk, and certainly not the bodily stagings and ecological arrangements within which the talk is carried on. However, it is not as if these other aspects of the situation play no role in the structuring of the interaction. Far from it. Their role is crucial to the whole way in which the event is organized. We owe Goffman a major debt for getting us to see this.
>
> (Kendon 1988c: 23)

People who engage in face-to-face interaction thus 'fashion the situations in which they participate through the ways in which they conduct themselves and read the conduct of others' (Drew and Wootton 1988: 5). There are procedures and conventions regulating rights and obligations that provide interactants with basic rules for playing their interaction game. Goffman compared them with traffic rules or syntactic rules in a language. These rules – based on social contract and social consensus, that is to say, on 'social order' – 'inform the interaction order and allow for a traffic of use' (Goffman 1983a: 6; see also 1971: xf.). The interactants have to come up with a shared agreement on their interaction situation. As Goffman points out,

> [t]his includes agreement concerning perceptual relevances and irrelevancies, and a 'working consensus' involving a degree of mutual considerateness, sympathy, and a muting of opinion differences ... At the same time a heightened sense of moral responsibility for one's acts also seems to develop.
>
> (Goffman 1963: 96ff.)

In 'interpersonal rituals' the social relationship between interactants are affirmed and supported. These rituals encompass accounts, apologies, 'tie-signs ... that indicate the nature of relationships between persons' and 'normal appearances ... [i.e.] signs ... that nothing in the world is out of the ordinary and routines may be followed as usual' (Goffman 1971: 63, 109, 194, 239). Goffman's reference to the interactants' 'sense of moral responsibility' in an encounter shows that for him interaction has important moral aspects and implications. And here his notions of 'self' and 'face' play an important role. Goffman defines 'face' as follows:

> Every person lives in a world of social encounters, involving him either in face-to-face or mediated contact with other participants. In each of these contacts, he tends to act

out what is sometimes called a *line* – that is, a pattern of verbal and nonverbal acts by which he expresses his view of the situation and through his evaluation of the participants, especially himself. ...

The term face may be defined as the positive social value a person effectively claims for himself by the line others assume he has taken during a particular contact. Face is an image of self delineated in terms of approved social attributes – albeit an image that others may share, as when a person makes a good showing for his profession or religion by making a good showing for himself.

(Goffman 1967: 5)

Goffman sees the self as 'a social product ... that ... depends upon validation [of individuals' performances in social situations] awarded and withheld in accordance with the norms of a stratified society'. These norms are constituted by the rules and rituals of the social order – which make the self also 'an object of social ritual' (Branaman 1997: xlvi, lxiii). However, for Goffman self is also a 'kind of player in a ritual game who copes honorably or dishonorably, diplomatically or undiplomatically, with the judgmental contingencies of the situation' (Goffman 1967: 31). Thus, although the self is seen first and foremost as being a social product, individuals are nevertheless able to strategically manipulate the social situations and especially the impressions they invoke in others – like an actor on a theatre stage. This Janus-like understanding of the self in Goffman's approach is captured by Branaman (1997: xlviii) when she notes: 'the self is the mask the individual wears in social situations, but it is also the human being behind the mask who decides which mask to wear'. Branaman concisely summarizes the interrelationship between the concepts of self and face in Goffman's thinking as follows:

It is through our attachment to self that we are attached to society. We maintain face by following social norms, showing deference for and affirming the dignity of others, and presenting ourselves in accordance with our own places in the status hierarchy. The main function of "face work" – interactional work oriented towards affirming and protecting the dignity of social participants – is to maintain the ritual order of social life.

(Branaman 1997: lxiii)

In his book *The Presentation of Self in Everyday Life* Goffman points out that social life and the structural properties of social encounters can be analysed from the perspective of the dramatic performance. There are actors who play their part with the aim to impress in one way or another an audience which consists of co-participants, observers or bystanders. Goffman describes a social encounter of two or more people as a structured event with a clear opening and closing phase:

The opening will typically be marked by the participants turning from their several disjointed orientations, moving together and bodily addressing one another; the closing by their departing in some physical way from the prior immediacy of copresence. Typically, ritual brackets will also be found, such as greetings and farewells, these establishing and terminating open, official joint engagement, that is, ratified participation. ... Throughout the course of the encounter the participants will be obliged to sustain involvement in what is being said and ensure that no long stretch occurs when no one ... is taking the floor.

(Goffman 1981: 130)

In what Goffman calls '*moments* of talk' one usually distinguishes the notions of hearer and speaker. With hearers – or listeners or recipients – Goffman differentiates between ratified participants – that is participants in an encounter addressed both verbally and visually and recognized by the speaker – and unratified participants or bystanders, who may either unintentionally 'overhear' what is said or who follow these moments of talk intentionally as eavesdroppers. Goffman points out that the relations between speaker, addressed and unaddressed recipients is 'complicated, significant, and not much addressed' (Goffman 1981: 131ff.).

Hearers or recipients of moments of talk are not only found in conversations, meetings, hearings and other situations in which persons come together. Talk can also take the form of what Goffman calls a 'platform monologue, as in the case of political addresses, ... lectures, dramatic recitations, poetry readings' and so on. These platform performances constitute another important interaction entity that can have a 'live audience', a 'broadcast audience' and even 'imagined recipients' – as in 'radio and TV talk' (Goffman 1981: 137f.). The largest interactional unit in Goffman's approach is constituted by 'celebrative social occasions' which Goffman defines as 'foregathering[s] of individuals admitted on a controlled basis, the whole occurring under the auspices of, and in honor of, some jointly appreciated circumstances' (Goffman 1983a: 7).

For the notion of speaker Goffman identifies three roles: the *animator*, the *author* and the *principal*. The *animator* is 'the talking machine ... an individual active in the role of utterance production ... Animator and recipient are part of the same level and mode of analysis ... not social roles in the full sense so much as functional nodes in a communication system'. The *author* is 'someone who has selected the sentiments that are being expressed and the words in which they are encoded', and the *principal* is 'someone whose position is established by the words that are spoken, someone whose beliefs have been told, someone who is committed to what the words say'. The animator is defined as 'a person active in some particular social identity or role ... as a member of a group, office, ... association or whatever'. The individual as animator 'speaks ... in the name of "we", not "I"... the "we" including more than self'. The configuration of these three roles constitutes the 'production format of an utterance' (Goffman 1981: 144f.).

Goffman decomposes, so to speak, the notion of hearer or recipient and speaker to point out that these 'commonsense notions ... are crude, ... concealing a complex differentiation of participation statuses and ... complex questions of production format'. This decomposition also reveals 'that the notion of a conversational encounter does not suffice in dealing with the context in which words are spoken ... the whole social situation, the whole surround, must always be considered' (Goffman 1981: 144ff.).

Moreover, Goffman points out that interactants in an encounter can change their social role in a very dynamic way. How Goffman's approach to the interaction order deals with these dynamics is summarized by Jim O'Driscoll:

In reality, of course, the participation status of those involved in talk is changing all the time, not just because *who* is talking and who they address can change but, more crucially, because of *what* is said. Part of Goffman's ritual model assumes that anything done in interaction always and inevitably carries implications about the character of the person who says it, that person's evaluation of other participants and the relationship between them ... To capture these potentially infinitely mutable personal circumstances, Goffman uses the term *footing*, which he defines as "the alignment we take up to ourselves and others present as expressed in the way we manage the production and reception of an utterance" (1981: 128). In addition, anything said also carries an implication about what sort of thing is going on, about how the speaker construes the experience. This is where Goffman's use of the concept of *frame* comes in. For him, a frame is "principles of organization which govern events ... and our subjective involvement in them" (Goffman 1974: 10). Now, it should be obvious that framing does not take place independently of the abovementioned concerns. When something is said which effectively claims a definition of the situation, it simultaneously makes claims about the participants and their relationships. Therefore, "a change in footing is another way of talking about a change in our frame for events" (1981: 128).

(O'Driscoll 2009: 88)

To analyse and capture these dynamics is extremely complex. Goffman explained why: 'As dramatists can put any world on their stage, so we can enact any participation framework and production format in our conversation' (Goffman 1981: 155).

Goffman himself tried to illustrate and analyse the complex structural properties of social interactions in his writings. In what follows, three examples in which he discussed and analysed forms of social interaction and the sequential ordering of actions are presented.

In his micro-analysis of contacts between socially acquainted persons, Goffman makes the following observations: If two people who know each other meet, 'each party of the relationship will be obliged to recall on sight the name of the other, along with some biographical detail' (Goffman 1983b: 41f.). This knowledge must be displayed when they greet each other. The closer the interactants know each other, the richer is their knowledge about each other's biography. Goffman illustrates this as follows:

> For example, if Marsha and Martha are adult close friends, then each is likely to know, and be expected to know, critical matters about the other's close others, enough so that each can efficiently report stories involving her own others. I might add that ceremonies of greeting and departure in our society often require reference to these 'other person's others', this being a case where what can be asked about ought to be asked about.
>
> (Goffman 1983b: 42)

Closely acquainted people also feel obliged to update each other with respect to changes in their life circumstances; they expect to receive such reports and feel entitled to make enquiries about such issues. However, it goes without saying that these enquiries are made with 'referential tact'. That is to say, they have to be phrased in such a way that they are inoffensive and not indelicate in the given situation.[2] Goffman illustrates this situation with the following example:

> Meeting John on the street, his friend has the right (indeed, often the obligation) to ask him how his wife Marsha is and to use her first name as a fully specifying designation; John will know which Marsha his friend is referring to and will have a ready answer. Meeting John on the street just after John (it is known) has broken up with Marsha, his friend omits the nicety, and not because John would not know who was being spoken of.
>
> (Goffman 1983b: 28)

On the basis of these considerations Goffman defines such a relationship between acquainted people as follows:

> [What] we think of as a relationship is, in one sense, merely a provision for the use of cryptic expressions, a provision of what is required in order to allude to things economically. Certainly our obligation to keep the names of our friends in mind, along with other pertinent social facts concerning them, is more than a means of celebrating and renewing our social relationship to them; it also ensues a shared orientation for reference and hence talk whenever we come into contact with them. What affirms relationships also organizes talk.
>
> (Goffman 1983b: 42)

Another example with which Goffman illustrates his approach of context microanalysis is the 'service transaction' in which

> a "server", in a setting prepared for the purpose, perfunctorily and regularly provides goods of some kinds to a series of customers of clients, typically either in exchange for money or as an intermediate phase in bureaucratic processing.
>
> (Goffman 1983a: 14)

Both interactants, the server and the served, find each other in the same social situation which is characterized by a specific institutionalized format. Goffman points out that the service transaction is characterized by at least two rules:

First, there is a basic understanding between the parties involved that everybody will be treated equally. This 'principle of equality' has important implications, of course:

> In order to deal with more than one candidate for service at a time in what can be perceived as an orderly and fair manner, a queuing arrangement is likely to be employed, this likely involving a first come first serve rule. This rule produces a temporal ordering that totally blocks the influence of such differential social statuses and relationships as candidates bring with them to the service situation – attributes which are of massive significance outside the situation ...
>
> (Goffman 1983a: 14)

When customers enter a 'service arena' it is in their own interest to find out as soon as possible how the 'local tracking system' works. Do they have to take a numbered slip from a machine? Do they have to join a queue? Must they monitor the persons who are already present as well as the person who enters the scene just after them? If multiple servers take care of sub-queues, they have to find out in which sub-queue they are and who will look after them. If their place in such a queue is respected, other queuers will have to respect the general queuing discipline, even if they may have special relationships with the server.

Second, Goffman points out that in these transactions people who are seeking service can expect that each of them

> will be treated with courtesy, for example, that the server will give quick attention to the service request, and execute it with words, gestures, and manner that somehow display approval of the asker and pleasure in the contact. Implied (when taken in conjunction with the equality principle) is that a customer who makes a very small purchase will be given no less a reception than one who makes a very large one.
> (Goffman 1983a: 14f.)

However, besides these two rules there are many other issues that are relevant in service transactions. There are conditions, for example, a person must meet to qualify for a candidate for service, like, for example, '[s]ituationally perceptible qualifications regarding age, sobriety, language ability, and solvency' (Goffman 1983a: 15). Not all service transactions require that the server and the person(s) served have eye-contact (see below) – that is why Goffman prefers to speak of service transactions and not of service encounters. However, he points out that in these transactions

> [t]he standard arrangement ... is for eyes to meet, the mutual obligation of a social encounter accepted, and civil titles used ... in the initial interchange, typically in utterance-initial or utterance-terminal position. In our society, this means a gender-marked vocative and a tinting of behavior that is thought to be suitable for the gender mix in the transaction ... If served is a pre-adult, then this too is likely to be reflected in server's vocative selection and "speech register".
> (Goffman 1983a: 15)

Server and served may also know each other by name and may have had a prior relationship. If this is the case,

> then the transaction is likely to be initiated and terminated by a relationship ritual: individually identifying terms of address are likely to be used along with the exchange of inquiry and well-wishing found in standard greetings and farewells between acquaintances. So long as these initial and terminal flurries of sociability are sustained as a subordinate involvement during the transaction, so long as other persons present do not feel their movement in the queue is being impeded, then no sense of intrusion into the application of equalitarian treatment is likely to be sensed. The management of personal relationships is thus bracketed.
> (Goffman 1983a: 15)

Goffman points out that 'all the various elements in the standard structure of serving can be ... breached in almost an infinite number of ways'. However, when this is done, it is done in 'the form of deniable acts' which can be disputed if the actors are challenged openly (Goffman 1983a: 15).

Going to the cinema and buying tickets is another scenario with which Goffman illustrates his approach to researching interaction. If one goes with one's partner to the movies, one goes to a ticket window, takes money out of one's purse and says to the ticket seller: 'Two please'. With this elliptic utterance one indicates that one wants tickets – and given the situation the ticket seller is completely aware of this, despite the information-wise rather underspecified utterance addressed to her or him. Goffman notes that the ticket seller appreciates that s/he was not asked to '*give*' the customer the tickets, 'but to *exchange* them for money'. This interaction requires no 'prior state of talk'. If one approaches the ticket window one has 'a right to start flat out with words regarding tickets'. The job of the person who sells the tickets obliges him or her to 'make sense out of cryptic utterances regarding tickets' because of the institutionalized service arrangement which s/he is part of. Goffman points out that the whole transaction of buying tickets at a movie can be carried out without an exchange of words and even without eye-contact (Goffman 1983b: 34f.). With examples like this Goffman supports his observation that

> the general constraint that an utterance must satisfy, namely, that it connects acceptably with what recipient has in, or can bring to, mind, applies in a manner to non-linguistic acts in wordless contexts ... [W]henever we come into contact with another ... we find ourselves with one central obligation: to render our behavior understandably relevant to what the other can come to perceive is going on. Whatever else, our activity must be addressed to the other's mind, that is, to the other's capacity to read our words and actions for evidence of our feelings, thoughts and intent. This confines what we say and do, but it also allows us to bring to bear all of the world to which the other can catch allusions.
>
> (Goffman 1983b: 50f.)

To sum up: Goffman's interaction research provided deep insights into the complex structural properties of human interaction in social situations. Social interaction is a social institution with its own rules and orders that constitute a 'syntax' which regulates interactional rights and obligations. Goffman showed that these rules – which also control the order of actions in interaction – are based on the social order constitutive for the interactants' community. Interactions are rooted in, and dependent on, specific contexts and create (new) contexts at the same time. Participants in co-present interaction permanently monitor and analyse each other's forms of behaviour; they make inferences regarding their own and the other's motivations, intentions and self-presentation, and they frame their encounters and permanently negotiate/renegotiate, construct/reconstruct and frame/reframe their roles as well as the interaction situation during these encounters, thus affirming and protecting their dignity – their face – to maintain the ritual and moral order of social life.

5.3 HAROLD GARFINKEL'S ETHNOMETHODOLOGY

Harold Garfinkel, one of Goffman's colleagues and friends, also investigated the social order, the sociology of daily life. He did so, however, in a specific framework for which he coined the label 'ethnomethodology'. He defined his approach as follows:

> I use the term *ethnomethodology* to refer to various policies, methods, results, risks, and lunacies with which to locate and accomplish the study of the rational properties of practical actions as contingent ongoing accomplishments of organized artful practices of everyday life.
>
> (Garfinkel 1972: 309)

He emphasized that ethnomethodology is

> concerned with the question of how, over the temporal course of their actual engagements, and 'knowing' the society only from within, members produce stable, accountable practical activities, i.e., social structures of everyday activities.
>
> (Garfinkel 1967: 185)

And he characterizes ethnomethodological studies as studies that analyse

> everyday activities as members' methods for making those same activities visibly-rational-and-reportable-for-all-practical-purposes, i.e., "accountable", as organizations of commonplace everyday activities. The reflexivity of that phenomenon is a singular feature of practical actions, of practical circumstances, of common sense knowledge of social structures, and of practical sociological reasoning. By permitting us to locate and examine their occurrence the reflexivity of that phenomenon establishes their study.
>
> (Garfinkel 1967: vii)

Thus, like Goffman, Garfinkel focuses his research on how ordinary members of a society or community use 'taken-for-granted, *commonsense* practices' (Firth 2009: 67) as means and (ethno)methods of practical reasoning to constitute, understand and make shared sense not only of the common context and the specific circumstances of their actions, but also of their social order, i.e. their social world. In doing so they heavily rely on the 'reflexive relation between the "facts" about society and the ways ... [they] use practical reasoning and commonsense knowledge to depict society' (Psathas 1994: 1162). Garfinkel's approach will be illustrated with four of his and his students' studies:

In a study on procedures followed for coding patients in a psychiatric clinic, for example, Garfinkel wanted to investigate how people who work in the clinic do these codings and how students examine the codings. Garfinkel (1972: 311) and his students demonstrated that the coders in the clinic 'were assuming knowledge of the very organized ways of the clinic that their coding procedures were intended to produce descriptions of'. Obviously this 'presupposed knowledge' was necessary for the coders to be satisfied with their categorizations made during the actual coding situations and to be convinced that their coding results represented 'what really happened'. But what did the coders actually do when they were made to follow the coding instructions? Garfinkel and his co-workers started from the assumption that '*whatever* they did could be counted correct procedure in *some* coding game'. Their task then was to find out how the coders played what kind of game to get the coding results documented in the folders. Garfinkel presents these results as follows:

> We soon found the essential relevance to the coders of such considerations as: "et cetera," "unless," "let it pass," and "factum valet."[3]
>
> For convenience call these considerations "ad hoc", and call their use in the coder's work of interrogating contents for answers to their questions "ad hocing". Coders used these same ad hoc considerations in order to recognize the relevance of the coding instructions to the organized activities of the clinic. Only when this relevance was clear were the coders satisfied that the coding instructions did analyze actually encountered folder contents in such a way as to permit the coders to treat folder contents as reports of "real events".
>
> (Garfinkel 1972: 312)

That is to say, the coders followed coding rules and coding instructions; however, they adapted them so that they made sense in specific cases, that is to say that they fitted the given data. With this study Garfinkel rejected Talcott Parsons' idea 'that rules "cause" or "explain" behavior'; instead, he emphasized 'the inherent "looseness" and "resourcefulness" of rules' and he 'demonstrated that their use in actual settings was empirically researchable as a topic in its own right' (Firth 2009: 70).

In another experiment Garfinkel (1972: 316) asked students to 'report common conversation by writing on the left side of a sheet what the parties actually said and on the right side what they and their partners understood that they were talking about'. It turned out that the students found the task impossible. Gumperz and Hymes summarize Garfinkel's interpretation of this result as follows:

> [The students] took the task to be one of remedying the sketchiness of the conversation by elaborating its contents, by appealing outside the speech event to what became, under prodding, an infinite regress of context. Their error was to assume a theory of signs in which the way something is said is divorced from what is being said ..., and in concentrating on the "what", neglecting the "how". In fact, the conversation (like any conversation) was an instance of one or more alternative ways of speaking; it was intelligible to its participants not because of some shared infinity of substantive knowledge as to what is being talked about but in the first instance because they agreed at the time on how the talking was being done and how it was to be interpreted. The fact that such momentary agreements can be reached, however, does not mean that content can be reconstructed later under different conditions.
>
> (Gumperz and Hymes 1972: 303)

This experiment supports the idea put forward by Garfinkel (1967: 4ff.) and Garfinkel and Sacks (1970) that not only deictic expressions (see Chapter Two) but all linguistic actions are indexical. With the notion of indexicality Garfinkel 'refers to the fact that for members, the meaning of what they say and do is dependent on the context in which their doing and saying occurs' (Psathas 1994: 1161). Firth points out that for Garfinkel

> understanding is *accomplished* not on the basis of pre-established shared meanings, but *procedurally* and *contextually* – in that what is said [and done, G. S.] is invariably assessed in a particular, local context, by particular persons, at a particular moment.
>
> (Firth 2009: 71)

In his famous 'breaching experiments' Garfinkel instructed students 'to engage an acquaintance or friend in an ordinary conversation and, without indicating that what the experimenter was saying was in any way out of the ordinary, to insist that the person clarify the sense of his commonplace remarks' (Garfinkel 1963: 220ff.). Two such interactions are reported here (see Garfinkel 1967: 42 and 44):

> Interaction 1:
>> The subject was telling the experimenter, a member of the subject's car pool, about having had a flat tire while going to work the previous day.
>> S: I had a flat tire.
>> E: What do you mean, you had a flat tire?
> She appeared momentarily stunned, then she answered in a hostile way:
>> 'What do you mean? What do you mean? A flat tire is a flat tire. That is what I meant. What a crazy question!'

> Interaction 2:
>> The victim waved his hand cheerily.
>> S: How are you?
>> E: How am I in regard to what? My health, my finance, my school work, my peace of mind, my...
>> S: (Red in face and suddenly out of control.)
>> I was just trying to be polite. Frankly I don't give a damn how you are.

Garfinkel's (1967: 36f.) explicit aim with these experiments was to make 'commonplace scenes visible' by starting 'with familiar scenes' and then 'make trouble'. With the experiments he made the students breach Alfred Schütz's (1962) 'idealization of the congruency of relevance' that contributes to making up his 'general thesis of reciprocal perspective'. Heritage summarizes the results of these experiments as follows:

> the subjects had expected that the experimenters would be drawing upon background knowledge of 'what everybody knows', supply a sense to their remarks that was 'empirically identical' with the sense intended by the [subjects]. The [subject] thus assumed, in each case, that both parties knew 'what he is talking about without any requirement of a check-out' (Garfinkel 1963: 220). In each case, the [subject] took for granted that the [experimenter] would supply whatever unstated understandings

would be required in order to make recognizable sense of his talk. This requirement ... pervades all interaction ... It is noticeable that the [experimenters'] breaches of this requirement resulted in interactional breakdowns which were extraordinarily rapid and complete ... Moreover, ... the [experimenters'] breaches were very rapidly and powerfully sanctioned ... [T]he [subject] treated the intelligible character of his own talk as something to which he was morally entitled and, correspondingly, treated the breaching move as illegitimate, deserving of sanction and requiring explanation. The experiment thus indicated that maintaining 'reciprocity of perspectives' (as one of the presuppositions of the attitude of daily life) is not merely a cognitive task, but one which each actor 'trusts' that the other will accomplish as a matter of moral necessity.

(Heritage 1984: 81f.)

Thus, these experiments revealed that 'interactants hold themselves and one another morally accountable for the "accommodative work" through which they make sense of their circumstances' (Heritage 1984: 84).

In a student counselling experiment, undergraduates were told to describe a problem they had and to ask the counsellor questions about it; the students were told that they had to design their questions as yes/no questions. The counsellor and the students were situated in adjoining rooms, connected by intercom. After every question/answer sequence the students were asked to switch off their intercom and to tape-record their reflections on the counsellor's answer. What the students did not know was that the counsellor gave his/her answers according to a random schedule. Nevertheless, it turned out that the students tried their very best to interpret the advice given as coherent answers to their questions given by a motivated counsellor (Garfinkel 1967: 76ff.). With this experiment Garfinkel wanted to illustrate his notion of the 'documentary method of interpretation' which he defined as consisting of

treating an actual appearance as "the document of", as "pointing to", as "stating on behalf of" a presupposed underlying pattern ... The method is recognizable for the everyday necessities of recognizing what a person is "talking about" given that he does not say exactly what he means.

(Garfinkel 1967: 78)

Thus, the documentary method provides interactants with the basis for the shared understanding of their actions. Firth points out that in this study the

'documentary method of interpretation' is one resource that enabled the students to make sense of otherwise incoherent actions. This 'method' and the ... notion of the 'natural attitude' ... are claimed to permeate all acts of mundane perception and cognition ... Garfinkel maintains that the 'natural attitude' is part of a member's 'commonsense assumptions' that underpin social interaction and the 'accommodative work' which the interaction necessitates. The assumptions include:

1. *Searching for a normal form* ... [W]hen discrepancies and/or ambiguities appear, people suspend doubt and search for an assumed 'normal form' that would account for the discrepancies.
2. *Doing the reciprocity of perspectives*. This entails sustaining the assumption that each participant would have the same experiences if they were to change places.
3. *Employing the et cetera principle*. This assumption entails participants filling in (observedly 'missing') information during social activities; in this way, participants let unclarities and anomalies 'pass' in the belief that they will be subsequently clarified ...

(Firth 2009: 74f.)

Garfinkel made at least three fundamental contributions to the study of social interaction:

First, he put the focus of this enterprise on practical commonsense knowledge which provides interactants with the basis for understanding their actions in their social world – their social order. Individuals, or members – in Garfinkel's terminology – use commonsense practices as shared ethnomethods of practical reasoning to constitute, and at the same time to make shared sense of and understand, their actions and their social world. Gumperz and Hymes point out that for Garfinkel

> [i]t is these modes of reasoning that should be the first order business in social research. The basis of culture, Garfinkel suggests, is not shared knowledge but shared rules of interpretation; not common substantive information, already acquired, but "common sense" knowledge of what can count as reasonable, factual, related, and the like.
>
> (Gumperz and Hymes 1972: 304)

Second, in doing so, Garfinkel pointed out 'the constitutive role of cognition in the organisation of social activities' by showing that interactants strive for accomplishing shared understanding procedurally and contextually, that they take their mutual efforts to reach this aim as a matter of moral necessity and that they use the documentary method of interpretation as a resource for making sense of seemingly incoherent actions (see Firth 2009: 93).

And third, in doing this he described 'the local, contingent and reflexive "work" through which concrete social settings, identities and activities are rendered recognizable and meaningful' (Firth 2009: 94). Gumperz and Hymes assess this as the fundamental contention of Garfinkel's work: 'the orderliness, rationality, accountability of everyday life is, as he puts it, a "contingent, ongoing accomplishment", a kind of "work" or "doing"' (Gumperz and Hymes 1972: 304).

5.4 HARVEY SACKS AND CONVERSATION ANALYSIS

Harvey Sacks was a student – and later a colleague – of both Goffman and Garfinkel. Garfinkel closely cooperated for an extended period with Sacks; they even published together (Garfinkel and Sacks 1970). Influenced by these two scholars, especially by their studies on practical reasoning, on the sequential ordering of actions, on interactional units as well as on talk in face-to-face interactions and the interactants' behaviour in conversation, Sacks developed the field of 'Conversation Analysis' (from here on abbreviated as CA) in close cooperation with Emanuel A. Schegloff and Gail Jefferson (see Schegloff 1992: xv, xxiii). This subsection presents the CA approach and some of its crucial aspects and insights.

In one of his papers Sacks explains what kinds of methodological considerations were responsible for his decision to study tape-recorded conversations:

> When I started to do research in sociology I figured that sociology could not be an actual science unless it was able to handle the details of actual events, handle them formally, and in the first instance be informative about them in the direct ways in which primitive sciences tend to be informative, that is, that anyone else can go and see whether what was said is so. And that is a tremendous control on seeing whether one is learning anything. So the question was, could there be some way that sociology could hope to deal with the details of actual events, formally and informatively? ... I wanted to locate some set of materials that would permit a test. ... It was not from any large interest in language or from some theoretical formulation of what should be studied that I started with tape-recorded conversation, but simply because I could get my hands on it and I could study it again and again, and also, consequentially, because others could look at what I had studied and make of it what they could, if, for example, they wanted to be able to disagree with me.
>
> (Sacks 1984: 26)

He was convinced that studying conversations – the actual and basic naturally occurring forms of language use in specific situations and contexts – would provide not only important insights into the 'details of actual events', but also into the speakers' practical commonsense knowledge and reasoning manifest in their conversational practices. Among the first conversation data Sacks studied were recordings of phone calls to the Suicide Prevention Center in Los Angeles. His repeated analyses of these and other more ordinary telephone calls confirmed his hypothesis that 'ordinary conversation [is] a deeply ordered, structurally organized phenomenon' (Clift *et al.* 2009: 40). These first analyses focused on the systematics of the organization of turn-taking for conversation in which the speakers co-construct meaning and social action, on how speakers manage to regulate who is speaking next and when and on the sequential order of social actions and activities during conversation. The following general features observed in conversations are crucial for the CA approach (see Sacks *et al.* 1974: 700ff.):

- The number of speakers involved in a conversation varies and speaker-change takes place.

- Usually one party talks at a time; however, it is also common that more than one interactant speak at a time, but these occurrences are rather brief.

- Speakers try to avoid overlaps and to minimize gaps between turns.

- Turn order and turn size vary.

- The length of a conversation, what parties say and the distribution of turns is not specified in advance.

- Talk can be continuous or discontinuous.

- Speakers use 'turn-allocation techniques', e.g. a current speaker may select a next speaker or parties involved in the conversation may 'self-select' in starting to talk.

- Turns consist of 'turn-constructional units (TCUs)' like, e.g. a word, a clause, or one or more sentences that are recognized by their interactants as meaningful. At the end of a TCU a next speaker may take a turn or the current speaker may produce a next TCU. That is to say, ends of TCUs are not only 'turn-completion points' (TCPs), but also 'transition-relevance places (TRPs)'.

- Problems that arise during speaking, hearing and understanding can be repaired by interactants in a conversation.

Sacks and his colleagues Schegloff and Jefferson illustrated and discussed these observations in their seminal 1974 paper on turn-taking in conversation with which they established CA as a subdiscipline of sociology in its own right. David Logue and Tanya Stivers characterize this subdiscipline as follows:

> As a theory of social interaction, Conversation Analysis holds that conversation is built out of sequences of actions. As such, language is not fundamentally concerned with 'meaning' but with implementing actions such as greeting, requesting, offering, inviting, complimenting, chastizing and insulting. Moreover, the theory asserts that people produce and recognize each other's social actions via a norm-governed system. Insofar as social interaction is norm-governed, people are expected to hold one another accountable for violations of these norms.
>
> (Logue and Stivers 2012: 1285)

Conversation analysts base their studies on audio- and video-recordings of naturally occurring conversations of almost all kinds[4] which they transcribe as minutely and carefully as possible, using a specifically developed transcription system (see, e.g. Heritage and Clayman 2010: 283ff.; Jefferson 2004)

> which is intended to capture in fine detail the temporal production of talk ... the characteristics of the sequencing of turns, including gaps, pauses, and overlaps; and elements of speech delivery such as audible breath and laughter, stress, enunciation, intonation and pitch, all of which have been shown to have interactional import ... [T]ranscripts aim to provide a detailed but accessible rendering of those features that ... prove to be the most relevant for analyzing the methods by which participants concertedly accomplish orderly and intelligible social interaction ... [T]ranscripts are available for inspection alongside the analyses themselves.
>
> (Clift *et al.* 2009: 43)

The following excerpt (1) from such a transcript (from Sacks *et al.* 1974: 702) illustrates some aspects of this transcription system:

(1)   Jeannette: <u>Oh</u> you know, Mittie- <u>Gor</u>don, eh- <u>Gor</u>don, Mittie's <u>hus</u>band died.
                      (0.3)
        Estelle: Oh whe::n.
        Jeannette: Well it was in the paper this morning.
        Estelle: It <u>wa</u>::s,
→ Jeannette: Yeah.

In this example underscoring indicates stressing, colons indicate prolongation, the numbers in brackets indicate the length of a pause (in this case, 0.3 seconds) and the arrow marks the line of interest for the analysis, in this example the start of a next speaker after a turn composed of a single word with no gap between the turns.

The observation that there is no, or only a very brief, gap between turns can especially be made in so-called *adjacency pairs* (Schegloff and Sacks 1973: 295), sequential units like, e.g. 'question–answer', greeting–greeting', 'offer–acceptance/refusal', 'invitation–acceptance/decline', which achieve this close ordering. Sacks, Schegloff and Jefferson (1974) inferred from this precise temporal alignment of turns that speakers (at least speakers of English) must anticipate the end of a speaker's turn, because the next speaker's preparation for articulating his or her turn requires some time. But what about speakers of other languages?

Psycholinguistic analyses of a corpus – or, in CA methodological terms, a collection – of Dutch two-party telephone conversations revealed that in 45 per cent of all speaker transitions the time between the end of a turn of a speaker and the start of a new turn of a next speaker, the so-called 'FLOOR TRANSFER OFFSET (FTO)' varies between –250 and 250 ms; 85 per cent of all speaker transitions have an FTO of –750 and 750 ms.[5] Thus, there are indeed only minimal gaps and overlaps in speaker transitions during conversation. This confirms 'that listeners do not wait until they DETECT the end of a speaker's turn; rather, they ANTICIPATE this moment' (de Ruiter *et al.* 2006: 516f.).

Some researchers have suggested that this ability to 'PROJECT the moment of completion of a current speaker's turn' is based on lexicosyntactic cues, others argue that prosodic features, especially intonation contours are decisive for this ability. These hypotheses were tested in an online experiment in which the 'presence of symbolic (lexicosyntactic) content and intonational contour of utterances recorded in natural [Dutch] conversations' was manipulated (de Ruiter *et al.* 2006: 515). Subjects were presented with natural words and no-words stimuli as well as with verbal stimuli where intonational contours were removed; then they were asked 'to press a button ... at the moment they thought the speaker would be finishing speaking' (de Ruiter *et al.* 2006: 523). They were encouraged to try to anticipate this moment. The results of these experiments are summarized as follows:

> When hearing the original recordings, subjects can anticipate turn endings with the same degree of accuracy attested in real conversation. With intonational contour

entirely removed (leaving intact words and syntax, with a completely flat pitch) there is no change in subjects' accuracy of end-of-turn projection. But in the opposite case (with original intonational contour intact, but with no recognizable words) subjects' performance deteriorates significantly. These results establish that the symbolic (i.e. lexicosyntactic) content of an utterance is necessary (and possibly sufficient) for projecting the moment of its completion, and thus for regulating conversational turn-taking. By contrast, and perhaps surprisingly, intonational contour is neither necessary nor sufficient for end-of-turn projection.

(de Ruiter *et al.* 2006: 515)

Jan Peter de Ruiter and his colleagues point out that their experiments show that grammar 'is not just a means for semantic representation of predicate-argument relations', but also 'an inherent temporal resource for listeners to chart out the course of the speaker's expression and to plan their own speech accordingly'. Speakers exploit lexicosyntactic options available in specific contexts of speech to 'actively foreshadow structure, thereby manipulating the unfolding course of the interaction itself, and literally controlling the interlocutor's processes of cognition and action'. This supports the hypothesis that language is 'structurally DESIGNED FOR strategic deployment in social interaction' (de Ruiter *et al.* 2006: 532).

CA research results – like the findings and observations reported so far – more or less explicitly claim to be valid for all languages. Is there any support for such a universal claim of CA, given the fact that most research so far has been done on English? Recently another group of scholars (Stivers *et al.* 2009) researched question–answer adjacency pairs across ten languages (Danish, Italian, Dutch, English, Japanese, Lao, Korean, Tzeltal, Hai//om, Yélî-Dnye). Research in CA has shown that we can differentiate between preferred and dispreferred answers in question-response systems in many (if not all) languages. Preferred answers to questions express agreement and they are delivered more quickly than dispreferred answers (see Enfield *et al.* 2010: 2616). Example (2) from Danish (Heinemann 2010: 2722) illustrates such a preferred answer (note the code switch to English after the first Danish answer '*MJah*'):

(2)	Line:	→1	*Ska'*	*vi*	*ta'*	*det*	*her*	*med?*
			Shall	we	take	this	here	with
			Should we take this with us?					

	Mette:	→2	>.mJah.<	.fnnt	*Let's do that.*
			>.mPRT.<	.fnnt	*Let's do that.*
			>.mYes.<	.fnnt	*Let's do that.*

Responses to questions that disconfirm and disagree are dispreferred actions which tend to be delayed and mitigated and they may sometimes be pursued for reconfirmation. Example (3) from Tzeltal (Brown 2010: 2646) illustrates such a dispreferred answer:

(3) A: *eej*   *lek*   *me*   *ay-Ø*   *in*   *ch'i*   *j-tatik-*
         eh   good   if   EXIST-3ABS   DEIC   PT   HON-'sir'
         ay-Ø   *ya*   *x-ala*   *ba-at*   *ya'tik*   *tz'in*
         EXIST-3ABS   INC   ASP-DIM   go-2A   today   PT
         Eh it's good if that's the case, sir, is there somewhere you are going to go
         now?
         (0.3)

     N: *ma'yuk-*   DISCONFIRMING ANSWER
         No(where)

     A: *ma'yuk-ix*   *a*   *[tz'in*   PURSUIT OF RECONFIRMATION
         None=ACS   DEIC   PT
         There's no(where) then.

     N: *[ma'yuk.*   CONFIRMATION
                                No(where).

The study of Stivers *et al.* (2009) restricted itself to the comparison of polar (yes–no)
questions, the commonest type of questions in nine of the ten languages researched.
The study of de Ruiter and his colleagues presented above which 'analysed a corpus of
Dutch conversation ... for timing across all types of turns and responses ... found no
differences between response times after questions and nonquestions'; therefore the
researchers in this project took the question-response sequences to be analysed as
representative for turn-taking in general. Their study confirmed that turn-taking in
conversation follows a 'minimal-gap minimal overlap' norm and supports the
assumption that turn-taking is 'a universal system with minimal cultural variability'
(Stivers *et al.* 2009: 10587f.):

> [T]he response timings for each language ... have a unimodal distribution with a mode
> offset for each language between 0 and +200 ms, and an overall mode of 0 ms. The
> medians are also quite uniform, ranging from 0 ms (English, Japanese, Tzeltal and Yélî
> Dnye) to +300 (Danish, Hai//om, Lao) ... The means display somewhat more variation
> ... Danish has the slowest response time on average (+469 ms) and Japanese has the
> fastest (+7 ms). The mean response offset for the full dataset is +208 ms, and the
> language-specific means fall within ≈250 ms either side of this cross-language mean,
> approximately the length of time it takes to produce a single English syllable ...
>
> (Stivers *et al.* 2009: 10587f.)

The differences in the response times are pragmatically explained: 'A speaker of Danish
avoids silence just as a speaker of Japanese avoids silence, but silence happens faster in
Japanese than in Danish' (Stivers: p.c.), or, in more scientific terms, 'what constitutes a
subjectively notable delay involves greater absolute duration in some languages than in
others' (Stivers *et al.* 2009: 10590). These slight differences seem to be culturally calibrated,
so to speak. In addition, the study showed that answers are produced faster and more

often than responses that do not answer the question (like, for example, '*I don't know*' or '*I can't remember*'). Confirmations are also produced faster and more often than disconfirmations (between 100 and 500 ms on average) – these findings confirm the distinction between preferred and dispreferred answers. Visible responses, like head nods, head shakes, shrugs, eye blinks and eyebrow flashes were even faster than speech, however, the researchers observed substantial variation in how frequently such responses were included in a response. In nine of the ten languages responses were given faster when speakers were looking at the person to whom they addressed the question, however, the variation in how often questioners gazed at addressees suggests that 'gaze may be more culturally variable than other behaviors' (Stivers *et al.* 2009: 10588). The overall result that 'responses tend to be neither in overlap nor delayed by more than half a second' seems to capture 'a universal feature of the interactional systems that underlie the use of languages' (Stivers *et al.* 2009: 10590).

At transition-relevance places speakers can either decide to keep the floor and start a new turn-constructional unit[6] or they can select a next speaker or they just can end their turn giving another interlocutor the chance to self-select him- or herself as next speaker. Excerpt (4) from Japanese (Tanaka 1999: 46) illustrates a case of speaker selection of next speaker:

(4)	M: (looking at T)							
	... *yappari*	*kan*	*ga*	*ii*	*n*	*desu*	*yo*	*ne::*
	after all	intuition	NOMP	good	NMLZ	COP	FP	FP
	... 'after all, ((you)) have a good sense of intuition'							

	Minasan		*no*	*baai*
	you ((plural))		P	case
	'in the case of people like you'			

dakara (.) .hh
'therefore'

	shize::n	*ni*	*wakatte* [*kite*
	naturally	P	come to understand
	'((it)) just comes naturally'		

              [

T:	[*Iya mendokusai*	*da*	*dake*	*(hh)*	*to*	*iu*	*oh*
	[no bothersome	DF	only		QUOTP	say	DF
	['No, it's just that ((I)) can't be bothered'						

  S: *hhh*

In this example participants have been talking about T and his ability to operate a computer without reading the manual with instructions. Tanaka (1999: 46) explains which next speaker selection techniques M is using and what is going on here:

M selects T as next speaker, both through her gaze direction (addressing device) and by complimenting the latter on his superior sense of intuition (the first pair part of an adjacency pair compliment / acceptance or rejection). T responds immediately, in this case by less favourably reformulating the activity referred to.

Example (5) from Guyanese Creole illustrates 'turn-initial overlap' (marked with a bracket [ ) because 'a next-speaker has not been selected by the previous turn in line 2 and both Pank and Nancy self-select' themselves 'at a recognizable transition-relevance place' as next speaker (Sidnell 2001: 1273):

(5)			
	1. Pank:	suna narai dadii. en=	Suna is Narain's father. And=
	2. John:	=shot yoo ass:.	=Shut your ass
	3. Pank:→	joo suna	Joe Suna,
		[	
	4.Nancy:→	joo. yea	Joe. Yes
	5.	Joo a harii da	Joe is Harry Suna's father
		[	[
	6. Pank	Harri	Harry
	7.	Suna da	Suna's father.

Sidnell interprets this excerpt as follows:

> Here Pank is making a claim about a genealogical link, and, after coming to a point of possible completion (recognizable by virtue of the prosody, the syntax and the content of the utterance) has begun to build an addition to the turn through the use of conjunctive *en* 'and'. John's disagreement effectively forestalls any further contribution Pank might make as an addition and creates an environment in which, upon its possible completion, a restatement of the claim or evidence of its veracity is expectably due – the alternation of claim and disagreement sustaining the sense of the larger course of action as an argument. Both Nancy and Pank attempt to occupy the slot provided for by John's turn and thus produce a minimal overlap before Pank drops out allowing Nancy to recycle his turn beginning in the clear ...
>
> (Sidnell 2001: 1274)[7]

Speakers cannot only select next speaker or self-select themselves as next speakers, interactants in a conversation can also repair 'troubles of speaking, hearing and understanding' (Sidnell 2009a: 3). These troubles are displayed in so-called 'trouble source turns' (TST); this is usually done with a question (see Egbert 1997: 612). If speakers realize that they have made a mistake, like having provided a wrong reference, they can immediately or after some delay make a self-repair. Examples (6) and (7) illustrate a 'self repair in transition space' and a self-repair after a gap but 'just in time to pre-empt other-correction'. These repairs were made by speakers of the Papuan language Yélî Dnye (Levinson 2007: 45):

(6)	M:	*ki*	*D:ââkî:a u*		*lama*	*ka*	*pyede* =	*aa*
		That	D	3.POSS	knowledge	is	sitting	er
		That D:ââkî:a knows all about it = er						

Nteniyé	u	lama
Nteniyé	3.POSS	knowledge

Nteniyé knows it.

(7) R: *mu* *Lêmonkê* *kêle*
This.nonvisible Lêmonkê (standing behind speaker) wasn't there then

P: (P looks around to check)

R: *ee!* (gestures 'not')
eh-
(1.0)
Yamî'n:aa
(I mean) Yamî'n:aa
[

P: *Yamî'n:aa*   < – Note P has delayed correction

Excerpt (8) illustrates how a TST of a speaker (lines 1–2) is repaired after a repair initiation turn (which is the first pair part of the adjacency pair [1PP] in line 5) by two responses from other parties present (which constitute the second pair part of the adjacency pair [2PP] in lines 7 and 8). This example of other-initiated repair is taken from a conversation of Germans speaking German with a Westphalian dialect accent (Egbert 1997: 621f.):

(8) TST 1 M: der mann war allerdings auch tscheche °glaub ich.°
but the husband was czech °i believe°

2 (0.2)
((dialect))

3 H: oh gott [wat n düennehne
oh god [what a mess
[

4 A: [( )

1PP 5 I: was war der?
what was he?

6 (.)

2PP 7 H: tscheche
czech

2PP 8 M: gebürtiger tscheche
a born czech

That repairs can be extremely important in certain contexts is documented by the following longer (slightly simplified) excerpt from a conversation between speakers of Lue ((L)) and Siamese ((S) = Central Thai) – two languages of the Tai-Kadai language family – recorded by Michael Moerman (1988: 125ff.) in a Thai-Lue village (note that there is a gap between the lines 8 and 32; about 30 seconds of the original transcript are omitted here):

(9)   ...

3   S_{((L))}   ma·   ãt   tî·   à·cá·n   bá·j   nï
come   record   CNJ   T   N   PRT
They came and recorded at Acan B's.

4   (.2)

5   MM_{((L))}   ə·[:::[
O[:::[h

6   S   á·w   á·w   bâ·   nŏ·   xá·w   xãp
PRV   PRV   T   N   PRN   sing
... had Ba Noo sing,

7   (.4)

8   á·w   ná·n   dá·   pá·j   pă·w   pĭ
PRV   T   N   PRV   blow   pipe
had Nan Daa play the pipe.

...

32   DO_{((S))}   khon   thî·   nǎj   kháp
person   where   sing
Where was the singer from

33   (.7)

34   DO   khon   bâ·n   nî·   lŷ·
person   village   this   QPRT
Someone from this village?

35   S_{((L))}   ãn- (·)   kun-   ãn   tí   jŭ·   hoŋja·
um   person   um   CNJ   to be   infirmary
tî   põ   a·ca·n   bá·j   hân   nɛ.
CNJ with   T   N   DEM   PRT
Um- (·) a guy – um who stays at the infirmary at Acan B's there.

36   (1)

37   B_{((L))}   Isa·
What

38   (.3)

39   B   wã   kun   xàp   na
say   person   sing   PRT
You talking about the singer?

40 S   mɛn   iɛ.
               That's right.

41   (.2)

42   bâ   nǒo   nân   nɛ.
               T   N   DEM   PRT
               That Ba Noo.

43 WS((L))   bâ   nǒo   Xî·   t[ŭ·t   nɛ[.
               T   N   leper PRT
               Ba Noo the   l[eper

44 S   [man   [pin   kun
                                            PRN   is   person
                                            phǎjǎ·ːt   nâŋkǎw   lɛː.
                                            sick   somewhat PRT
                                            bâ   nân ko
                                            T   DEM CNJ
                                            [He[is sort of siːck, that guy.

45 B?   hmm

46 S   man há   jŭ   káp a
         PRN usually be   with
         [ca·n bá·j.[
         T   N
        A [can B.

47 WS   [bâ nǒo [lŭ·k
         T   N   child
         mɛ·thâ·w mun
         T   N
         bâ·nce·ŋbá·n
         N
         [Ba Noo[the son of
         Mɛthaw Mun of Chiengban

48   nɛ·   tá·
              PRT T
              uncle

49 B   ə·ːː
              Oːːh

50 S   bâ   nǒo   nân
              T   N   DEM
              That Ba Noo.

This is an excerpt from a conversation between some inhabitants of a Thai-Lue village and the district officer (DO) about recordings of Lue folksongs. Moerman (1988: 20ff.) analyses it as follows: In lines 3, 6 and 8 the speaker S introduces the missionary Acan B in whose house the recordings were made, and the artists, a singer and a piper. Thirty seconds later (line 32) the DO asked about the whereabouts of the singer, his question is not immediately answered and so the DO continues his turn-constructional unit with another repair initiating question (line 34) proposing a possible answer with his question. S informs him that the singer stays at the infirmary at Acan B's place. The speaker's repair (in line 35) initiates another repair with increasing specificity in the question (in lines 37–39) asked by a village elder. S repeats his earlier reference form together with a demonstrative, and after S's self-repair his wife adds (in an other-repair) the singer's eponym (in line 43) – 'the leper'. Moerman points out that many villagers have the same name, therefore eponyms – kind of nicknames – are often added to names to accomplish more specific person reference. However, in this case S immediately overlaps his wife's turn (in line 44) and corrects his wife utterance that could be misunderstood as a medical diagnosis by the downplaying and downgrading phrase 'He is sort of sick'. With this turn S disagrees, dismisses and challenges his wife's turn, obscuring the eponym she used. Moerman interprets S's turn as an obliterative overlap:

> When overlaps *are* obliterative, when, as here, one speaker clearly places his talk so as to blot out the talk of another, the intruder's precise placement discloses him to have been attending the talk he overlaps very closely indeed. It is not faulty listening or imperfect participation. The mechanical image is of pinpoint bombing, not careless condition, of turns.
>
> (Moerman 1988: 21)

Moerman provides the following ethnographic background information that explains and justifies S's intervention here. S is a client of the missionary who looks after and protects the singer Noo, who has a harmless skin ailment, but not leprosy. S knows that some people already have complained about Noo to the DO. If the DO would regard Noo as a true leper, he could remove him from the missionary's compound to a leper colony. Thus, his wife's harmless person reference with an eponym could have had serious consequences.[8] In the ongoing conversation S and his wife elaborate their reference to Noo (overlapping in lines 46 and 47), tell the DO more about Noo's whereabouts and kin-relations and S finishes the sequence with the final neutral phrase 'That Ba Noo' (in line 50 which repeats line 42 again). Moerman comments on this excerpt as follows:

> The entire drama took less than ten seconds to perform. Its specifiable moves and units of action – turns, repairs, adjacency pairs, sequences – were conversationally organized. But we never merely exchange turns of talk. In all conversation, people are living their lives, performing their roles, enacting their culture. The motives and meanings of all talk are thick with culture. To understand what the moves mean requires (or recalls) cultural knowledge. The techniques and texture of conversation analysis precisely

located the motivated, ongoing, actual operation of major social institutions. In "The Leper", naming practices, the authority of officials, loyalty to patrons, identificatory social memberships were momentarily and momentously invoked and enlivened. This does not mean that the social institutions and cultural patterns produced the talk. But they are implicated in its meaning. The immediacy and complexity of every real social event precludes producing, interpreting, or accounting for it by some single set of rules (like those for repair, turn-taking, loyalty, or kinship).

(Moerman 1988: 22)

In addition to the ability of people engaged in conversation to make (other-initiated or self-) repairs, interlocutors can also manipulate the actions in the sequences of turns. Goodwin and Heritage (1990: 296) point out that Schegloff (1992: xxix) referred to this ability with the term '"strategic/sequential" dimension of actions' and elaborate as follows: 'This approach focuses on the ways alternative forms of an action shape the possibilities for different types of response, and on how these various forms can be manipulated to achieve specific outcomes'. It was mentioned above that CA differentiates between preferred and dispreferred responses. Excerpt (3) above illustrated a dispreferred response to a question. Excerpt (10) provided by Sidnell (2010: 78f.) illustrates general features of dispreferred responses in more detail:

(10) 01 A Uh if you'd care to come and visit a little while
     02   This morning I'll give you a cup of coffee.
     03 B hehh Well that's awfully sweet of you. I don't
     04   think I can make it this morning. .hh uhm I'm
     05   running an ad in the paper and-and uh I have to
     06   stay near the phone

Sidnell (2010: 78f.) points out that in B's response we observe delays 'by prefacing the turn with audible breathing ("hehh") and "well" and "that's awfully sweet of you"' (line 3), palliatives, i.e. 'some kind of appreciation, apology and/or token agreement by which the ... "negative" valence of the turn is mitigated' – in excerpt (10) these palliatives are the appreciation 'that's awfully sweet of you' and 'I don't think ...' (lines 3–4) – and the explanation and justification for why the 'dispreferred response is being produced' – in this case, why 'an invitation is being declined'.

As Clift *et al.* point out, these

design features of dispreferred responses can be used as a resource for the maintenance of social solidarity in talk-in-interaction ... [The] means of 'marking' a dispreferred response can provide a source for a first speaker to revise the original first pair-part in such a way as to try to avoid disagreement or rejection.

(Clift *et al.* 2009: 49)

There are a number of means speakers can use to do this. So-called 'presequences' like 'Are you doing anything tonight?' preface actions like requests and invitations. As

Goodwin and Heritage (1990: 297) point out, presequences 'enable parties to abort a projected interaction sequence in which conflict, disagreement, or rejection might emerge ... [If] the projected sequence is not aborted in this way an affiliative outcome [i.e. agreement, acceptance, etc. (G. S.)] becomes highly likely'. Excerpt (11) presented in Sidnell (2010: 80; see also Levinson 1983: 320) illustrates how a speaker treats a two second long silence after the preparation of a request as an indication of a dispreferred answer and 'partially withdraws the (pre-)request by reversing the valence of the question with "probably not"':

(11) 01   So I was wondering would you be in your office
       02   on Monday (.) by any chance?
       03→   (2s)
       04   Probably not.

The CA approach has researched a number of other phenomena, like openings and closings of conversations, storytelling and narrative in conversations. However, this brief overview can only deal with some of the topics that are constitutive for this paradigm. The research on turns (TCUs) and turn-taking, gaps and overlaps, repair, adjacency pairs and action organization or sequencing that are briefly sketched out here illustrates that conversation is an emerging, yet highly orderly activity 'in which participants co-construct meaning and social action in an exquisitely timed choreography of interlocking communicative moves', as Mark Dingemanse (p.c.) put it.

5.5 CONCLUDING REMARKS

John Heritage's appraisal of Schegloff provides a passage that succinctly summarizes this chapter:

> Goffman insisted that social interaction is to be conceived as a social institution in its own right, with its own normative organization and moral obligations, which, in turn, are linked to other aspects of the social world through face, role and identity ... Goffman conceived social interaction as the product of a set of moral rights and rituals – a "syntax" as he once put it ... irreducible to individual psychology. It was this conception which ... mandated ... the study of social interaction – what Goffman ... later termed the "interaction order" – as a subject matter in its own right.
>   Garfinkel's researches developed the proposition ... that shared understanding and mutual intelligibility among humans are possible only through approximate, revisable ... practical and shared methods of reasoning whose results are unavoidably inscribed in courses of social action. ...
>   Building from these perspectives, CA focuses on the competencies which persons use and rely on to co-construct orderly and mutually understandable courses of action. Accepting John Austin's supposition that we "do things with words", CA has developed a program of research by mapping the resources with which members of the social

world produce, recognize, understand and manipulate social interactions. Its basic assumption is that while the resources for the construction of conduct are highly institutionalized ..., they also serve as the building blocks for highly particularized courses of conduct, and for specifically meaningful activities fitted to the singular characteristics of particular persons and contexts.

(Heritage 2003: 3)

What does this chapter tell us about the anecdote reported in the introduction to this volume? I was obviously unaware of the Trobriand Islanders' interaction order, its normative organization and its moral obligations which coerce persons greeted with the ritualized question *Ambe?* – 'Where are you going to?' to respond in the culturally appropriate way. My inadequate responses were forms of misbehaviour: I unwittingly and unwillingly did a breaching experiment, but this 'experiment' finally provided me with the necessary inside knowledge of how to behave and react properly in this greeting situation. Once I understood the Trobrianders' set of moral rights and rituals and had learned (about) their shared methods of reasoning, I could answer the question constructing my turn in such a way that my response provided the information expected by the persons who greeted me. Now the question-response adjacency pair was co-constructed in an orderly and meaningful way within the frame of the Trobrianders' interaction order.

5.6 EXERCISE/WORK SECTION

- Compare Eibl-Eibesfeldt's ideas about 'universal interaction strategies' with Levinson's 'interaction engine' and Goffman's 'interaction order'. Elaborate on similarities and differences between these concepts.

- Observe, describe and analyse a 'social encounter' of your own choice. If possible, document it on videotape. Try to unveil the underlying interaction order and detect and describe the methods of reasoning shared by the interactants.

- Contact a friend and ask the person whether s/he would like to conduct a kind of 'special' experiment with you. If s/he agrees, do a Garfinkel 'breeching experiment' for about ten minutes or so and then interview (and record) your friend and ask how s/he felt and what s/he thought about you and the situation. If you realize that your friend cannot handle the stress during this situation, abort the experiment immediately, but – if possible – interview her or him.

- Videotape your friends or family having dinner together (see 1.7) or a talk show (see 2.6, 3.5) or use the documentation of dyadic interactions you videotaped for your phatic communion experiment (see 4.6), try to transcribe 30 seconds of interactions with the CA transcription system as minutely as possible and analyse the transcript with respect to turn construction, turn-taking, gaps and overlaps, repairs, adjacency pairs and action sequencing.

5.7 SUGGESTIONS FOR FURTHER READING

Couper-Kuhlen and Ono (2007); Goffman (1959, 1969); C. Goodwin (1993); M. Goodwin (2006); Reynolds (2011); Roberts *et al.* (2011); Schegloff (1988, 2007); Senft (1999); Sidnell (2009b); Streeck *et al.* (2011); Takanashi and Sung-Yul Park (2011).

NOTES

1   Note that here Goffman employs linguistic analogies with respect to the analysis of interaction.

2   Referential tact manifests that interactants respect 'the moral norms of considerateness which bind individuals qua interactants. Delicacy, courtesy, modesty, politeness – these are the sort of attributes that are involved' (Goffman 1983b: 28).

3   This refers to the Latin maxim: '*Quod fieri non debuit, factum valet*', i.e. '*What ought not to be done is valid when done*'.

4   For an overview see Clift *et al.* (2009: 41ff.).

5   Negative FTO values indicate an overlap between the turns.

6   Another strategy speakers may use to 'secure rights to produce an extended turn-at-talk' are so-called 'prefaces', for example phrases like '*Let me tell you something*' that preannounces a speaker's intention to keep the floor for a while (see Sidnell 2001: 1281f.).

7   It goes without saying that we also observe competitive overlap (interruption). For an example see Sidnell (2001: 1278).

8   For cross-linguistic/cross-cultural studies on person reference in interaction see Enfield and Stivers (2007).

Pragmatics and politics

Language, social class, ethnicity and education and linguistic ideologies

6.1 INTRODUCTION

The 1960s were not only a decade of cold, hot and civil wars, conflicts, riots, (nuclear and other) threats, radical political changes, assassinations, and student revolts but also the years in which the USA won the space race with the Soviet Union and in which the anti-Vietnam-War movement and the Civil Rights movement in the USA (and elsewhere) gained more and more strength. In addition, this period of time is also known as the 'Swinging Sixties' in which the young generation, in a kind of cultural revolution, radically changed the ways of living typical for the rather conservative 1950s. They abolished former taboos – especially with respect to sexuality and the rights of women – and questioned unlegitimized authority in all public and private domains. This development was strongly influenced by Marxist ideas and other ideologies of a so-called 'New Left' which tried to abolish social inequalities and overcome the social class structure in the Western capitalist societies. It was a decade of both an overall politicalization of private and public spheres and a liberalization and emancipation from so far unquestioned social norms and other pressures towards social conformity – especially in the Western world.

This prevailing political atmosphere had its reverberations in the scientific discourse, too, of course, especially within the humanities. Thus, it is no coincidence that this decade saw the rise of sociolinguistics, which had its origins mainly in the Anglo-Saxon world with protagonists like, for example, Uriel Weinreich, Charles Ferguson, Joshua Fishman, Dell Hymes, John Gumperz, and William Labov. In the 1976 translation of his monograph *Sociolinguistics*, Norbert Dittmar characterizes the status this discipline had gained as follows:

> In the last decade sociolinguistics has become a powerful factor in promoting emancipation. Attempts have been made to attenuate conflicts in schools and to remove the obvious inequality of opportunity of broad sections of the working classes and peripheral social groups by systematically exposing the connection between speech form and class structure, and by application of the insights gained to specific social contexts.

> (Dittmar 1976: 1)

Among the most influential scholars within the field of sociolinguistics of this time were the British sociologist and former teacher Basil Bernstein and the American linguist William Labov.[1]

Basil Bernstein developed a 'code theory' which was 'based on the claim that children and teachers from different class backgrounds spoke in different codes, and that this produced ... a failure of communication' (Good 1999: 9). Bernstein's research had not only political but also pedagogical consequences which resulted in so-called 'compensatory' education programmes. Despite the fact that Bernstein (1970a and b) himself argued against these programmes, his code theory was characterized as a 'verbal deprivation theory' or 'deficit hypothesis' by scholars like Labov (1970a: 153), who confronted it with sociolinguistic approaches that were referred to as the 'difference hypothesis' or as the 'variability concept'.

The first part of this chapter presents a brief survey of Bernstein's code theory and Labov's variability concept and the controversy between the followers of these two approaches which had strong implications for linguistic pragmatics.

The discussion of Bernstein's and Labov's contributions to sociolinguistics illustrates how linguistic research contributed to increase the researchers' awareness of the political impact of their studies. This observation is taken up in the second part of the chapter in which I discuss the topic of linguistic ideologies and their role for linguistic pragmatics. After a brief discussion of the concept – based on Michael Silverstein's (1979) pioneering paper on 'Language structure and linguistic ideologies' and on Jef Verschueren's (2012) work *Ideology in Language Use* – three exemplary case studies of research on language ideologies will be presented.

6.2 BASIL BERNSTEIN'S CODE THEORY

Bernstein's code theory is a social theory which attempts to reveal the interrelationship between speech, socialization within the family, social class and school. In 1959 he published a paper in which he differentiates between a 'public' and a 'formal language'; later he speaks of

> [t]wo general types of code ... *elaborated* and *restricted*. They can be defined, on a linguistic level, in terms of the probability of predicting for any one speaker which syntactic elements are to be used to organize meaning across a representative range of speech. The codes themselves are functions of a particular form of social relationship, or more generally of social structures ...
>
> The most general condition for the emergence of the [restricted] code is a social relationship based upon a common, extensive set of closely related identifications and expectations self-consciously held by the members ... The meanings are likely to be concrete, descriptive or narrative rather than analytical or abstract ...
>
> An elaborated code, where prediction is much less possible ... is likely to arise in that social relationship which raises the tension in its members to select verbal arrangement from their linguistic resources which closely fits specific referents. This situation will arise where the intent of the other person cannot be taken for granted, having the

consequence that meanings will have to be expanded and raised to the level of verbal explicitness. Here verbal planning, unlike the case in the restricted code, promotes a higher level of syntactic organization and lexical selection. The preparation and delivery of relatively explicit meaning is the major function of this code.

(Bernstein 1967: 127ff.)

Thus, codes are learned by children in their sociocultural environment, that is first of all in their families. Bernstein (1972: 174) differentiates two types of families; the status-oriented and the person-oriented family. As Dittmar (1976: 25) points out, the 'status-oriented type admits of few alternatives in communication; it is therefore described ... as a "closed role system", which is characteristic for the genesis of the "restricted" speech code' whereas the person-oriented family offers 'many alternatives ... in communication'. This 'open role system' 'produces the elaborated speech code'. Restricted codes are context-dependent, predictable and therefore 'particularistic', whereas elaborated codes are context independent, much less predictable and thus 'universalistic' (Bernstein 1972: 163). Bernstein (1967: 128) points out that '[r]estricted codes are not necessarily linked to social class'. However, in non-verbal and verbal intelligence tests as well as in a number of experiments[2] he claims to have found correlations between speech codes and social class which verify the following hypothesis:

Children socialized within middle class and associated strata can be expected to possess *both* an elaborated and a restricted code; while children socialized within some sections of the working class strata, particularly the lower working class, can be expected to be limited to the restricted code.

(Bernstein 1967: 131)

Thus Bernstein claimed that children who were socialized mainly in a restricted code are limited in their communicative skills (hence the criticism of the code theory as being a deficit hypothesis); usually these children are members of the lower classes; on the other hand, children who acquired and were socialized in an elaborate code are verbally skilled speakers who can deal with all kinds of communicative situations; usually these children grow up in middle class families.

This has consequences for the school career of middle and lower class children. Success at school requires the use of the elaborate code which is transmitted there. This constitutes a big disadvantage for children of the lower classes: 'If a child is to succeed as he progresses through school, it becomes critical for him to possess, or at least be oriented towards, an elaborated code' (Bernstein 1967: 131). This educational inequality – for Bernstein (1961: 308) 'a wastage of working-class educational potential' – perpetuates the inequality between the classes in the Western capitalist system:

The code theory asserts that there is a social class regulated unequal distribution of privileging principles of communication ... and that social class, indirectly, effects the classification and framing of the elaborated code transmitted by the school so as to facilitate and perpetuate its unequal acquisition. Thus the code theory ... draws attention to the relations between macro power relations and micro practices of transmission, acquisition and evaluation and the positioning and oppositioning to which these practices give rise.

(Bernstein 1990: 118f.)

Bernstein's research was politically explosive and had pedagogical consequences, both in Europe and, especially, in North America. A number of so-called 'compensatory' education programmes were developed and carried out, like the 'Operation Headstart' programme in the USA (see Dittmar 1976: 87, 94f.). Dittmar – from a Marxist point of view – explains this as follows:

The reasons for the rapid success of Bernstein's socialization theory are self evident: it names factors preventing full utilization of cultural reserves and proposes a way of rectifying this without calling into question the structure of authority and production in a capitalist society.

(Dittmar 1976: 85)

Throughout the 1960s, 1970s and 1980s Bernstein's theory and his and his followers' empirical research on the interrelationship between language, social class and socialization and the compensatory education programmes were heavily criticized (see Dittmar 1976: Chapters Two and Three; also Good 1999: 9). The failure of the compensatory programmes in the USA – despite their considerable financial costs – falsified 'the hopes of State and industrial interests in relation to compensatory programmes' (Dittmar 1976: 87) and supported scholars who refuted the basic theoretical conception of the code theory on which these programmes were based. Dittmar pointed out that 'the controversy about the Deficit Hypothesis ... can be regarded ... as the catalyst for the defects of this theory in the academic and social sphere' (Dittmar 1976: 87). For Labov (1970a: 180), the 'essential fallacy of the verbal deprivation theory lies in tracing the educational failure of the child to his personal deficiencies'; he argued that compensatory programmes were doomed to fail because they were 'designed to repair the child, rather than the school'; on the basis of his linguistic research he pleaded to change the institution 'School' so that school education could offer equal opportunities to all pupils, regardless of their social class background. The next section provides a brief survey of the variability concept and William Labov's contributions to it.

6.3 WILLIAM LABOV AND THE VARIABILITY CONCEPT

The variability concept is rooted in the tradition of American, British and Prague structuralism and influenced by the traditional linguistic disciplines that are concerned with the analysis of speech variation, such as dialectology, anthropological linguistics and research on languages in contact. It starts from a completely different theoretical position than the code theory and uses much more adequate descriptive methods for analysing different language varieties than Bernstein and his followers who were trained psychologists and education researchers.

The difference hypothesis assumes that language varieties are functionally equivalent 'in relation to the possibilities of expression and the logical capacity for analysis' and aims at the 'explanation of all linguistic differentiations caused by the intervention of social and regional parameters, and of their correlations with the social structure' (Dittmar 1976: 103). Thus, contrary to the directed hypotheses of research in the code theory paradigm that try to explain the role of differently evaluated speech codes for the social success of its speakers at school by considering just a limited number of social parameters, the research hypotheses within the variability concept are undirected. The speech behaviour described in the variability concept paradigm is not observed in formal test situations (mostly) in school contexts, but in naturally occurring social interactions on the basis of participant observation and other, specially developed methods of data gathering (see Labov 1970b, 1972d). The aim is to discover socially determined speech norms, both on the micro level – where forms of verbal interaction between individuals are analysed – and on the macro level – where the distribution and function of speech varieties in a society are researched (see Dittmar 1976: 103). Language is studied in its social context with a strong emphasis on the specific speech situation and the social background and significance of the communicative interaction and the speakers involved. In addition, questions about the pragmatic functions of language varieties are in the focus of the variability concept.

For the purposes pursued here, this section will concentrate only on a few of Labov's papers which refute the deficit hypothesis and compensatory education programmes, especially in ghetto schools. Labov starts his paper on 'The logic of nonstandard English' with the observation that these programmes are based on the assumption that the Black children in these schools 'show a cultural deficit as a result of an impoverished environment in their early years. As far as language is concerned, the deficit theory appears as a concept of "verbal deprivation"' (Labov 1970a: 153). Labov supports this assessment with quotes from Bereiter *et al.*'s (1966) and Bereiter and Engelmann's (1966) publications on this topic which are based on Bernstein's code theory. Labov writes:

> Bereiter's program for an academically oriented preschool is based upon their premise that Negro children must have a language with which they can learn, and their empirical finding that these children come to school without such a language. In his work on four-year-old Negro children from Urbana, Bereiter reports that their communication was by gestures, 'single words', and 'a series of badly connected words or phrases' such as *They mine* and *Me got juice*. He reports that Negro children could not ask questions, that 'without exaggeration ... these four-year-olds could make no statements of any kind'. Furthermore, when these children were asked 'Where is the book?', they did not know enough to look at the table where the book was lying in order to answer. Thus Bereiter concludes that the children's speech forms are nothing more than a series of emotional cries, and he decides to treat them 'as if the children had no language at all'. He identifies their speech with his interpretation of Bernstein's restricted code: 'the language of culturally deprived children ... is not merely an underdeveloped version of standard English, but is a basically non-logical mode of expressive behavior' (Bereiter *et al.*, 1966. p. 113).
>
> (Labov 1970a: 156f.)

Labov debunks 'the notion of "verbal deprivation" [as] a part of the modern mythology of educational psychology' and sets out to 'clear away' this 'illusion ... and provide a more adequate notion of the relations between standard and non-standard dialects'. He shows that the 'empirical' findings reported by Bereiter and his co-workers are based on 'a poor understanding of the nature of language' (Labov 1970a: 154) and points out that the interview data gathered and presented by Bereiter to illustrate and justify his analysis are based on the

> asymmetrical situation ... where anything [the child] says can literally be held against him. He has learned a number of devices to avoid saying anything in this situation ... If one takes this interview as a measure of the verbal capacity of the child, it must be as his capacity to defend himself in a hostile and threatening situation ... The verbal behavior which is shown by the child ... is ... the result of regular sociolinguistic factors operating upon adult and child in this asymmetrical situation.
>
> (Labov 1970a: 158)

On the basis of his own data and data gathered by his collaborators, Labov illustrates that 'in many ways working-class speakers are more effective narrators, reasoners, and debaters than many middle-class speakers who temporize, qualify, and lose their argument in a mass of irrelevant detail' (Labov 1970a: 164). His comparative analysis of Standard English and what he calls Non-standard Negro English (NNE) reveals that both dialects follow distinct grammatical rules and a logic of their own and he points out that '[a]ll linguists who work with NNE recognize that it is a separate system, closely related to Standard English but set apart from the surrounding white dialects by a number of persistent and systematic differences' (Labov 1970a: 184). The fact that the data and insights on the NNE gathered and gained by linguists like Labov differ so much from the claims of educational psychologists like Bereiter and Engelmann is due to the different theoretical and methodological approaches to this variety of American English. The insights gained by research done within the framework of the variability concept reveal the inadequacy and fallacies of the deficit hypothesis and its 'ignorance of the most basic facts about human language and the people who speak it' (Labov 1970a: 187). Labov concludes his plea for an appropriate treatment of the non-standard dialect of Black schoolchildren as follows: 'That educational psychology should be strongly influenced by a theory so false to the facts of language is unfortunate; but that children should be the victims of this ignorance is intolerable' (Labov 1970a: 187). Insights like this illustrate that at least at this point of the controversy scholars like Labov were completely aware of the political importance and impact of their research.

The highly political controversy about how to assess and understand the speech behaviour of Blacks in the USA pedagogically, socially and linguistically motivated Labov and other linguists working within the theoretical framework of the variability concept to continue and intensify their research on this variety of American English. The various labels they used to refer to this language variety – Non-standard Negro English (NNE) – Black English Vernacular (BEV) – Afro-American (Vernacular) English (AA(V)E) – African American Language (AAL) – mirror the political impact this research had over the years, as well as the various political and linguistic ideologies with respect to the 'politically' correct reference to this variety. In a number of studies Labov (1972a) described the structure – the grammatical and semantic rules – of AAL in which he explained, for example, why a sentence like

> It ain't no cat can't get in no coop

does not mean:

> *'There isn't any cat that cannot get into any [pigeon] coop.'

but, according to the grammatical and semantic rules of the AAL:

> 'There isn't any cat that can get into any [pigeon] coop.'
>
> (Labov 1972a: 130).

Moreover, Labov studied the use of AAL in ritual insults (see 3.3.1 above) and in stories of personal experience (see also Dittmar 1976: 226–235) and analysed this language in its specific social setting in New York City. He impressively illustrates not only the creative power of the grammar of the language spoken by the Blacks in South Central Harlem, but also the 'great verbal skills' its speakers display, for example in ritual insults that are 'well-organized speech event(s) which [occur] with great frequency in the verbal interaction of black adolescents ... and [occupy] long stretches of their time' (Labov 1972b: 305). Despite their low level of achievement in school, the Black adolescents who get engaged in ritual insults show (off) their highly-developed linguistic competence and capabilities within this form of interaction with members of their peer group. Detailed and minute studies like these contributed to finishing the hot and often highly ideological controversy between the supporters of the code theory and their opponents, who argued on the basis of the variability concept. The outcome of the dispute was finally a matter of a good theory driving out a bad one.[3]

That ideology also played a role for the Black adolescents in Harlem themselves and not only for the linguists who researched their verbal behaviour was illustrated by Labov in his article on 'The linguistic consequences of being a lame'. The Harlem adolescents refer to 'isolated children who grow up without being members of any vernacular peer group' as 'lames'. Therefore they do not have the grammatical competence and the verbal skills to adequately interact with members of these groups. They all simply 'lack the knowledge which is necessary to run any kind of game in the vernacular culture', as Labov (1972c: 84) points out. Thus, 'language is one of the most striking and salient emblems of lame status' (Labov 1972c: 108). This reveals that the speakers of AAL have developed a language ideology which excludes, segregates and denounces individuals whose Black English (BE) language variety is closer to Standard English (SE) than to the BE spoken in the vernacular culture. Labov's research results in the following insights:

> *Categorical or semi-categorical rules of BE are weakened to variable rules by the Lames; variable rules that are in strong use in BE are reduced to a low level by the Lames.*

Whenever there is a contrast between SE and BE, the language of the lames is shifted dramatically to SE. In many cases, this leads to a close alignment between the Lames and white non-standard vernaculars.

(Labov 1972c: 98)

However, as Labov points out, these 'lames' are quite often consultants of linguists and anthropologists, because these 'marginal men ... are detached from their own society far enough to be interested and accessible to the language, the problems and preoccupations of the investigator'. As consultants they cannot but give 'an inaccurate or misleading account of the vernacular culture' (Labov 1972c: 110). It is evident that this is an important insight for anthropological, linguistic and pragmatic research:

[A]n accurate description of a language will demand some knowledge of the social structure of its users. We must be able to find our way through the various intersecting patterns of the normally heterogeneous society if we are to locate the most uniform and consistent forms of the grammar, since an understanding of variation requires a realistic assessment of the invariance that accompanies it.

(Labov 1972c: 108)

This knowledge is only gained by studying the speakers' actual use of language in social interactions.

The deficit versus difference hypothesis controversy resulted in innovative methodological tools and theoretical as well as practical insights which are extremely important for present-day research on endangered languages and efforts to revitalize them. Projects that aim to document and revitalize endangered languages require descriptive competence and sociolinguistic – or, if you like, ethnographic and pragmatic – expertise to gain insights into why a language is endangered and what effects this process has on the speakers' attitudes towards their language. This knowledge puts linguists engaged in these endeavours into the position to decide whether there are chances to reverse language shift in progress that will otherwise lead to language loss. The attitudes of speakers of endangered language are very much shaped by their own language ideologies and by those of others (see Senft 2010c). In the next subsection of this chapter we will have a closer look at language ideologies and their implications for research in pragmatics.

6.4 LANGUAGE IDEOLOGIES

In his pioneering paper on 'Language structure and linguistic ideologies' Michael Silverstein (1979: 193) defined '... ideologies about language, or linguistic ideologies, [as] any sets of beliefs about language articulated by the users as a rationalization or justification of perceived language structure and use'. These language ideologies are 'expressed in native metapragmatic theories or ethno-metapragmatics ... as rationalizations about the use of language' (Silverstein 1979: 207f.). In their 1994 survey article on research on language ideology and language attitudes, Kathryn Woolard and Bambi Schieffelin review 'the full range of scholars' notions of ideology: from seemingly neutral cultural conceptions of language to strategies for maintaining social power, from unconscious ideology read from speech practices by analysts to the most conscious native-speaker explanations of appropriate language behavior' (Woolard and Schieffelin 1994: 58).

In his recent monograph on *Ideology in Language Use* Jef Verschueren elaborates on the concept of ideology as follows: He points out that '... ideology is associated with *underlying patterns of meaning, frames of interpretation, world views*, or *forms of everyday thinking and explanation*.' For him a language ideology 'is a fully integrated *sociocultural-cognitive phenomenon*' that represents its speakers' 'general way of thinking about language', which 'involves a specific form of intersubjectivity or sharing ..., as well as affect and stance' (Verschueren 2012: 7ff.). He defines the concept of ideology (in general) in four main theses (printed in bold in the original) which run as follows:

> We can define as ideological any basic pattern of meaning or frame of interpretation bearing on or involved in (an) aspect(s) of social 'reality' (in particular in the realm of social relations in the public sphere), felt to be commonsensical, and often functioning in a normative way.
>
> (Verschueren 2012: 10)

In an additional comment to this thesis Verschueren points out that

> *the common-sense ... nature of ideological meaning is manifested in the fact that it is rarely questioned ... Its not being questioned means that the meaning concerned is often ... carried along implicitly rather than being formulated explicitly.*
>
> (Verschueren 2012: 12f.)

The next three theses run as follows:

> Ideology ... may be highly immune to experience and observation.
>
> (Verschueren 2012: 14)

> (One of) the most visible manifestation(s) of ideology is LANGUAGE USE or DISCOURSE, which may reflect, construct and/or maintain ideological patterns.
>
> (Verschueren 2012: 17)

> Discursively reflected, constructed, and or supported ideological meaning may serve the purposes of framing, validating, explaining, or legitimating attitudes, states of affairs, and actions in the domain in which they are applicable.
>
> (Verschueren 2012: 19)

Verschueren illustrates his definition of ideology in language use with a corpus of history textbooks from the late nineteenth to the twentieth century. In what follows the concept of *linguistic ideology* will be illustrated with examples from the Solomon Islands and from Rapa Nui (Easter Island) and with ideologies underlying honorific language use.

6.4.1 Language ideologies in two Pacific speech communities

In their anthology *Consequences of Contact: Language Ideologies and Sociocultural Transformations in Pacific Societies* Miki Makihara and Bambi B. Schieffelin (2007; see Senft 2010b) try to explain why the Pacific has been an area of enormous contemporary linguistic, cultural, political and social diversity. Much of this diversity can be explained by the different contact situations Pacific communities have experienced with both former and present-day colonial and postcolonial powers, governments and religious institutions, as well as by more recent influences such as globalization, urbanization, militarization and environmental change. Systematic research on the indigenous languages spoken in the Pacific did not start until the end of the nineteenth century. By now, scholars within the social and cognitive sciences have realized that language and speech practices in Pacific societies play a central role in the construction of self and for these communities' social and political realities. Language diversity is understood as a marker of social identity. However, the fact that contact and trade languages and *lingua francas* (most of which have now become creoles) developed, shows the need for shared translocal languages in the area as well. The consequences of contact history for the diversity of the languages spoken in the Pacific were fundamental; unfortunately, they were also quite often fatal. Indigenous languages spoken in the Pacific area have been dying ever since earliest contacts with European languages. Missionaries and government officials introduced literacy and Western scripts with the first translations of (parts of) the Bible into a usually randomly selected variety of one of the local languages. This resulted in the marginalization, if not death, of other dialects not only of the chosen local language but more often than not also of its neighbouring languages and in the abandonment of the very few indigenous scripts, like the Rongorongo script of the Rapa Nui. Writing was suddenly taken as being more authoritative than speaking. These new notions about language also introduced new language ideologies into the various speech communities which re-shaped indigenous ways of feeling, thinking and speaking about language. The featuring of the following two representative contributions to Makihara's and Schieffelin's anthology illustrate the importance of language ideologies for an adequate understanding of the strong interrelationship between linguistic and cultural processes in contact situations for two speech communities in the Pacific.

6.4.1.1 *Language ideologies in Honiara, Solomon Islands*

In her essay on 'Linguistic paths to urban self in postcolonial Solomon Islands' Christine Jourdan (2007) describes and analyses the urban modalities of language use by residents of Honiara, the capital city of the Solomon Islands, with the aim of showing how contact has affected urban definitions of self and identity. In multilingual Honiara – there are more than 70 languages spoken in the Solomons – cultural and linguistic contact, together with ideologies of change and progress, has created the need for a definition of urban identity which feeds on ideologies of tradition, custom, modernization and social roles and options, and which is revealed through language choice and verbal practice. Language choice is not only an expression of the speaker's identity and agency. The attention speakers pay to language selection also reveals a great deal about their need constantly to redefine their sociality, as well as about the situatedness of the speakers' social selves in situations of culture contact. Jourdan provides some background information on the effects of contact on the linguistic situation of the Solomon Islands prior to and during colonization and on postcolonial Honiara. She points out that multilingualism has always been a feature of Solomon Island societies. Although the dominant language ideology of the colonial times used to be characterized by linguistic hegemony and hierarchy, the linguistic and social parameters of this multilingual situation have changed in recent times. The colonial sociolinguistic hierarchy, with English – the official language – at the top and local vernaculars and Solomons Pijin – the *lingua franca* – at the bottom, has been reorganized.[4] Jourdan points out that Honiarans now use different language varieties to index their position in the urban world, to indicate ethnic identities and to illustrate their social sophistication. Thus, their language choice reveals the situated and contextual construction of their social selves. In present-day Honiara, languages not only mark ethnicity, but also social class, age group, and urban identity. Honiarans have constructed a hierarchy of languages which is context-dependent:

- if they want to emphasize their ethnic selves, the vernaculars are placed at the top;

- if they want to index their gendered selves, Pijin and vernaculars come first;

- and if they want to index that they are young urban people they stress Pijin as the language for daily interaction and English as the language of social advancement.

Thus, the language ideology that was dominant in pre-colonial times characterized by reciprocal multilingualism and the language ideology that was dominant in colonial times characterized by linguistic hegemony and hierarchy have both been replaced by multiple ideologies which compete with one another. These insights are crucial for a sound analysis of language use in Honiara.

6.4.1.2 *Language ideology of the Rapa Nui*

Miki Makihara's (2007) essay on 'Linguistic purism in Rapa Nui political discourse' examines ideologies of code choice and language revitalization embedded in forms of political discourse among the bilingual, indigenous Polynesian community of Rapa Nui (or Easter Island), which Chile annexed in 1888. Since then the Rapa Nui language has been marginalized and endangered by the spread of Spanish, the national language of Chile. However, Rapa Nui political leaders have challenged this situation first by expanding syncretic Rapa Nui-Spanish speech styles into the public and political domain. More recently, they have developed an ideology of linguistic purism and constructed purist Rapa Nui linguistic codes for political discourse in order to re-emphasize the value of their Polynesian language and to voice their ethnic identity within the Chilean nation. After a brief summary of the historical, sociolinguistic and political contexts of these developments relating them to the island's particular history of contact, Makihara presents and analyses two excerpts taken from a forum to debate aspects of the Rapa Nui Indigenous Law and from a meeting with a continental government official. The following example, taken from the first excerpt (Makihara 2007: 55), illustrates the use of syncretic Rapa Nui, which is 'characterized by the simultaneous presence of multiple varieties of Rapa Nui and Spanish within and across individual utterances' (Makihara 2007: 50). It was taken from a debate about indigenous law between the president of a self-proclaimed council of elders (C) and the Rapa Nui governor (G); parts of the utterances in which speakers switch from Rapa Nui to Spanish are underlined:

C. *E tiaki ena a mātou, ki tū <u>compromiso</u>*
We (EXCL) are waiting for the <u>commitment</u>

era o te <u>gobierno</u> pe nei ē he aŋa mai e
by the <u>government</u> that they would elaborate

rāua i te <u>declaración</u>. Ko kī 'ana ho 'i e
a <u>declaration</u>. A (his fellow participant) told

A. ko garo 'a 'ā e koe pe nei ē, mo tu 'u
you and you heard that when the

mai o ra <u>decracione</u> (<u>declaración</u>), ki
<u>declaration</u> arrives, and when we (excl.) see

u 'i atu e mātou 'ana titika he <u>buka</u> (<u>busca</u>)
that it is correct, we (incl) would <u>look</u> for

a tātou i te <u>manera</u>, he aŋa te
the <u>way</u> to make a new

<u>rey</u> (<u>ley</u>) āpī, <u>o que se yó</u>, o he <u>junta</u>
<u>law</u> , <u>or what do I know</u>, or <u>combine</u>

ararua <u>rey</u>, <u>no sé</u>.
two <u>laws</u>, <u>I don't know</u>.
...

G: <u>No</u>, ko <u>acuerdo</u> 'āpa 'i a tātou.
G:<u>No</u>, (it's that) we (INCL) <u>agreed.</u>

<u>Mira</u>, <u>el problema</u> i te <u>hora</u> nei to 'oku mana' u
<u>Look</u>, <u>the problem</u> of the <u>moment</u> in my opinion

es el siguiente ...
is the following ...

Te me'e o te <u>*subsecretario*</u> *i* <u>*pia*</u> mai ki a au
(This is) what the <u>under-secretary</u> <u>asked</u> me;

'<u>*mire señor, usted vaya a la Isla de Pascua y*</u>
'<u>look sir, you go to Easter Island and</u>

<u>*materialize este acuerdo.*</u>
<u>materialize this agreement.</u>

(Makihara 2007: 55)

Makihara points out that this example, with the 'frequent inter- and intrasentential codeswitching between Rapa Nui and Spanish, Rapa Nui interferences and the ... use of Spanish borrowings' is not only typical for the 'syncretic speech in political debate' but also 'very similar to everyday Rapa Nui speech' (Makihara 2007: 56).

The next example taken from the second excerpt illustrates the use of purist Rapa Nui (Makihara 2007: 58). This time the very same president of the council of elders addresses monolingual Spanish-speaking Chilean senators in purist Rapa Nui, which was then 'translated' into Spanish by another leader of the council:

C: *Te mātou me'e haŋa, ke hakanoho i te*
C: What we (EXCL) want is to stop all that is

me'e ta 'ato 'a nei o te <u>*hora*</u> *nei e makenu*
moving at this <u>moment</u>, that we don't

mai ena, 'ina he aŋiaŋi mai. Te rua, te
understand. Secondly, the land

henua ko hape 'a. <u>*Tiene que*</u> *hakatitika*
(arrangement) is incorrect. They <u>have to</u>

rāua i te rāua me'e, he hakahoki mai i te tātou henua.
straighten out their deed and return our (INCL) land.

This part of the council leader's speech was translated – or rather transformed – into Spanish by another leading member of the elders' council as follows:

T: *Nosotros solicitamos como legitimos representantes del pueblo de Rapa Nui,*
T: We solicit as legitimate representatives of the Rapa Nui people,

que por intermedio de ustedes, ver la posibilidad da parar todo proyecto que
that through your intermediation, to see the possibility of stopping every project that

esté destinado al desarrollo de Isla de Pascua. Pues nos falta una cosa muy
is destined for the development of Easter Island. Because we need one very

principal que es la tierra, por eso estamos aqui para que ustedes transmitan
principal thing, which is the land, that is why we are here so that you transmit

al supreme gobierno nuestra inquietud, para que vean la solución de
to the supreme government, so that they see the solution to

reconocer y restituir nuestra propiedad a la tierra que es la base de todo
recognize and return our [title (G. S.)] to the land, which is the base for all

el desarrollo de la isla. Sin la tierra no podemos hacer nada.
development of the island. Without the land we cannot do anything.

(Makihara 2007: 58)

The Rapa Nui speech and the Spanish translation had two audiences – the Chilean senators and the Rapa Nui participants. Makahira explains what was actually going on during these speeches:

> The message to the senators in purist Rapa Nui speech was largely symbolic, aimed at highlighting the cultural differences between the representatives of the state and the Rapa Nui, and at adding weight to Rapa Nui claims of self-representation and ancestral rights over their land. The propositional content of the main leader's Rapa Nui speech, however, also targets his fellow Rapa Nui as explicitly addressed recipients of the message. The speaker frequently uses the inclusive first person pronoun *tātou* ('we' or 'our' including you) to refer to Rapa Nui (except for one occasion...[see first line of the excerpt above; G. S.]), and he refers to the senators and Chileans in general as *rāua* 'they'. He represents claims and requests addressed to the Chilean audience explaining them to the Rapa Nui audience and calls on the Rapa Nui to unite [in another part of his speech not presented here] ... In his translation [the other Rapa Nui leader] ... goes well beyond the original in establishing the identities of the parties involved and the relationships between them: ... the speakers as "legitimate representatives of the Rapa Nui people" ..., the addressees as "honorable senators" ...[as] intermediaries who should "transmit [the Rapa Nui] concern to the supreme government" ... Through the use of ... contextualization cues and politeness markers [the translator] skillfully establishes a horizontal alignment between Chileans and Rapa Nui...
>
> The juxtaposition of the speaker and the translator and of two clearly separated languages, and especially the choice of purist Rapa Nui, contributed greatly to the communicative effectiveness of the performance.

(Makahira 2007: 60)

The use of purist Rapa Nui in this meeting had two important functions: on the one hand it emphasized the ethnic, political and linguistic boundaries between the Chileans and the Rapa Nui, and on the other hand it had an important bonding function for the Rapa Nui, because the purist language use is a symbol for their unity and a historical coherence before and after the independence of the island community from Chile. The existence of purist Rapa Nui could be supportive for language revitalization and maintenance projects. However, syncretic Rapa Nui is the dominant variety in everyday life and in real discussions of substance in political discourse. The purist registers developed by political activists for Rapa Nui are only used as a means to unite the indigenous community of the Rapa Nui symbolically against outsiders and to voice their own ethnic identity.

6.4.2 Language ideologies of honorific language

In his seminal paper on linguistic ideology Michael Silverstein (1979: 216ff.) provided an analysis of 'the so-called "linguistic etiquette" of Javanese' based on Clifford Geertz's ethnographic masterpiece *The Religion of Java* (1976 [= 1960]) to illustrate his concept of language ideology. In 1998 Judith Irvine published a revised and enlarged version of her 1992 paper on 'Ideologies of honorific language' in which she compared 'Javanese, Wolof ... Zulu ... [and] ChiBemba ... with regard to honorific expressions and the social and cultural frameworks relevant thereto' (Irvine 1992: 251). She defines honorifics as 'means of expressing respect (or disrespect)' (Irvine 1992: 251) which are manifest in 'specially conventionalized forms' (Irvine 1998: 51) which signal 'deference' in a way that also 'requires some further set of shared understandings about the expression's significance and pragmatic potential' (Irvine 1998: 53). She aims to answer the question whether 'one can identify any cultural concomitants of linguistic systems in which honorifics occur' (Irvine 1998: 51).

Already the choice of the languages analysed – Javanese is a Western Austronesian language, whereas, Wolof, Zulu and ChiBemba are Niger-Congo languages – reveals that the presence of honorifics is found in unrelated speech communities around the world. And a closer look at the social structure of the four speech communities allows her to refute the prevalent hypothesis that 'court life and/or entrenched class differences are ... necessary and sufficient conditions for the existence of linguistic honorifics'. Irvine argues that 'the relationship between the distribution of social and linguistic forms is more productively sought in cultural ideologies of language [paying] special attention to the language ideologies that link ideas about language with ideas about social rank, respect and appropriate conduct'. She highlights the 'connection with power relations and interests that are central in a social order' which is connoted with the concept 'ideology' as a relevant characteristic of honorific language (Irvine 1998: 52).

In her first analysis of the Javanese honorifics she shows that in this language respectful expression operates through a complex system of lexical alternants. She illustrates the six language levels of Javanese – the four higher levels of Krama and Madya and the two lower levels of Ngoko – with the following examples taken from Joseph Errington (1988: 90f.; see Irvine 1992: 253):

| KRAMA: | 1. | *menapa* | *nandalem* | *mundhut* | *sekul* | *semanten* |
| | 2. | *menapa* | *panjenengan* | *mendhet* | *sekul* | *semanten* |

MADYA:	3.	*napa*	*sampeyan*	*mendhet*	*sekul*	*semonten*
	4.	*napa*	*sampeyan*	*njupuk*	*senga*	*semonten*

NGOKO:	5.	*apa*	*sliramu*	*mundhut*	*sega*	*semono*
	6.	*apa*	*kowe*	*njupuk*	*sega*	*semono*

Gloss	Question marker	you	take	rice	that much

Did you take that much rice?

In the Niger-Congo language Zulu spoken in South Africa there is a respect vocabulary which is known as *hlonipha*. Irvine (1992: 253) provides examples of ordinary and *hlonipha* lexical alternants provided by Doke and Vilakazi (1958); some of these are presented below (the graphemes 'c' and 'x' represent clicks):

	ORDINARY	HLONIPHA
'graze, weave'	*aluka*	*acuka*
'be rejected'	*jaba*	*gxaba*
'house'	*indlu*	*incumba*
'our'	*-ithu*	*-itšu*
'thy'	*-kho*	*-to*

Besides the *hlonipha* respect vocabulary, Zulu has another type of deferential expression, *bonga* – 'praise'. Irvine (1998: 58) points out that these two types are 'ideologically linked with different social contexts (family and court)[5] and with different users (women and men)'. In former times *hlonipha* words allowed Zulu women to 'avoid uttering the name of the husband's father' as well as words that sounded like this name. Irvine (1998: 60) also points out that '*hlonipha* forms were also used by men to avoid using the name of the mother-in-law, though the custom was not as strict for men as it was for women'. The use of *hlonipha* also required specifc forms of behaviour, such as the avoidance of eye-contact, restraining one's affectivity and covering one's body.

The *bonga* type of deferential expression is used to 'express gratitude' and refers to 'an exuberant poetic style of male public oratory, usually addressed to important political figures ... at public gatherings'; there are 'male professional praise-poets' who perform praises characterized by 'vivid detailed imagery and a sense of spontaneous enthusiasm' (Irvine 1998: 59). The *bonga* type, however, does not rely on honorifics in the form of isosemantic (i.e. same-sensed) alternants.

Irvine summarized her description of the Zulu types of deferential expressions as follows:

> [T]he Zulu expressive system includes an utterer-focused, ecstatic, high-affect, engaged style without honorifics, and an addressee- or bystander-focused, flat-affect, disengaged, avoidance style with honorifics.

> (Irvine 1998: 59)

The Niger-Congo language ChiBemba, spoken in Zambia, expresses respect through its noun class system (Irvine 1992: 254). Languages with noun class systems divide nouns into different classes, each of which requires a different set of agreement markers on verbs, adjectives, possessive pronouns, numerals, etc. In the ChiBemba system most human nouns belong to class 1 in the singular and class 2 in the plural. Nouns in class 1 with singular reference can be marked for honorification by being shifted in form and agreement to class 2 (in a similar way as in French, for example, where we have the second person plural pronoun *vous* which can be used as a honorific plural form instead of the second person singular form *tu*); however, given this fact, there is no corresponding way of marking honorification in the plural. This is illustrated with the following examples:

(a) not respectful

umo	*umukalamba*	*waandi*	*aleelya*	*isabi*
1	1	1	1	9a
one	older-sibling	my	subject-tense-eat	fish

'One of my older siblings is eating fish.'
([more literally (G. S.)], 'My one older sibling is eating fish.')

(b) respectful

Bamo	*abakalamba*	*baandi*	*baaleelya*	*isabi*
2	2	2	2	9a
one	older-sibling	my	subject-tense-eat	fish

'One of my older siblings is eating fish.'
(([more literally (G. S.)], 'My one older sibling is eating fish.')

(c) ambiguous

babili	*abakalamba*	*baandi*	*baaleelya*	*isabi*
2	2	2	2	9a
two	older-sibling	my	subject-tense-eat	fish

'Two of my older siblings are eating fish.'
([more literally (G. S.)], 'My two older siblings are eating fish.')

There are some nouns which are habitually given honorification in this way; assigning them to class 1 (or one of a number of other singular classes) gives rise to interpretations of disrespect or insult. Irvine (1992: 254) provides the following examples based on the noun stem *-kaši* 'wife':

		CLASS	VALUE
abakaši	'(respectable) wife'	2	honorific (because plural, G. S.)
umukaši	'wife'	1	disrespectful
akakaši	'(insignificant) wife'	12	insult
ičikaši	'(gross) wife'	7	insult
ilikaši	'egregious[?] wife'	5	"a little derogatory"

The Niger-Congo language Wolof, spoken in Senegal, the Gambia and a few other West African countries, does not have a comparable system of alternant expressions but marks respect and deference with two speech registers which are characterized by different prosodic patterns. These patterns 'are nonsegmentable and operate more on the level of utterance meaning than on the level of sentence meaning' (Irvine 1998: 55). The two speech registers are called *waxu géér* 'noble speech' and *waxu gewel* 'griot speech'.[6] Irvine (1992: 255) characterizes the prosodic patterns of these two varieties as follows:

	waxu géér 'NOBLE SPEECH'	*waxu gewel* 'GRIOT SPEECH'
Pitch	low	high
Volume	soft	loud
Tempo	slow	fast
Voice	breathy	clear
Contour	pitch nucleus last	pitch nucleus first
Dynamic range	narrow	wide

Other characteristic features that differentiate these two registers are semantic differences and rhetorical elaborations.

Now what about the linguistic ideologies that underlie these four systems of honorific language? In Java the *priyayi*'s, the traditional elite's, conception of their language is characterized by:

> ideas about subtlety and refinement on the one hand and violence and anger on the other ... The 'higher' ... levels are considered to be governed by an ethic of proper order, peace and calm ... The 'lower' levels ... are 'the language one loses one's temper in' ... Yet in some ways the point is really what happens not to one's own temper but to one's addressee's. The language levels are addressee-focused ... Polite conduct toward a respected addressee is conduct that is stylized, depersonalized, and flat-affect ... Still, the use of 'high' deferential styles also implies the speaker's own refinement as shown by her/his ability to efface emotion, sensitivity to the stability of others, and pragmatic delicacy.
>
> (Irvine 1992: 256)

The Wolof language ideology is characterized by ideas similar to those mentioned for the Javanese *priyayi*, however, the use of the two varieties – noble speech and griot speech –

> is not limited to the social ranks they are named for. Both registers are used on some occasions by almost everyone. Still, their use always conveys a sense that the participants in the speech situation inhabit contrasting ranks, even if only metaphorically. Normatively, "griot speech" is the way low-ranking griots address high-ranking nobles. Any person may employ this register to flatter an addressee; yet, in so doing, a speaker engages in griot-like, hence low-ranking, conduct. The Wolof linguistic

ideology ... identifies the register system primarily with the speaker ..., elevating the addressee only by implication ... Wolof nobles avoid using the "griot speech" register ... on public, formal occasions. Instead, they hire a lower-ranking intermediary, usually a griot, to speak on their behalf. The noble sponsor of the speech thus manages to get the addressee flattered while nevertheless suggesting his or her own high rank by refraining from engaging in affectively charged speech ...

(Irvine 1998: 58)

Irvine (1998: 59) notes that the Wolof 'griot speech' variety reminds one of the Zulu praise-oratory style described above, because 'both deliver praise through dramatic, heightened affect [and] semantically elaborated discourse', however, she emphasizes that 'Wolof and Zulu differ in that the Zulu linguistic ideology does not connect praise-performance with low caste, or with particularly low rank of any sort. Speaking *bonga* style does not compromise the speaker's status'. Irvine also points out that there is a

logical parallel between the Zulu *hlonipha* style and the higher levels ... of Javanese. Both involve lowered affect, euphemism, neutralization to certain contrasts and conspicuous conventionality. The Zulu system, then, incorporates both patterns of talk described ... for Wolof and Javanese.

(Irvine 1998: 59)

Irvine summarizes her comparison of the honorific systems of the four languages as follows:

grammatical honorifics accompany linguistic ideologies that specify flattened affect, conventionality, and avoidance of engagement with the concrete or the sensory as a way to express respect for *others* (rather than ways to express one's *own* rank). Put another way, honorifics are embedded in an ideology in which a low-affect style can be other-elevating. They are connected with the management of affectivity and conventionality, and with the ways these relate to rank and power. What kinds of rank and power are concerned varies from one system to another ...

(Irvine (1992: 261)

Irvine concludes the 1998 version of her paper with the caveat that linguistic ideologies are not only found in allegedly 'exotic' languages but actually almost everywhere – 'even' in linguistics:

Some generations ago, linguists sometimes singled out honorific language in Africa and Asia for ridicule or criticism as the signs of what they took to be false pride, decadent overrefinement, or slavish deference to oriental despotism. That they did so says more about those linguists' attitudes toward indigenous social hierarchies than it says about the language in question or their cultural contexts.

(Irvine 1998: 64)

6.5 CONCLUDING REMARKS

This chapter put the rise of sociolinguistics in the historical context of the 1960s, when the discussion of class structure of capitalist societies with its social inequalities dominated not only political discourse, but also scientific debates, especially within the humanities. The dispute between proponents of Bernstein's code theory and Labov's variability concept topicalized paradigmatically the relationship between social class and speech form. Research within the frame of the difference hypothesis revealed that the classification of the speech of the lower classes as a 'restricted' code was not only based on inadequate methods of data gathering and on a lack of linguistic expertise, but also on language ideologies of researchers who were members of the (upper) middle class. They attempted to remedy proclaimed verbal deficits of children of the lower classes with compensatory education programmes aimed at 'repairing' the child, but not the school as an institution that represented and propagated first and foremost middle class interests. This inadequate approach to the problem politicized the proponents of the variability concept. They demonstrated that a proper understanding and assessing of the verbal skills of lower class children, especially of Black children in the urban centres of the USA, needed research of how they use their language in their social contexts. It is only there that one can gather adequate cultural knowledge based on participant observation and the proper linguistic data which enable linguists to detect the rule-governed grammatical structure of these children's vernacular. It was probably at this point that the boundary between pragmatics and sociolinguistics started to blur (see Foley 1997: 29). Sociolinguistics, like pragmatics, became interested in actual language use and verbal interactions between speakers in various social contexts. The proponents of the variability concept finally won their struggle against the supporters of the code theory – and this finally affected the educational politics of the USA, sanctioned even by court decisions.

These studies, however, also revealed that language varieties are important status emblems, not only for members of the middle classes, but also for the Black adolescents studied by Labov and his colleagues. They used their vernacular and their ideas about it as a means to constitute group identity on the one hand and to segregate others who could not adequately command the verbal skills characteristic for their verbal interactions on the other hand. Thus language use as well as language ideology were crucial for the creation of sociocultural identity. To understand these sociolinguistic patterns turned out to be crucial for linguists, especially for and in their choice of consultants who are adequate representatives of the speech community to be researched.

A closer look at language ideologies in other speech communities confirmed that ideologies are normative for the regulation of social relations between specific speech groups in public interactions. As emblems of social identity they not only mark group membership and solidarity – and thus have an important bonding function – they also index a speaker's position within her or his speech community with respect to social rank. Moreover, linguistic ideologies also have the function to legitimize power relations between members of the speech communities and the distribution of power within a society as a whole. They thus control the political conditions within speech communities and proper conduct and behaviour of their members. The understanding of a society's linguistic ideologies is crucial for a proper understanding and adequate linguistic analysis of a number of verbal interactions and phenomena to be observed in group relations within the speech community.

What does this chapter tell us about the anecdote reported in the introduction to this volume? The Trobriand Islanders obviously have a linguistic ideology that regulates their greeting behaviour. Whoever is greeted with the question *Ambe* – 'Where (are you going to)?' has to respond respectfully and truthfully according to the ideology that sets the norm for this verbal interaction. The ideology also prescribes that this reaction is expected from each and every member of the community, disregarding any hierarchical differences within the Trobrianders' socially highly stratified society. Once I had understood this hierarchy levelling – and at the same time highly bonding – function of this form of greeting, I could also understand other little rituals I observed in the village, like the giving and taking of tobacco. It quite often happened that people who had just asked me for tobacco and paper and who could hardly wait till they could smoke their hand-rolled cigarette were approached by other people who had waited in the background and now asked them for a smoke. I observed that they, almost bewildered, puffed what they had thought was 'their' cigarette three or four times and then passed it on to the person who had requested it. This behaviour is also based on a normative ideology, albeit a cultural one, which is again binding upon everyone even across clan boundaries: it prescribes the almost immediate passing on of something like a cigarette to someone who asks for it. This norm strengthens group coherence and group identity by testing the validity of group-specific ideologies over and over again in marginal everyday interactions: It contributes to the continuity of the group solidarity, strengthens social harmony within the group and increases the social bond between the members of the community and is thus politically highly important (see Senft 1995: 218f.).

6.6 EXERCISE/WORK SECTION

- What are the main characteristics of the linguistic ideology/ideologies which are fundamental for the code theory on the one hand and the difference hypothesis on the other?

- Discuss the pros and cons of being a monolingual/multilingual speaker in a multilingual society.

- What is a 'standard language' and who defines this standard? Why do speakers of languages develop different varieties, dialects, registers, technical languages, etc. of their 'standard' language?

- Which language policies – informed by linguistic insights – should guide verbal education in different school levels? Justify the proposals made.

- Gather audio-data from three or more speakers with foreign or regional (dialect) accents, look for a group of linguistic laypersons, let them hear excerpts of your data and ask them to characterize the speakers of these varieties of your language. After these assessments, ask the laypersons about the reasons for their judgements and characterize the linguistic ideologies that guided their assessments.

- Conduct a small research project (based on participant observation combined with brief interviews) on the forms of address used in your university in official and unofficial situations. How do students address each other? How do students address their lecturers/professors – and vice versa? How do lecturers/professors/ deans address each other? Which linguistic ideologies underlie these systems of address? Can these systems be used to make inferences about hierarchical structures within a university? And what are the linguistic ideologies underlying these forms of address?

- Collect data (speeches, TV-spots, newscasts, newspaper articles, advertisements, etc.) which mirror linguistic ideologies, reveal the ideologies and thus justify your choice of data.

6.7 SUGGESTIONS FOR FURTHER READING

Basso, K. (1970); Baugh (1983); Blommaert (1999, 2011); Çap (2010); Fairclough (2001); Fenigsen (2003); Finegan (1980); Garland (2008); Giles *et al.* (1987); Haviland (2011); Kroskrity, Schieffelin and Woolard (1992); McElhinny (2003); Morgan (1994); Mufwene (1992); Schieffelin, Woolard and Kroskrity (1998); Webster (2008); Wodak (1997).

NOTES

1 Dittmar (1976) provides an excellent survey both of Bernstein's code theory and its reception in the USA and of Labov's variability concept and its influence on sociolinguistics and implications for American educational politics.
2 For a critical survey see Dittmar (1976: Chapter 2).
3 This was also acknowledged in the so-called Ann Arbor Decision: 'In July 1979, United States District Judge Charles W. Joiner decided that there was a failure on the part of the Ann Arbor School Board ... to provide leadership and help for its teachers in learning about the existence of "Black English" as a home and community language of many Black students and that it had also failed to suggest to these same teachers ways and means of using that knowledge in teaching Black children code-switching skills for reading standard English. He decided that inattention to the relationship between Black English and standard English was not rational in light of existing knowledge on the subject' (Monteith 1980: 556). See also Romaine (1995: 495).
4 The following text passage from Jourdan and Maebiru (2002: xxii) – adapted to a kind of interlinearized transcription – should provide a flavour of Solomon Pijin:

Taem wa, taem Merika hemi landim longo Solomone, ia hem nao, oloketa
During the war, when the Americans landed in the Solomons, that's it, all these

waetemane mifala wawaka longo oloketa bifoa, oloketa givim onda fo mifala tuu.
white men with whom we used to work, gave us orders.

Mifala kamu, ia, mifala baeleke kam fo 'Aoke nomoa. Wokabaoti nomoa long loti fo
We came, yes, we walked all the way to Auki. Walked on the road to

'Aoke.
Auki.

5   Note that Irvine (1998: 61) points out 'that the respect vocabulary arose not in connection with the state, but in the power dynamics of [Zulu] family and affinal relations'.

6   'Griot' is an expression that refers to storytellers, praise singers, poets, etc. in West Africa.

Understanding pragmatics

Summary and outlook

7.1 INTRODUCTION

This chapter will take up the three central threads mentioned in the introduction to this volume to point out how they indeed bind the six chapters of this book into a complex whole. After this summary of the central concerns of pragmatics, which is guided by the leitmotif that 'the heart of the pragmatic enterprise [is] the description of language as social action' (Clift *et al.* 2009: 50), the volume ends with an outlook on recent developments within the discipline that try to 'emancipate' pragmatics from its domination 'by views of language derived from Euro-American languages and ways of speaking' (Hanks *et al.* 2009a: 1).

7.2 SUMMARY

It was pointed out in the introduction that this volume has the following three central threads that bind the chapters into a complex whole:

1. Languages are used by their speakers in social interactions; they are first and foremost instruments for creating social bonds and accountability relations. The means by which languages create these bonds and relations vary across languages and cultures.

2. Speech is part of the context of the situation in which it is produced, language has an essentially pragmatic character and 'meaning resides in the pragmatic function of an utterance' (Bauman 1992: 147).

    •   Speakers of a language follow conventions, rules and regulations in their use of language in social interactions.

    •   The meaning of words, phrases and sentences is conveyed in certain kinds of situative contexts.

    •   The speakers' uses of language fulfil specific functions in and for these speakers' communicative behaviour.

3. Pragmatics is the transdiscipline that studies these language- and culture-specific forms of language use.

The anecdote reported on the first pages of the volume was taken as exemplary for 'understanding pragmatics' because it introduced the central concerns of this transdiscipline. From the point of view of the six disciplines taken as being most relevant for pragmatics it was shown at the end of every chapter how this anecdote illustrates not only cultural differences in language use and understanding, but also how cultural, situative and interpersonal context and culture-specific conventions contribute to meaning in actual language use.

Keeping these fundamental insights in mind, the six chapters are briefly summarized as follows:

Chapter One pointed out that philosophers and linguists doing pragmatics understand:

- speech as the performing of actions in specific contexts; these actions have meaning and force and achieve certain effects which co-constitute and create social reality;

- that speech is primarily 'an instrument for the creation of accountability relations' (Seuren 2009: 140); and

- that one of the primary functions of a language is social binding where the resulting pact or '*social contract*' is based on conventions and on the social competence of its speakers.

Chapter Two revealed that psychologists and linguists doing pragmatics emphasize:

- that deictic verbal references in speech constitute a collaborative task for speakers and hearers who interact with each other;

- that gestures that accompany speech are especially designed for addressees to establish not only social bonds but also to convey more or less complex additional information in social interaction; and

- that these references and gestures vary across languages and cultures.

Chapter Three illustrated how human ethologists and linguists doing pragmatics have shown:

- that humans have developed complex behaviour patterns which were differentiated through processes of ritualization into communicative behaviour signals;

- that these signals are used to develop social contact with others and to establish and maintain a social bond between the senders of the signals and their partners in social interactions;

- that some of the more complex signals have become social rites which increase the predictability of human behaviour and provide security and order in human interaction and that they are therefore highly important for group maintenance;

- that humans have developed highly complex and very culture-specific rituals with important functions of bonding which convey harmony, sympathy, trust and solidarity;

- that the familiarity with such forms of ritualized behaviour is the prerequisite for getting access to a group because all its members have to be on 'common ground' if they want to interact adequately with each other;

- that given all these signals, rites and rituals, speech is just one part – although an important one – of human interaction, which is fundamentally multimodal in nature; and

- that despite the huge variety of these signals, rites and rituals it is possible to hypothesize that they could all be based on a finite set of conventionalized basic interaction strategies that might be universal.

Chapter Four emphasized that ethnologists and linguists doing pragmatics point out:

- that they understand speech as a mode of behaviour, a mode of action in which the meaning of an utterance is constituted by its function in certain contexts;

- that one of the primary forms of language is realized in phatic communion, a form of language use that has primarily bonding functions;

- that the situative context and the interactants' common cultural knowledge provide the necessary information for understanding phatic expressions as a means to consolidate the relationship between the interactants;

- that the meaning of an utterance, thus, can only be understood in relation to the speech event in which it is embedded;

- that the rules that guide the communicative behaviour of members of a specific speech community can vary immensely; they have to be learned to achieve communicative competence within this community;

- that achieving linguistic and cultural competence in a speech community requires the understanding of how it structures, patterns and regulates its ways of speaking;

- that research on the interrelationship between language, culture and cognition treats language primarily as an instrument of thought; however, although language contributes in shaping thinking for non-verbal problem solving instances, it remains problematic to argue that it is only language that influences thought in general.

Chapter Five reported that sociologists and linguists doing pragmatics agree:

- that social interaction constitutes an institutional order with norms, rights and obligations that rule and regulate the interactants' conduct and behaviour;

- that there are procedures and conventions regulating rights and obligations that provide interactants with rules and rituals for 'playing' their interaction 'game'; the rules are based on social contract and social consensus;

- that participants in interactions are aware of the norms valid in their society and that they cooperate in maintaining the ritual and moral 'interaction order' of their social life;

- that the study of interaction must consider the whole social situation, the specific contexts in which they are rooted and on which they depend;

- that members of a community use commonsense practices and shared rules of interpretation as a means of practical reasoning to constitute, understand and make sense of their social world; and

- that conversation in interaction is a highly – and probably universally – ordered and structurally organized activity 'in which participants co-construct meaning and social action in an exquisitely timed choreography of interlocking communicative moves' (Mark Dingemanse [p.c.]); the understanding of the meaning of these moves in specific speech communities, however, requires cultural knowledge.

Chapter Six has shown that politically aware linguists point out:

- that an adequate description of a language demands knowledge of the social structure of its speakers; therefore, language must be studied in its social context with a strong emphasis on the specific speech situation and the social background and significance of the communicative interaction and the speakers involved;

- that language varieties are emblems of social identity; they not only mark group membership and solidarity, and thus have important bonding functions, they also index a speaker's position within her or his speech community with respect to social rank; moreover, they also segregate others who lack an adequate command of the verbal skills that are characteristic for the group members' verbal interactions;

- that language use and language ideology are crucial for the creation of sociocultural identity and normative for the regulation of social relations between specific speech groups in public interactions;

- that linguistic ideologies also have the function to legitimize power relations between group members and the distribution of power within a speech community as a whole. They control the political conditions within speech communities and proper conduct and behaviour of their members;

- that the understanding of a society's linguistic ideologies is crucial for a proper understanding and adequate linguistic analysis of a number of verbal interactions and phenomena to be observed in group relations within a speech community.

These characteristic features of some of the core domains of the discipline provide ample evidence for the fact that linguistic pragmatics is rather a 'transdiscipline' that brings together and interacts with a rather broad variety of other disciplines within the humanities. These disciplines share with pragmatics the fundamental interest in human social (inter)action and the joint creation of meaning. Being a transdiscipline, pragmatics is also cross-linguistically and cross-culturally oriented; therefore it focuses on culture-specific and language-specific differences in actual language use and understanding. Here the question of how cultural, situative and interpersonal context and culture- and language-specific norms and conventions contribute to meaning (and understanding) in actual language use are central.

The cross-linguistic/cross-cultural orientation of pragmatics has revealed that the theories developed in this field are predominantly rooted in West-European and Anglo-American traditions. Thus, in some cases, theories which claim to have universal validity – like the theories of Searle and Grice discussed in Chapter One – are falsified when they are confronted with non-Indo-European languages. This has led to increased 'skepticism in relation to the universality of theories and findings' within pragmatic circles which resulted in the recent emerging of the '"emancipatory pragmatics" movement ... which focuses precisely on the cultural embeddedness of analytical concepts and which ... consciously applies specific non-western notions of language use in theory building and empirical research' (Verschueren 2011: 5). In the final section of this book some basic ideas of this new movement are presented in a brief outlook on future developments within pragmatics.

7.3 A BRIEF OUTLOOK ON FUTURE DEVELOPMENTS WITHIN THE DISCIPLINE: EMANCIPATORY PRAGMATICS

In their programmatic essay 'Towards an emancipatory pragmatics' William Hanks, Sachiko Ide and Yasuhiro Katagiri ask the following provocative questions:

> What would happen ... were we to apply a concept like the Japanese *wakimae* "discernment" to a language like Yukatec Maya or English? Could we productively use the Maya concept of the speaker's body space, called *iknal*, to describe Japanese, Thai, Lao or IGui? ... What could honorific usage and interpretation in Thai or Japanese tell us about languages like English or Finnish? On first appearance, these may seem quixotic questions, since the concepts cited are deeply rooted in their own specific cultures, and applying them directly to another appears inappropriate. Yet, when Euro-American concepts like information exchange and speech act forces are applied to languages like Maya, Thai, Japanese and so on, they are assumed to be appropriate. This discrepancy is indicative of the mostly one-way flow of received theory and description, from Euro-America to the rest. The result is that different non-Western languages tend to be compared and juxtaposed only in a metalanguage that is itself resolutely Western. We question that unidirectional flow in order to provincialize standard theory, to show that it is ultimately a projection of a particular, historically specific view of the world.
>
> (Hanks *et al.* 2009a: 2)

With the emancipatory pragmatics movement these scholars and a gradually growing group of other researchers want to 'break free from the constraints of established paradigms and to multiply the sources of theory' (Hanks *et al.*: 2009a: 2). They see their approach to pragmatics as 'emancipatory ... in the sense of freeing analysis from the confines of theoretical orthodoxies grounded in dominant thought and practice' (Hanks *et al.* 2009a: 2).[1] Their project is – necessarily – both interdisciplinary and transdisciplinary, with a strong focus on cross-linguistic/cross-cultural difference of language use and multimodal interactions between members of the speech communities being investigated. The contributions in two special issues of the *Journal of Pragmatics* (see Hanks *et al.* 2009b; Hanks *et al.* 2012) provide interesting and promising examples for this new direction in pragmatics.

NOTE

1   For a discussion of the term 'emancipatory pragmatics' see Mey (2012: 705f.).

References

Please note that publications marked with an asterisk (*) were suggested for further reading.

Abercrombie, David. 1956. *Problems and Principles*. London: Longmans.

Agar, Michael. 1994. *Language Shock – Understanding the Culture of Conversation*. New York: William Morrow.

Ameka, Felix and James Essegbey. 2006. Elements of the grammar of space in Ewe. In: Stephen C. Levinson and David Wilkins (eds.), *Grammars of Space*, 359–399. Cambridge, UK: Cambridge University Press.

Anderson, Stephen R. and Edward L. Keenan. 1985. Deixis. In: Timothy Shopen (ed.), *Language Typology and Syntactic Description. Volume III. Grammatical Categories and the Lexicon*, 259–308. Cambridge, UK: Cambridge University Press.

Anscombe, Gertrude Elizabeth M. 1957. *Intention*. Oxford, UK: Basil Blackwell.

*Antonopoulou, Eleni and Kiki Nikiforidou. 2002. Deictic motion and the adoption of perspective in Greek. *Pragmatics* 12: 273–295.

*Auer, Peter and Aldo di Luzio (eds.). 1992. *The Contextualization of Language*. Amsterdam: John Benjamins.

Austin, John L. 1961. *Philosophical Papers*. Oxford, UK: Oxford University Press.

——1962. *How to Do Things with Words*. The William James Lectures at Harvard University in 1955. Edited by J. O. Urmson and Marina Sbisà. Oxford, UK: Clarendon Press [= 1976, Oxford University Press].

Ayer, Alfred J. 1936. *Language, Truth and Logic*. London: Victor Gollancz Ltd.

* Baker, Anne, B. van den Bogaerde and Onno Crasborn (eds.). 2003. *Cross-linguistic Perspectives in Sign Language Research*. Hamburg, Germany: Signum.

*Baron-Cohen, Simon. 2003. *Mind Reading, the Interactive Guide to Emotions*. Cambridge, UK: University of Cambridge, Jessica Kingsley Publishers.

Basso, Ellen B. 1985. *A Musical View of the Universe: Kalapalo Myth and Ritual Performances*. Philadelphia, US: University of Pennsylvania Press.

*——2008. Epistemic deixis in Kalapalo. *Pragmatics* 18: 215–252.

Basso, Ellen B. and Gunter Senft. 2009. Introduction. In: Gunter Senft and Ellen B. Basso (eds.), *Ritual Communication*. Oxford, UK: Berg.

*Basso, Keith H. 1970. "To give up on words" – Silence in western Apache culture. *Southwestern Journal of Anthropology* 26: 213–230.

——1979. *Portraits of "the Whiteman": Linguistic Play and Cultural Symbols among the Western Apache*. Cambridge, UK: Cambridge University Press.

*Batic, Gian Claudio (ed.). 2011. *Encoding Emotions in African Languages*. München, Germany: Lincom.

*Baugh, John. 1983. *Black Street Speech. Its History, Structure and Survival*. Austin, US: University of Texas Press.

Bauman, Richard. 1992. Text and discourse in anthropological linguistics. In: William Bright (ed.), *International Encyclopedia of Linguistics*, 145–147. New York: Oxford University Press.

Bauman, Richard and Joel Sherzer (eds.). 1974. *Explorations in the Ethnography of Speaking.* Cambridge: Cambridge University Press.

*Bazzanella, Carla. 1990. Phatic connectives as interactional cues in contemporary spoken Italian. *Journal of Pragmatics* 14: 629–647.

Bell, Charles. 1806. *Essays on the Anatomy of Expression in Painting.* London: Longman, Reese, Hurst & Orme.

Bennardo, Giovanni. 2002. *Representing Space in Oceania – Culture in Language and Mind.* Canberra: Pacific Linguistics.

Bereiter, Carl and Siegfried Engelmann. 1966. *Teaching Disadvantaged Children in the Pre-school.* Englewood Cliffs, US: Prentice Hall.

Bereiter, Carl, Siegfried Engelmann, Jean Osborn and P. A. Reidford. 1966. An academically oriented preschool for culturally deprived children. In: Fred M. Hechinger, (ed.), *Pre-school Education Today*, 105–137. New York: Doubleday.

Berger, Peter L. and Thomas Luckmann. 1966. *The Social Construction of Reality: A Treatise in the Sociology of Knowledge.* New York: Doubleday.

Bernstein, Basil. 1959. A public language. Some sociological implications of a linguistic form. *British Journal of Sociology* 10: 311–326.

——1961. Social class and linguistic development: a theory of social learning. In: Albert Henry Halsey, Jean Floud and C. Arnold Anderson (eds.), *Education, Economy and Society*, 288–314. New York: Free Press.

——1967. Elaborated and restricted codes: An outline. In: Stanley Lieberson (ed.), *Explorations in Sociolinguistics*, 126–133. Bloomington, US: Indiana University Press [fourth edition; 1973].

——1970a. A critique of the concepts of 'compensatory education'. In: David Rubinstein and Colin Stoneman (eds.), *Education for Democracy*, 110–121. Harmondsworth: Penguin.

——1970b. Education cannot compensate for society. *New Society*, 26 February: 344–347.

——1972. Social class, language and socialization. In: Pier Paolo Giglioli (ed.), *Language and Social Context*, 157–178. Harmondsworth: Penguin.

——1990. *Class, Code and Control Vol. 4: The Structuring of Pedagogic Discourse.* London: Routledge.

Birdwhistell, Ray L. 1970. *Kinesics and Context.* Philadelphia, US: University of Pennsylvania Press.

*Blanco Salgueiro, Antonio. 2010. Promises, threats, and the foundation of speech act theory. *Pragmatics* 20: 213–228.

Bloch, Maurice. 1976. Review of Richard Bauman and Joel Sherzer (eds.), 1974. *Explorations in the Ethnography of Speaking.* Cambridge, UK: Cambridge University Press. *Language in Society* 5: 229–234.

*Blommaert, Jan. 1999. *Language Ideological Debates.* Berlin: Mouton de Gruyter.

*——2011. The long language-ideological debate in Belgium. *Journal of Multicultural Discourses* 6: 241–256.

Blum-Kulka, Shoshona, Juliane House and Gabriele Kasper (eds.). 1989. *Cross-Cultural Pragmatics: Requests and Apologies.* Norwood, NJ: Ablex.

Boas, Franz. 1911. Introduction. In: Franz Boas (ed.), *Handbook of American Indian Languages.* Bureau of American Ethnology, Bulletin 40, Part 1, 1–83. Washington DC: Government Printing Office.

Bohnemeyer, Jürgen. 2001. Deixis. In: Neil J. Smelser and Paul B. Baltes (eds.), *International Encyclopedia of the Social and Behavioral Sciences.* Vol 5, 3371–3375. Amsterdam: Elsevier.

Bohnemeyer, Jürgen and Christel Stolz. 2006. Spatial reference in Yucatek Maya: A survey. In: Stephen C. Levinson and David Wilkins (eds.), *Grammars of Space*, 273–310. Cambridge, UK: University of Cambridge Press.

*Boroditsky, Lera. 2001. Does language shape thought? Mandarin and English speakers' conceptions of time. *Cognitive Psychology* 43: 1–22.

Boroditsky, Lera and Alice Gaby. 2010. Remembrances of times east: Absolute spatial representations of time in an Australian Aboriginal community. *Psychological Science*. http://pss.sagepub.com/content/21/11/1635.full.

Branaman, Ann. 1997. Goffman's social theory. In: Charles Lemert and Ann Branaman (eds.), *The Goffman Reader*, xlv–lxxxii. Oxford: Blackwell.

Brown, Penelope. 2010. Questions and their responses in Tzeltal. *Journal of Pragmatics* 42: 2627–2648.

Brown, Penelope and Stephen C. Levinson. 1978. Universals in language usage: Politeness phenomena. In: Esther N. Goody (ed.), *Questions and Politeness: Strategies in Social Interaction*, 56–311. Cambridge, UK: Cambridge University Press.

——1993. *Linguistic and Nonlinguistic Coding of Spatial Arrays: Explorations in Mayan Cognition*. CARG Working paper No. 24. Nijmegen, The Netherlands: MPI for Psycholinguistics.

Bühler, Karl. 1934. *Sprachtheorie: Die Darstellungsfunktion der Sprache*. Jena, Germany: Fischer. [= 1965. Stuttgart, Germany: Gustav Fischer Verlag].

——1990. *Theory of Language: The Representational Function of Language*. Translated by Donald Fraser Goodwin. Amsterdam: John Benjamins. [Translation of Bühler (1934)].

*Burenhult, Niclas. 2003. Attention, accessibility, and the addressee: The case of the Jahai demonstrative 'ton'. *Pragmatics* 13: 363–379.

*Çap, Piotr. (2010) *Legitimisation in Political Discourse: A Cross-Disciplinary Perspective on the Modern US War Rhetoric*. (second revised edition). Newcastle, UK: Cambridge Scholars Publishing.

*Castelfranchi, Cristiano and Marco Guerini. 2007. Is it a promise or a threat? *Pragmatics & Cognition* 15: 277–311.

Chagnon, Napoleon. 1968. *Yanomamö – the Fierce People*. New York: Holt, Rinehart and Winston.

*Charnock, H. Ross. 2009. Overruling as a speech act: Performativity and normative discourse. *Journal of Pragmatics* 41: 401–426.

Chen, Rong. 1993. Responding to compliments. A contrastive study of politeness strategies between American English and Chinese speakers. *Journal of Pragmatics* 20: 49–75.

Cheepen, Christine. 1988. *The Predictability of Informal Conversation*. London: Continuum International Publishing.

Chomsky, Noam. 1965. *Aspects of the Theory of Syntax*. Cambridge, Mass., US: MIT Press.

Chu, Mingyuan and Sotaro Kita. 2011. The nature of gestures' beneficial role in spatial problem solving. *Journal of Experimental Psychology: General*. 140: 102–115.

Church, R. Breckinridge and Susan Goldin-Meadow. 1986. The mismatch between gesture and speech as an index of transitional knowledge. *Cognition* 23: 43–71.

Clark, Herbert H. 1973. Space, time, semantics, and the child. In: Timothy E. Moore (ed.), *Cognitive Development and the Acquisition of Language*, 27–63. New York: Academic Press.

——1979. Responding to indirect speech acts. *Cognitive Psychology* 11: 430–477.

——1996a. *Using Language*. Cambridge, UK: Cambridge University Press.

——1996b. Communities, commonalities and communication. In: John Gumperz and Stephen C. Levinson (eds.), *Rethinking Linguistic Relativity*, 324–355. Cambridge, UK: Cambridge University Press.

*Clark, Herbert H. and Thomas B. Carlson. 1982. Hearers and speech acts. *Language* 58: 332–373.

Clark, Herbert and Deanna Wilkes-Gibbs. 1986. Referring as a collaborative process. *Cognition* 22: 1–39.

Clift, Rebecca, Paul Drew and Ian Hutchby. 2009. Conversation analysis. In: Sigurd D'hondt, Jan-Ola Östman and Jef Verschueren (eds.), *The Pragmatics of Interaction*, 40–54. Amsterdam: John Benjamins.

Connolly, Bon and Robin Anderson. 1987. *First Contact*. New York: Viking.

Corazza, Eros. 2010. Indexicals and Demonstratives. *Handbook of Pragmatics Online*. 19 pp. Amsterdam: John Benjamins. http://www.benjamins.com/online/hop/

Coulmas, Florian. 1981. "Poison to your soul" – Thanks and apologies contrastively viewed. In: Florian Coulmas (ed.), *Conversational Routine. Explorations in Standardized Communication Situations and Prepatterned Speech*, 69–91. The Hague: Mouton.

*Couper-Kuhlen, Elizabeth and Tsuyoshi Ono (eds.). 2007. Turn continuation in cross-linguistic perspective. *Pragmatics* (special issue) 17: 505–660.

*Coupland, Justine (ed.). 2000. *Small Talk*. London: Longman.

*Crary, Alice. 2002. The happy truth: J. L. Austin's *How to Do Things with Words. Inquiry* 45: 59–80.

Daikuhara, Midori. 1986. A study of compliments from a cross-cultural perspective: Japanese vs. American English. *The PENN Working Papers in Educational Linguistics* – Fall 1986: 87–106.

Darnell, Regna. 2009. Franz Boas. In: Gunter Senft, Jan-Ola Östman and Jef Verschueren (eds.), *Culture and Language Use*, 41–49. Amsterdam: John Benjamins.

Darwin, Charles. 1872. *The Expression of Emotion in Man and Animals*. London: Murray.

*Davis, Wayne A. 1998. *Implicature: Intention, Convention and Principle in the Failure of Gricean Theory*. Cambridge, UK: Cambridge University Press.

De Jorio, Andrea. 2000. *Gesture in Naples and Gesture in Classical Antiquity*. A translation of *La mimica degli antichi investigata nel gestire napoletano* – Gestural Expression of the Ancients in the Light of Neapolitan Gesturing (1832), and with an Introduction and Notes by Adam Kendon. Bloomington, US: Indiana University Press.

de León, Lourdes. 1990. *Space games in Tzotzil: creating a context for spatial reference*. Berlin, Nijmegen (The Netherlands): Mimeo.

de Ruiter, Jan Peter, Holger Mitterer and Nick Enfield. 2006. Projecting the end of a speaker's turn: A cognitive cornerstone of conversation. *Language* 82: 515–535.

*Demir, Özlem Ece, Wing-Chee So, Asli Özyürek and Susan Goldin-Meadow. 2011. Turkish- and English-speaking children display sensitivity to perceptual context in the referring expressions they produce in speech and gesture. *Language and Cognitive Processes*. Available online 25 October 2011. DOI: 10.1080/01690965.2011.589273.

Denny, J. Peter. 1978. Locating the universals in lexical systems for spatial deixis. *Papers from the Parasession on the Lexicon, Chicago Linguistic Society. April 14–15, 1978*, 71–84. Chicago, US: Chicago Linguistic Society.

——1985. Was ist universal am raumdeiktischen Lexikon? In: Harro Schweizer (ed.), *Sprache und Raum*, 111–128. Stuttgart, Germany: Metzler.

Deutsch, Robert. 1977. *Spatial Structurings in Everyday Face-to-Face Behavior*. New York: Orangeburg (The Association for the Study of Man-Environment Relations, Inc.).

*Diessel, Holger. 1999. *Demonstratives. Form, Function and Grammaticalization*. Amsterdam: John Benjamins.

Dittmar, Norbert. 1976. *Sociolinguistics – A Critical Survey of Theory and Application*. London: Arnold. [originally published 1973 in German, translated by Peter Sand, Pieter Seuren and Kevin Whiteley].

Dixon, Robert M. W. 2003. Demonstratives. A cross-linguistic typology. *Studies in Language* 27: 61–112.

Doke, Clement and B. W. Vilakazi. 1958. *Zulu–English Dictionary.* (second edition). Johannesburg: Witwatersrand University Press.

Drew, Paul and Anthony Wootton. 1988. Introduction. In: Paul Drew and Anthony Wootton (eds.), *Erving Goffman – Exploring the Interaction Order,* 1–13. Cambridge, UK: Polity Press.

*Drew, Paul and John Heritage (eds.). 2006. *Conversation Analysis* (4 volumes). London: Sage.

Duchenne, Guillaume B. A. 1876. *Mécanisme de la physiognomie humaine ou analyse électro-physiologique de l'expression des passions.* Paris: J. B. Baillière et Fils.

*Dumont, Jean-Paul. 1977. From dogs to stars: The phatic function of naming among the Panare. In: Ellen B. Basso (ed.), *Carib-Speaking Indians: Culture, Society and Language,* 89–97. Tucson, US: The University of Arizona Press.

Dunbar, Robin. 1993. Coevolution of neocortex size, group size and language in humans. *Behavioral and Brain Sciences* 16: 681–735.

——1996. *Grooming, Gossip and the Evolution of Language.* London: Faber and Faber.

*——2007. Mind the bonding gap: constraints on the evolution of hominin societies. In: Stephen Shennan (ed.), *Pattern and Process in Cultural Evolution,* 223–234. Berkeley, US: University of California Press.

——2009. Why only humans have language. In: Rudolf Botha and Chris Knight (eds.), *The Prehistory of Language,* 12–35. Oxford: Oxford University Press.

Duncan, Susan D. 2005. Gesture in signing: A case study from Taiwan Sign Language. *Language and Linguistics* 6: 279–318.

*Duncan, Susan D., Justine Cassell and Elena T. Levy (eds.). 2007. *Gesture and the Dynamic Dimension of Language – Essays in Honor of David McNeill.* Amsterdam: John Benjamins.

Dundes, Alan, Jerry W. Leach and Bora Özkök. 1972. The strategy of Turkish boys' verbal dueling rhymes. In: John Gumperz and Dell Hymes (eds.), *Directions in Sociolinguistics: The Ethnography of Communication,* 130–160. New York: Holt, Rinehart and Winston.

Duranti, Alessandro. 1988. Ethnography of speaking: toward a linguistics of the praxis. In: Frederick J. Newmeyer (ed.), *Linguistics: The Cambridge Survey. Volume IV Language: The Socio-Cultural Context,* 210–228. Cambridge, UK: Cambridge University Press.

——(ed.). 2004. *A Companion to Linguistic Anthropology.* Oxford, UK: Blackwell.

Duranti, Alessandro and Charles Goodwin (eds.). 1992. *Rethinking Context. Language as an Interactive Phenomenon.* Cambridge, UK: Cambridge University Press.

Egbert, Maria M. 1997. Some interactional achievements of other-initiated repair in multiperson conversation. *Journal of Pragmatics* 27: 611–634.

*Egner, Inge. 2006. Intercultural aspects of the speech act of promising: Western and African practices. *Intercultural Pragmatics* 3: 443–464.

Ehlich, Konrad. 1993. Deixis. In: Helmut Glück, (ed.), *Metzler Lexikon Sprache,* 123–124. Stuttgart, Germany: Metzler.

Ehrich, Veronika. 1992. *Hier und Jetzt: Studien zur lokalen und temporalen Deixis im Deutschen.* Tübingen, Germany: Niemeyer.

*Eibl-Eibesfeldt, Irenäus. 1968. On the ethology of the human greeting behavior. I. Observations on Bali natives, Papuans and Samoans along with comparative remarks. *Zeitschrift für Tierpsychologie* 25: 727–744.

——1971a. Eine ethologische Interpretation des Palmfruchtfestes der Waika (Venezuela) nebst einigen Bemerkungen über die bindende Funktion von Zwiegesprächen. *Anthropos* 66: 767–778.

*——1971b. Ethology of human greeting behavior. II. Greeting behavior and some other patterns of friendly contact in the Waika (Yanomama). *Zeitschrift für Tierpsychologie* 29: 196–213.

——1973a. The expressive behaviour of the deaf-and-blind-born. In: Mario von Cranach and Ian Vine (eds.), *Social Communication and Movement. Studies of Interaction and Expression in Man and Chimpanzee*, 163–194. London: Academic Press.

——1973b. Das Palmfruchtfest der Waika. In: Irenäus Eibl-Eibesfeldt (ed.), *Der vorprogrammierte Mensch. Das Ererbte als bestimmender Faktor im menschlichen Verhalten*, 223–241. Vienna: Fritz Molden.

*——1979. Human ethology: concepts and implications for the sciences of man. *Behavioural and Brain Sciences* 2: 1–57.

——1989. *Human Ethology*. New York: Aldine de Gruyter [second edition (paperback) 2008].

*——1996. *Love and Hate*. New York: Aldine de Gruyter.

Eibl-Eibesfeldt, Irenäus and Gunter Senft. 1987. Studienbrief "Rituelle Kommunikation" – Kommunikation – Wissen – Kultur. Hagen, Germany: Fernuniversität – Gesamthochschule Hagen, Fachbereich Erziehungs und Sozialwissenschaften.

Ekman, Paul. 1973. Cross-cultural studies of facial expressions. In Paul Ekman (ed.), *Darwin and Facial Expression – A Century of Research in Review*, 169–222. New York: Academic Press.

——1979. About brows: emotional and conversational signals. In: Mario von Cranach, Klaus Foppa, Wolfgang Lepenies and Detlev Ploog (eds.), *Human Ethology – Claims and Limits of a New Discipline*, 169–202. Cambridge, UK: Cambridge University Press.

——1994. Strong evidence for universals in facial expressions: A reply to Russell's mistaken critique. *Psychological Bulletin* 115: 268–287.

Ekman, Paul and Wallace V. Friesen. 1975. *Unmasking the Face. A Guide to Recognizing Emotions from Facial Expressions*. Englewood Cliffs, US: Prentice Hall.

——1978. *Facial Action Coding System*. Palo Alto, US: Consulting Psychologists Press.

Emmorey, Karen. 2001. *Language, Cognition and the Brain. Insights into Sign Language Research*. Hillsdale, US: Erlbaum.

Endicott, Kirk M. 1991. *An Analysis of Malay Magic*. Singapore: Oxford University Press.

Enfield, Nicholas J. 2001. Lip pointing: A discussion of form and function with reference to data from Laos. *Gesture* 1: 185–212.

——2003. Demonstratives in space and interaction: Data from Lao speakers and implications for semantic analysis. *Language* 79: 82–117.

Enfield, Nicholas J. and Tanya Stivers (eds.). 2007. *Person Reference in Interaction: Linguistic, Cultural, and Social Perspectives*. Cambridge, UK: Cambridge University Press.

*Enfield, Nicholas J., Sotaro Kita and Jan Peter de Ruiter. 2007. Primary and secondary pragmatic functions of pointing gestures. *Journal of Pragmatics* 39: 1722–1741.

Enfield, Nicholas J., Tanya Stivers and Stephen C. Levinson. 2010. Question-response sequences in conversation across ten languages. An Introduction. *Journal of Pragmatics* 42: 2615–2619.

Erickson, Frederick. 1975. One function of proxemic shifts in face-to-face interaction. In: Adam Kendon, Richard M. Harris and Mary Ritchie Key (eds.), *Organization of Behavior in Face-to-Face Interaction*, 175–187. The Hague: Mouton.

Errington, J. Joseph. 1988. *Structure and Style in Javanese*. Philadelphia, US: University of Pennsylvania Press.

Evans, Nicholas and Stephen C. Levinson. 2009a. The myth of language universals: Language diversity and its importance for cognitive science. *Behavioral and Brain Sciences* 32: 429–492.

——2009b. With diversity in mind: Freeing the language sciences from universal grammar [Author's response]. *Behavioral and Brain Sciences* 32: 472–484.

*Fairclough, Norman. 2001. *Language and Power* (second edition). London: Longman.

Feld, Steven. 1982. *Sound and Sentiment. Birds, Weeping, Poetics and Song in Kaluli*. Philadelphia, US: University of Pennsylvania Press.

*Fenigsen, Janina. 2003. Language ideologies in Barbados: Processes and paradigms. *Pragmatics* 13: 457–481.

Fillmore, Charles J. 1975. *Santa Cruz Lectures on Deixis 1971*. Bloomington, US: Indiana University Linguistics Club.

——1982. Towards a descriptive framework for spatial deixis. In: Robert Jarvella and Wolfgang Klein (eds.), *Speech, Place, and Action*, 31–59. Chichester, UK: John Wiley.

*Finegan, Edward. 1980. *Attitudes Toward English Usage: A History of the War of Words*. New York: Teacher's College Press.

Firth, Alan. 2009. Ethnomethodology. In: Sigurd D'hondt, Jan-Ola Östman and Jef Verschueren (eds.), *The Pragmatics of Interaction*, 66–78. Amsterdam: John Benjamins.

Fitch, Kristine L. and Gerry Philipsen. 1995. Ethnography of speaking. In: Jan Blommaert, Jan-Ola Östman and Jef Verschueren (eds.), *Handbook of Pragmatics – Manual*, 263–269. Amsterdam: John Benjamins.

Foley, William. 1997. *Anthropological Linguistics – An Introduction*. Oxford: Blackwell.

*Frake, Charles O. 1980. *Language and Cultural Description. Essays by Charles O. Frake*. Selected and introduced by Anwar S. Dil. Stanford, US: Stanford University Press.

French, David. 1963. The relationship of anthropology to studies in perception and cognition. In: S. Koch (ed.), *Psychology: A Study of a Science*, Vol 6, 388–428. New York: McGraw-Hill.

Garber, Philip, Martha W. Alibali and Susan Goldin-Meadow. 1998. Knowledge conveyed in gesture is not tied to hands. *Child Development* 69: 75–84.

Garfinkel, Harold. 1963. A conception of, and experiments with, 'trust' as a condition for stable concerted actions. In: O. J. Harvey (ed.), *Motivation and Social Interaction*, 187–238. New York: Ronald Press.

——1967. *Studies in Ethnomethodology*. Englewood Cliffs, US: Prentice Hall.

——1972. Remarks on ethnomethodology. In: John J. Gumperz and Dell Hymes (eds.), *Directions in Sociolinguistics – The Ethnography of Communication*, 309–324. New York: Holt, Rinehart and Winston.

Garfinkel, Harold and Harvey Sacks. 1970. On formal structures of practical actions. In: John C. McKinney and Edward A. Tiryakian (eds.), *Theoretical Sociology: Perspectives and Developments*, 337–366. Appleton-Century-Crofts.

*Garland, Jennifer N. 2008. The importance of being Irish: National identity, cultural authenticity, and linguistic authority in an Irish language class in the United States. *Pragmatics* 18: 253–276.

Gazdar, Gerald. 1979. *Pragmatics. Implicature, Presupposition, and Logical Form*. New York: Academic Press.

Geertz, Clifford. 1976. *The Religion of Java*. Chicago, US: University of Chicago Press [first published in 1960: Glencoe, US: The Free Press].

*Gentner, Dedre and Susan Goldin-Meadow (eds.). 2003. *Language in Mind: Advances in the Study of Language and Thought*. Cambridge, US: MIT Press.

*Giles, Howard, Miles Hewstone, Ellen B. Ryan and Patricia Johnson. 1987. Research on language attitudes. In: Ulrich Ammon, Norbert Dittmar, Klaus J. Mattheier (eds.), *Sociolinguistics: An International Handbook of the Science of Language and Society*, Vol. 1: 585–597. Berlin: Mouton de Gruyter.

*Goffman, Erving. 1959. *The Presentation of Self in Everyday Life*. New York: Doubleday Anchor.

——1961. *Encounters: Two Studies in the Sociology of Interaction*. Indianapolis, US: Bobbs-Merrill.

——1963. *Behavior in Public Places: Notes on the Social Organizations of Gatherings*. New York: Free Press.

——1967. *Interaction Ritual: Essays on Face-to-Face Behavior*. New York: Doubleday.
*——1969. *Strategic Interaction*. Philadelphia, US: University of Pennsylvania Press.
——1971. *Relations in Public: Microstudies of the Public Order*. New York: Harper and Row.
——1974. *Frame Analysis – An Essay on the Organization of Experience*. New York: Harper and Row.
——1981. *Forms of Talk*. Oxford, UK: Basil Blackwell.
——1983a. The interaction order. *American Sociological Review* 48: 1–17.
——1983b. Felicity's condition. *The American Journal of Sociology* 89: 1–53.
*Goldin-Meadow, Susan. 2003. *Hearing Gesture: How Our Hands Help Us Think*. Cambridge, MA, US: Harvard University Press.
——2006. Nonverbal communication: The hand's role in talking and thinking. In: William Damon and Richard M. Lerner (eds.), *Handbook of Child Psychology. Sixth Edition. Volume Two: Cognition, Perception and Language* edited by Deanna Kuhn and Robert Siegler, 336–369. New York: John Wiley.
Good, David A. 1999. Communicative success vs. failure. *Handbook of Pragmatics Online*. Amsterdam: John Benjamins.
*Goodwin, Charles. 1993. Recording human interaction in natural settings. *Pragmatics* 3: 181–209.
Goodwin, Charles and John Heritage. 1990. Conversation analysis. *Annual Review of Anthropology* 19: 283–307.
*Goodwin, Marjorie H. 2006. *The Hidden Life of Girls: Games of Stance, Status, and Exclusion*. Malden, US: Blackwell.
Gossen, Gary H. 1974. *Chamulas in the World of the Sun: Time and Space in a Maya Oral Tradition*. Cambridge, US: Harvard University Press.
Grammer, Karl, Wulf Schiefenhövel, Margret Schleidt, Beatrice Lorenz and Irenäus Eibl-Eibesfeldt. 1988. Patterns of the face: The eyebrow flash in crosscultural comparison. *Ethology* 77: 279–299.
Green, Keith. 1995. Deixis: A re-evaluation of concepts and categories. In: Keith Green (ed.), *New Essays in Deixis. Discourse, Narrative, Literature*, 11–25. Amsterdam: Rodopi.
Greenwood, John D. 2003. Wundt, Völkerpsychologie, and experimental social psychology. *History of Psychology* 6: 70–88.
*Grenoble, Lenore. 1998. *Deixis and Information Packaging in Russian Discourse*. Amsterdam: John Benjamins.
Grice, H. Paul. 1967. *Logic and Conversation*. Unpublished MS. of the William James Lectures, Harvard University.
——1975. Logic and conversation. In: Peter Cole and Jerry L. Morgan (eds.), *Syntax and Semantics. Vol. 3: Speech Acts*, 41–58. New York: Academic Press.
——1978. Further notes on logic and conversation. In: Peter Cole (ed.), *Syntax and Semantics. Vol. 9: Pragmatics*, 113–127. New York: Academic Press.
*——1981. Presupposition and conversational implicature. In: Peter Cole (ed.), *Radical Pragmatics*, 183–197. New York: Academic Press.
*——1989. *Studies in the Way of Words*. Cambridge, MS, US: Harvard University Press.
*Guidetti, Michèle and Jean-Marc Colletta (eds.). 2010. Gesture and multimodal development. Special Issue *Gesture* 10 (2).
*Gullberg, Marianne and Kees de Bot (eds.). 2010. *Gestures in Language Development*. Amsterdam: Benjamins.
Gumperz, John J. 1979. The sociolinguistic basis of speech act theory. In: J. Boyd and S. Ferra (eds.), *Speech Acts Ten Years After*, 101–121. Milan, Italy: Versus.
——1982. *Discourse Strategies*. Cambridge, UK: Cambridge University Press.

Gumperz, John J. and Dell Hymes (eds.). 1964. The ethnography of communication. *Special Issue of American Anthropologist* 66 (6) Part II.

——(eds.). 1972. *Directions in Sociolinguistics: The Ethnography of Communication*. New York: Holt, Rinehart and Winston.

*Habermas, Jürgen. 1984. *The Theory of Communicative Action. Reason and the Rationalization of Society* (translated by Thomas McCarthy). Boston, US: Beacon Press.

*——1987. *The Theory of Communicative Action. Lifeworld and System* (translated by Thomas McCarthy). Boston, US: Beacon Press.

Haiman, John. 1998. *Talk is Cheap. Sarcasm, Alienation and the Evolution of Language*. New York: Oxford University Press.

Hall, Edward T. 1968. Proxemics. *Current Anthropology* 9: 83–95, 106–108.

Hanks, William F. 1987. Markedness and category interactions in the Malagasy deictic system. *University of Chicago Working Papers in Linguistics*, Vol. 3 (January 1987): 109–136.

*——2009. Fieldwork on deixis. *Journal of Pragmatics* 41: 10–24.

Hanks, William F., Sachiko Ide and Yasuhiro Katagiri. 2009a. Towards an emancipatory pragmatics. Introduction to the Special Issue. *Journal of Pragmatics* 41: 1–9.

Hanks, William F., Sachiko Ide and Yasuhiro Katagiri (eds.). 2009b. Towards an Emancipatory Pragmatics Part One. Special Issue. *Journal of Pragmatics* 41: 1–196.

——(eds.). 2012. Towards an Emancipatory Pragmatics. Part Two. Special Issue. *Journal of Pragmatics* 44: 563–708.

*Harnish, Robert M. (ed.). 1994. *Basic Topics in the Philosophy of Language*. New York: Harvester Wheatsheaf.

*——2009. Internalism and externalism in speech act theory. *Lodz Papers in Pragmatics* 5: 9–31.

*Harré, Rom (ed.). 1988. *The Social Construction of Emotion*. Cambridge, UK: Cambridge University Press.

Harris, Stephen G. 1984. *Culture and Learning: Tradition and Education in North-East Arnhem Land*. Canberra: Australian Institute of Aboriginal and Torres Strait Islander Studies.

*Hassall, Tim. 1999. Request strategies in Indonesian. *Pragmatics* 9: 585–606.

*Haugh, Michael. 2002. The intuitive basis of implicature: Relevance theoretic implicitness versus Gricean implying. *Pragmatics* 12: 117–134.

Haviland, John B. 1979. Guugu Yimidhirr. In: Robert W. W. Dixon and Berry J. Blake (eds.), *Handbook of Australian Languages*, Vol I, 27–180. Amsterdam: John Benjamins.

——1993. Anchoring, iconicity, and orientation in Guugu Yimithirr pointing gestures. *Journal of Linguistic Anthropology* 3: 3–45.

——1998. Guugu Yimidhirr cardinal directions. *Ethos* 26 (1): 7–24.

*——2000. Pointing, gesture space and mental maps. In: David McNeill (ed.), *Language and Gesture*, 13–46. Cambridge, UK: Cambridge University Press.

——2009. Little rituals. In: Gunter Senft and Ellen B. Basso (eds.), *Ritual Communication*, 1–19. Oxford, UK: Berg.

*——2011. Ideologies of language: Some reflections on language and U.S. law. In: Bambi B. Schieffelin and Paul B. Garrett (eds.), *Anthropological Linguistics – Critical Concepts in Language Studies Vol 3: Talking about Language*, 172–194. London: Routledge.

Heeschen, Volker. 1982. Some systems of spatial deixis in Papuan languages. In: Jürgen Weissenborn and Wolfgang Klein (eds.), *Here and There. Cross-linguistic Studies on Deixis and Demonstration*, 81–109. Amsterdam: John Benjamins.

——1998. *An Ethnographic Grammar of the Eipo Language Spoken in the Central Mountains of Irian Jaya (West New Guinea), Indonesia*. Berlin: Dietrich Reimer.

Heeschen, Volker, Wulf Schiefenhövel and Irenäus Eibl-Eibesfeldt. 1981. Requesting, giving and taking: The relationship between verbal and nonverbal behavior in the speech community of the Eipo, Irian Jaya (West New Guinea). In: Mary Ritchie Key (ed.), *The Relationship between Verbal and Nonverbal Communication*, 139–165 (+ 21 plates). The Hague: Mouton.

Heinemann, Trine. 2010. The question-response system of Danish. *Journal of Pragmatics* 42: 2703–2725.

Henrich, Joseph, Steven J. Heine and Ara Norenzayan. 2010a. The weirdest people in the world? *Behavioral and Brain Sciences* 33: 61–83.

——2010b. Beyond WEIRD: Towards a broad-based behavioral science. *Behavioral and Brain Sciences* 33: 111–135.

Heritage, John. 1984. *Garfinkel and Ethnomethodology*. Cambridge, UK: Polity Press.

——2003. Presenting Emanuel Schegloff. In: Carlo L. Prevignano and Paul J. Thibault (eds.), *Discussing Conversation Analysis. The Work of Emanuel Schegloff*, 1–10. Amsterdam: John Benjamins.

Heritage, John and Steven Clayman. 2010. *Talk in Action. Interaction, Identities and Institutions*. Chichester, UK: Wiley-Blackwell.

Hjortsjö, Carl-Herman. 1969. *Man's Face and Mimic Language*. Malmö, Sweden: Studentlitteratur.

Hockett, Charles F. 1973. *Man's Place in Nature*. New York: McGraw-Hill.

*Holler, Judith and Katie Wilkin. 2009. Communicating common ground: How mutually shared knowledge influences speech and gesture in narrative talk. *Language and Cognitive Processes* 24: 267–289.

*Holzinger, Katharina. 2004. Bargaining through arguing: An empirical analysis based on speech act theory. *Political Communication* 21: 195–222.

Hookway, C. J. 1998. Charles Sanders Peirce. In: Jacob L. Mey and R. E. Asher (eds.), *Concise Encyclopedia of Pragmatics*, 1084–1086. Amsterdam: Elsevier.

*Horn, Laurence R. 2004. Implicature. In: Laurence R. Horn and Gregory Ward (eds.), *The Handbook of Pragmatics*, 3–28. Oxford, UK: Blackwell.

Huang, Yan. 2007. *Pragmatics*. Oxford, UK: Oxford University Press.

Hudson, Joyce. 1985. Selected speech act verbs in Walmatjari. In: G. Hutter and K. Gregerson (eds.), *Pragmatics in Non-Western Practice*, 63–83. Dallas, US: Summer Institute of Linguistics.

*Hunt, Earl and Franca Agnoli. 1991. The Whorfian hypothesis: A cognitive psychology perspective. *Psychological Review* 98: 377–389.

Hymes, Dell H. [1962] 1978. The ethnography of speaking. In Joshua Fishman (ed.), *Readings in the Sociology of Language*, 99–138. The Hague: Mouton [first published in 1962 in: T. Gladwin and W. C. Sturtevant (eds.), *Anthropology and Human Behavior*. 13–53. Washington DC, US: Anthropological Society of Washington].

——1972a. Models of the interaction of language and social life. In: John J. Gumperz and Dell Hymes (eds.), *Directions in Sociolinguistics: The Ethnography of Communication*, 35–71. New York: Holt, Rinehart and Winston.

——1972b. On communicative competence. In. J. B. Pride and Janet Holmes (eds.), *Sociolinguistics*, 269–293. Harmondsworth, UK: Penguin.

——1974. Ways of speaking. In: Richard Bauman and Joel Sherzer (eds.), *Explorations in the Ethnography of Speaking*, 433–451. Cambridge, UK: Cambridge University Press.

Hyslop, Catriona. 1993. *Towards a Typology of Spatial Deixis*. BA (honours)-thesis. Canberra: Australian National University.

Irvine, Judith. 1992. Ideologies of honorific language. *Pragmatics* 2: 251–262.

——1998. Ideologies of honorific language. In: Bambi B. Schieffelin, Kathryn A. Woolard and Paul Kroskrity (eds.), *Language Ideologies*, 51–67. New York: Oxford University Press. [revised and expanded reprint of Irvine (1992)]

Iverson, Jana M. and Susan Goldin-Meadow. 2005. Gesture paves the way for language development. *Psychological Science* 16: 368–371.

Izard, Carroll E. and Patricia M. Saxton. 1988. Emotions. In Richard C. Atkinson, Richard J. Herrnstein, Gardner Lindzey and R. Duncan Luce (eds.), *Stevens' Handbook of Experimental Psychology. Second Edition, Volume 1: Perception and Motivation*. 627–676. New York: John Wiley & Sons.

Jahoda, Gustav. 1995. In pursuit of the emic-etic distinction: Can we ever capture it? In: Nancy Rule Goldberger and Jody Bennett Veroff (eds.), *The Culture and Psychology Reader*, 128–138. New York: New York University Press.

Jakobson, Roman. 1960. Linguistics and poetics. In: Thomas A. Sebeok (ed.), *Style in Language*, 350–377. Boston, US: MIT Press.

Jefferson, Gail. 2004. Glossary of transcript symbols with an introduction. In: Gene H. Lerner (ed.), *Conversation Analysis: Studies from the First Generation*, 13–31. Amsterdam: John Benjamins.

Jourdan, Christine. 2007. Linguistic paths to urban self in postcolonial Solomon Islands. In: Miki Makihara and Bambi B. Schieffelin (eds.), *Consequences of Contact: Language Ideologies and Sociocultural Transformations in Pacific Societies*, 30–48. New York: Oxford University Press.

Jourdan, Christine and Ellen Maebiru. 2002. *Pijin – A Trilingual Cultural Dictionary (Pijin – English – French)*. Canberra: Pacific Linguistics.

*Jucker, Andreas. 2009. Speech act research between armchair, field and laboratory: The case of compliments. *Journal of Pragmatics* 41: 611–635.

*Kasher, Asa (ed.). 1998. *Pragmatics: Critical Concepts Vol. 2: Speech Act Theory and Particular Speech Acts*. London: Routledge.

*Kataoka, Kuniyoshi. 2004. Co-construction of a mental map in spatial discourse: A case of Japanese rock climbers' use of deictic verbs of motion. *Pragmatics* 14: 409–438.

Keenan (Ochs), Elinor. 1976. The universality of conversational postulates. *Language in Society* 5: 67–80.

Kelly, Spencer D. 2001. Broadening the units of analysis in communication: Speech and nonverbal behaviours in pragmatic comprehension. *Journal of Child Language* 28: 325–349.

Kelly, Spencer D., Asli Özyürek and Eric Maris. 2010. Two sides of the same coin: Speech and gesture mutually interact to enhance comprehension. *Psychological Science* 21: 260–267.

Kendon, Adam. 1972. Some relationships between body motion and speech. In: Aron W. Siegman and Benjamin Pope (eds.), *Studies in Dyadic Communication*, 177–210. New York: Pergamon Press.

——1977. Spatial organization in social encounters: The F-formation system. In: Adam Kendon (ed.), *Studies in the Behavior of Social Interaction*, 179–208. Bloomington, US: Indiana University Press.

——1980. Gesticulation and speech: Two aspects of the process of utterance. In: Mary Ritchie Key (ed.), *The Relationship of Verbal and Nonverbal Communication*, 207–227. The Hague: Mouton.

——1988a. How gestures can become like words. In: Fernando Poyatos, (ed.), *Cross-Cultural Perspectives in Nonverbal Communication*, 131–141. Toronto: Hogrefe.

*——1988b. *Sign Languages of Aboriginal Australia: Cultural, Semiotic and Communicative Perspectives*. Cambridge, UK: Cambridge University Press.

——1988c. Goffman's approach to face-to-face interaction. In: Paul Drew and Anthony Wootton (eds.), *Erving Goffman: Exploring the Interaction Order*, 14–40. Cambridge, UK: Polity Press.

——1995. Gestures as illocutionary and discourse structure markers in Southern Italian conversation. *Journal of Pragmatics* 23: 247–279.

——2000. Language and gesture: unity or duality? In: David McNeill, (ed.), *Language and Gesture*, 47–63. Cambridge, UK: Cambridge University Press.

——2004. *Gesture: Visible Action as Utterance*. Cambridge, UK: Cambridge University Press.

Kendon, Adam and Cornelia Müller. 2001. Introducing GESTURE. *Gesture* 1: 1–7.

Key, Mary Ritchie. 1977. *Nonverbal Communication. A Research Guide and Bibliography*. Metuchen, US: Scarecrow.

Kiefer, Ferenc. 1979. What do conversational maxims explain? *Linguisticae Investigationes* 3: 57–74.

Kita, Sotaro. 2009. Cross-cultural variation of speech accompanying gesture: A review. *Language and Cognitive Processes* 24: 145–167.

Kita, Sotaro and James Essegbey. 2001. Pointing left in Ghana – How a taboo on the use of the left hand influences gestural practice. *Gesture* 1: 73–95.

Kita, Sotaro and Sachiko Ide. 2007. Nodding, aizuchi, and final particles in Japanese conversation: How conversation reflects the ideology of communication and social relationships. *Journal of Pragmatics* 39: 1242–1254.

Kita, Sotaro and Asli Özyürek. 2003. What does cross-linguistic variation in semantic coordination of speech and gesture reveal? Evidence for an interface representation of spatial thinking and speaking. *Journal of Memory and Language* 48: 16–32.

Koerner, E. F. Konrad. 2000. Towards a 'full pedigree' of the Sapir-Whorf hypothesis: From Locke to Lucy. In: Martin Pütz and Marjolijn H. Verspoor (eds.), *Explorations in Linguistic Relativity*, 1–23. Amsterdam: John Benjamins.

*Krauss, Robert M. 1998. Why do we gesture when we speak? *Current Directions in Psychological Science* 7: 54–59.

Kroskrity, Paul V., Bambi B. Schieffelin and Kathryn Woolard (eds.). 1992. Special Issue on Language Ideologies. *Pragmatics* 2: 235–453.

Kuipers, Joel C. 1998. *Language, Identity and Marginality in Indonesia. The Changing Nature of Ritual Speech on the Island of Sumba*. Cambridge, UK: Cambridge University Press.

Labov, William. 1970a. The logic of nonstandard English. In: Frederick Williams (ed.) *Language and Poverty – Perspectives on a Theme*, 153–189. Chicago, US: Markham.

——1970b. The study of language in its social context. *Studium Generale* 23: 30–87.

——(ed.), 1972a. *Language in the Inner City: Studies in the Black English Vernacular*. Philadelphia, US: University of Pennsylvania Press.

——1972b. Rules for ritual insults. In: William Labov (ed.), *Language in the Inner City: Studies in the Black English Vernacular*, 297–353. Philadelphia, US: University of Pennsylvania Press.

——1972c. The linguistic consequences of being a lame. In: William Labov (ed.), *Language in the Inner City: Studies in the Black English Vernacular*, 255–292. Philadelphia, US: University of Pennsylvania Press.

——1972d. Some principles of linguistic methodology. *Language in Society* 1: 97–120.

Lakoff, Robin T. 1995. Conversational logic. In: Jef Verschueren, Jan-Ola Östman and Jan Blommaert (eds.), *Handbook of Pragmatics*, 190–198. Amsterdam: John Benjamins.

Laver, John. 1975. Communicative functions of phatic communion. In: Adam Kendon, Richard M. Harris and Mary Ritchie Key (eds.), *Organization of Behavior in Face-to-Face Interaction*, 215–238. The Hague: Mouton.

——1981. Linguistic routines and politeness in greeting and parting. In: Florian Coulmas (ed.), *Conversational Routine. Explorations in Standardized Communication Situations and Prepatterned Speech*, 289–304. The Hague: Mouton.

Lee, Penny. 1996. *The Whorf Theory Complex: A Critical Reconstruction*. Amsterdam: John Benjamins.

——2010. Benjamin Lee Whorf. In: Jan-Ola Östman and Jef Verschueren (eds.), *Handbook of Pragmatics Online*. Amsterdam: John Benjamins. URL: http://www.benjamins.com/online/hop/

Levelt, Willem J. M., Graham Richardson and Wido La Heu. 1985. Pointing and voicing in deictic expressions. *Journal of Memory and Language* 24: 133–164.

Levinson, Stephen C. 1983. *Pragmatics*. Cambridge, UK: Cambridge University Press.

*——1989. A review of Relevance [book review of Dan Sperber and Deirdre Wilson, *Relevance: Communication and Cognition*]. *Journal of Linguistics* 25: 455–472.

——1997. Deixis. In: Peter V. Lamarque (ed.), *Concise Encyclopedia of Philosophy of Language*, 214–219. Oxford, UK: Elsevier.

——2000. *Presumptive Meanings. The Theory of Generalized Conversational Implicature*. Cambridge, MA, US: The MIT Press.

——2003. *Space in Language and Cognition*. Cambridge, UK: Cambridge University Press.

——2006. On the human 'interaction engine'. In: Nicholas J. Enfield and Stephen C. Levinson (eds.), *Roots of Human Sociality: Culture, Cognition and Interaction*, 39–69. Oxford, UK: Berg.

——2007. Optimizing person reference – perspectives from usage on Rossel Island. In: Nicholas J. Enfield and Tanya Stivers (eds.), *Person Reference in Interaction. Linguistic, Cultural and Social Perspectives*, 29–72. Cambridge, UK: Cambridge University Press.

Levinson, Stephen C. and Nicholas Evans. 2010. Time for a sea-change in linguistics: Response to comments on 'The myth of language universals'. *Lingua* 120: 2733–2758.

*Levinson, Stephen C. and Pierre Jaisson (eds.). 2006. *Evolution and Culture*. Cambridge, US: MIT Press.

Levinson, Stephen C., Eric Pederson and Gunter Senft. (1997). Sprache und menschliche Orientierungsfähigkeiten. In: *Jahrbuch der Max-Planck-Gesellschaft*, 322–327. München: Generalverwaltung der Max-Planck-Gesellschaft.

Levy, Robert I. (ed.). 1983. Self and emotion. Special Issue of *Ethos* 11.

Liddell, Scott. 2003. *Grammar, Gesture and Meaning in American Sign Language*. Cambridge, UK: Cambridge University Press.

*Liebal, Katja, Cornelia Müller and Simone Pika (eds.). 2005. Gestural communication in nonhuman and human primates. Special Issue. *Gesture* 5.

*Liszkowski, Ulf. 2010. Deictic and other gestures in infancy. *Acción psicológica* 7: 21–33.

Logue, David M. and Tanya Stivers. 2012. Squawk in interaction: a primer of conversation analysis for students of animal communication. *Behaviour* 149: 1283–1298.

*Lorenz, Konrad. 1977. *Behind the Mirror – A Search for a Natural History of Human Knowledge*. New York: Harcourt Brace Jovanovich.

*Lucy, John A. 1997. Linguistic relativity. *Annual Review of Anthropology* 26: 291–312.

Lyons, John. 1977. *Semantics*. Vol. 1. Cambridge, UK: Cambridge University Press.

——1982. Deixis and subjectivity: Loquor, ergo sum? In: Robert Jarvella and Wolfgang Klein (eds.), *Speech, Place, and Action*, 101–124. Chichester, UK: John Wiley.

Makihara, Miki. 2007. Linguistic purism in Rapa Nui political discourse. In: Miki Makihara and Bambi B. Schieffelin (eds.), *Consequences of Contact: Language Ideologies and Sociocultural Transformations in Pacific Societies*, 49–69. New York: Oxford University Press.

Makihara, Miki and Bambi B. Schieffelin (eds.). 2007. *Consequences of Contact. Language Ideologies and Sociocultural Transformations in Pacific Societies*. New York: Oxford University Press.

Malinowski, Bronislaw. 1920. Classificatory particles in the language of Kiriwina. *Bulletin of the School of Oriental Studies*, London institution, Vol. I, part IV: 33–78.

——1922. *The Argonauts of the Western Pacific. An Account of Native Enterprise and Adventure in the Archipelagoes of Melanesian New Guinea*. London: Routledge & Kegan Paul.

——1935. *Coral Gardens and their Magic*. 2 Vols. London: Allen & Unwin.

——1936. The problem of meaning in primitve languages. In: C. K. Ogden and I. A. Richards, *The Meaning of Meaning. A Study of the Influence of Language upon Thought and of the Science of Symbolism*. Supplement I, 296–336. London: Kegan Paul, Trench, Trubner. [fourth revised edition; first edition: 1923]

——1974. *Magic, Science and Religion and Other Essays*. London: Souvenir Press.

*Malotki, Ekkehart. 1983. *Hopi Time: A Linguistic Analysis of the Temporal Concepts in the Hopi Language*. Berlin: Mouton de Gruyter.

Margetts, Anna. 2004. Spatial deixis in Saliba. In: Gunter Senft (ed.), *Deixis and Demonstratives in Oceanic Languages*, 37–57. Canberra: Pacific Linguistics.

Markus, Hazel R. and Shinobu Kitayama. 1991. Culture and self: Implications for cognition, emotion and motivation. *Psychological Review* 98: 224–253.

*Martínez-Flor, Alicia and Esther Usó-Juan (eds.), 2010. *Speech Act Performance: Theoretical, Empirical and Methodological Issues*. Amsterdam: John Benjamins.

Maynard, Senko K. 1993. *Kaiwabunseki* [conversation analysis]. Tokyo: Kuroshio.

*McElhinny, Bonnie. 2003. Fearful, forceful agents of the law: Ideologies about language and gender in police officers' narratives about the use of physical force. *Pragmatics* 13: 253–284.

McNeill, David. 1985. So you think gestures are nonverbal? *Psychological Review* 92: 350–371.

——1992. *Hand and Mind. What Gestures Reveal about Thought*. Chicago, US: Chicago University Press.

——2000. Introduction. In: David McNeill, (ed.), *Language and Gesture*, 1–10. Cambridge, UK: Cambridge University Press.

——2005. *Gesture and Thought*. Chicago, US: Chicago University Press.

——2006. Gesture and communication. In: Keith Brown (ed.-in-chief), *Encyclopedia of Language and Linguistics* (second edition), 58–76. Amsterdam: Elsevier.

Métraux, Rhoda. (1968). Bronislaw Malinowski. In *International Encyclopedia of Social Sciences* Vol. 9., 541–549. New York: Crowell Collier and Macmillan.

Mey, Jacob L. 1993. *Pragmatics – An Introduction*. Oxford, UK: Blackwell.

——1994. Pragmatics. In: R. E. Asher and J. M. Y. Simpson (eds.), *The Encyclopedia of Language and Linguistics*, Vol. 6, 3260–3278. Oxford, UK: Pergamon Press.

——2012. Anticipatory pragmatics. *Journal of Pragmatics* 44: 705–708.

Moerman, Michael. 1988. *Talking Culture: Ethnography and Conversation Analysis*. Philadelphia, US: University of Pennsylvania Press.

Monteith, Mary K. 1980. Implications of the Ann Arbor decision: Black English and the reading teacher. *Journal of Reading* 23: 556–559.

*Morgan, Marcyliena. 1994. Theories and politics in African American English. *Annual Review of Anthropology* 23: 325–345.

Morris, Charles W. 1938. Foundations of the theory of signs. In: Otto Neurath, Rudolf Carnap and Charles W. Morris (eds.), *International Encyclopedia of Unified Science*, 77–138. Chicago, US: University of Chicago Press.

Morris, Desmond. 1978. *Manwatching – A Field Guide to Human Behaviour*. London: Triad Granada.

Morris, Desmond, Peter Collett, Peter Marsh and Marie O'Shaughnessy. 1979. *Gestures, their Origins and Distribution*. New York: Stein and Day.

*Mufwene, Salikoko S. 1992. Ideology and facts on African American English. *Pragmatics* 2: 141–166.

*Muhawi, Ibrahim. 1999. The Arabic proverb and the speech community: Another look at phatic communion. In: Yasir Suleiman (ed.), *Language and Society in the Middle East and North Africa. Studies in Variation and Identity*, 259–290. Richmond, UK: Curzon.

*Mulamba, Kashama. 2009. Social beliefs for the realization of the speech acts of apology and complaint as defined in Ciluba, French and English. *Pragmatics* 19: 543–564.

*Naruoka, Keiko. 2006. The interactional functions of the Japanese demonstratives in conversation. *Pragmatics* 16: 475–512.

Neumann, Ragnhild. 2004. The conventionalization of the Ring Gesture in German discourse. In: Cornelia Müller and Roland Posner (eds.), *The Semantics and Pragmatics of Everyday Gestures*, 217–224. Berlin: Weidler.

Newman, Stanley S. 1964. Linguistic aspects of Yokuts style. In: Dell Hymes (ed.), *Language in Culture and Society*, 372–377. New York: Harper and Row.

*Niemeier, Susanne and René Dirven (eds.). 2000. *Evidence for Linguistic Relativity*. Amsterdam: John Benjamins.

Núñez, Rafael E. and Eve Sweetser. 2006. With the future behind them: Convergent evidence from Aymara language and gesture in the crosslinguistic comparison of spatial construal of time. *Cognitive Science* 30: 401–450.

O'Driscoll, Jim. 2009. Erving Goffman. In: Sigurd D'hondt, Jan-Ola Östman and Jef Verschueren (eds.), *The Pragmatics of Interaction*, 79–95. Amsterdam: John Benjamins.

Östman, Jan-Ola. 1988. Adaptation, variability, and effect: Comments on IPrA Working Documents 1 & 2. *IPrA Working Document* 3: 5–40.

Özyürek, Asli. 1998. An analysis of the basic meaning of Turkish demonstratives in face-to-face conversational interaction. In: S. Santi, I. Guaitella, C. Cave and G. Konopczynski (eds.), *Oralité et Gestualité: Communication multimodale, Interaction*, 609–614. Paris: L'Harmattan.

——2000. The influence of addressee location on spatial language and representational gestures of direction. In: David McNeill (ed.), *Language and Gesture*, 64–83. Cambridge, UK: Cambridge University Press.

——2002. Do speakers design their co-speech gestures for their addressees? The effects of addressee location on representational gestures. *Journal of Memory and Language* 46: 688–2002.

Özyurek, Asli and Sotaro Kita. 1999. Expressing manner and path in English and Turkish: Differences in speech, gesture, and conceptualization. In: Martin Hahn and Scott C. Stoness (eds.), *Proceedings of the 21st Annual Conference of the Cognitive Science Society*, 507–512. Mahwah, US: Lawrence Erlbaum. [Özyurek and Özyürek are variants of writing the name of the same person].

——2001. *Interacting with demonstratives: Encoding of joint attention as a semantic contrast in Turkish and Japanese demonstrative systems*. Istanbul, Nijmegen (The Netherlands): Mimeo.

*Özyurek, Asli, Sotraro Kita, Shanley Allan, Amanda Brown, Reyhan Furman and Tomoko Ishizuka. 2008. Development of cross-linguistic variation in speech and gesture: Motion events in English and Turkish. *Developmental Psychology* 44: 1040–1054.

Pagliai, Valentina. 2009. The art of dueling with words: Toward a new understanding of verbal duels across the world. *Oral Tradition* 24: 61–88.

Park, Duk-Soo. 2006. Phatic expressions in Korean. In: Ho-Min Sohn (ed.), *Korean Language in Culture and Society*, 155–163. Honolulu: University of Hawai'i Press.

Parker, Dorothy. 1944. *The Portable Dorothy Parker*. New York: Viking Press.

Payrató, Lluís. 2004. Notes on pragmatic and social aspects of everyday gestures. In: Cornelia Müller and Roland Posner (eds.), *The Semantics and Pragmatics of Everyday Gestures*, 103–113. Berlin: Weidler.

Pederson, Eric. 2006. Spatial language in Tamil. In: Stephen C. Levinson and David Wilkins (eds.), *Grammars of Space*, 400–436. Cambridge, UK: Cambridge University Press.

*——2007. Cognitive linguistics and linguistic relativity. In: Dirk Geeraerts and Hubert Cuyckens (eds.), *The Oxford Handbook of Cognitive Linguistics*, 1012–1044. Oxford, UK: Oxford University Press.

Pederson, Eric and David Wilkins. 1996. A cross-linguistic questionnaire on 'demonstratives'. In: Cognitive Anthropology Research Group (eds.), *Manual for the 1996 Field Season*, 1–13. Nijmegen, The Netherlands: Mimeo.

Pederson, Eric, Eve Danziger, David G. Wilkins, Stephen C. Levinson, Sotaro Kita and Gunter Senft. 1998. Semantic typology and spatial conceptualization. *Language* 74: 557–589.

*Perniss, Pamela, Roland Pfau and Markus Steinbach (eds.). 2007. *Visible Variation: Comparative Studies on Sign Language Structure*. Berlin: Mouton de Gruyter.

Pike, Kenneth L. 1954. *Language in Relation to a Unified Theory of the Structure of Human Behaviour*. Part I. Glendale, US: Summer Institute of Linguistics.

Pinker, Steven. 1989. *Learnability and Cognition. The Acquisition of Argument Structure*. Cambridge, US: MIT Press.

Ploeg, Anton. 2004. The German Eipo Research Project. *Le Journal de la Société des Océanistes* 118: 35–79. [URL: http://jso.revues.org/263].

Psathas, George. 1994. Ethnomethodology. In: R. E. Asher and J. M. Y. Simpson (eds.), *The Encyclopedia of Language and Linguistics*, Vol. 3, 1160–1164. Oxford, UK: Pergamon Press.

*Pullum, Geoffrey K. 1991. *The Great Eskimo Vocabulary Hoax and Other Irreverent Essays on the Study of Language*. Chicago, US: University of Chicago Press.

Putnam, Hilary. 1975. The meaning of 'meaning'. In: K. Gunderson (ed.), *Language, Mind and Knowledge*, 131–193. Minneapolis, US: The University of Minnesota Press.

Reiss, Nira. 1985. *Speech Act Taxonomy*. Amsterdam: John Benjamins.

*Reynolds, Edward. 2011. Enticing a challengeable in arguments: Sequence, epistemics and preference organisation. *Pragmatics* 21: 411–430.

*Roberts, Felicia, Piera Margutti and Shoji Takano. 2011. Judgements concerning the valence of inter-turn silence across speakers of American English, Italian and Japanese. *Discourse Processes* 48: 331–354.

Romaine, Suzanne. 1995. Sociolinguistics. In: Jef Verschueren, Jan-Ola Östman and Jan Blommaert (eds.), *Handbook of Pragmatics – Manual*, 489–495. Amsterdam: John Benjamins.

Rosaldo, Michelle Z. 1983. The shame of headhunters and the autonomy of self. *Ethos* 11: 135–151.

——2011. The things we do with words. Ilongot speech acts and speech act theory in philosophy. In: Bambi B. Schieffelin and Paul B. Garrett (eds.), *Anthropological Linguistics –Critical Concepts in Language Studies. Volume II: Thinking about Language: Part II*, 78–115. London: Routledge. [first published 1982 in *Language in Society* 11: 203–237].

Rousseau, Jean-Jacques. 1762. *Du Contrat Social ou Principes du Droit Politique*. Amsterdam: Marc Michel Rey.

Russell, Bertrand. 1905. On denoting. *Mind*, N.S. 14: 479–493.

Russell, James A. 1994. Is there universal recognition of emotion from facial expression? A review of the cross-cultural studies. *Psychological Bulletin* 115: 102–141.

* Russell, James A. and José M. Fernández-Dols (eds.). 1997. *The Psychology of Facial Expressions*. Cambridge, UK: Cambridge University Press.

Sacks, Harvey. 1984. Methodological remarks. In: J. Maxwell Atkinson and John Heritage (eds.), *Structures of Social Action: Studies in Conversation Analysis*, 21–27. Cambridge, UK: Cambridge University Press.

Sacks, Harvey and Emanuel A. Schegloff. 1979. Two preferences in the organization of reference to persons in conversation and their interaction. In George Psathas (ed.), *Everyday Language: Studies in Ethnomethodology*, 15–21. New York: Irvington.

Sacks, Harvey, Emanuel A. Schegloff and Gail Jefferson. 1974. A simplest systematics for the organization of turn-taking in conversation. *Language* 50: 696–735.

Sadock, Jerrold M. 1978. On testing conversational implicature. In: Peter Cole (ed.), *Syntax and Semantics. Vol. 9: Pragmatics*, 281–297. New York: Academic Press.

*——2004. Speech acts. In: Laurence R. Horn and Gregory Ward (eds.), *The Handbook of Pragmatics*, 394–406. Oxford, UK: Blackwell.

Sandler, Wendy and Diane Lillo-Martin. 2006. *Sign Language and Linguistic Universals*. Cambridge, UK: Cambridge University Press.

Sapir, Edward. 1929. The status of linguistics as a science. *Language* 5: 207–214.

——1931. Conceptual categories in primitive languages. *Science* 74: 578.

*Sauter, Disa A., Frank Eisner, Paul Ekman and Sophie K. Scott. 2010. Cross cultural recognition of basic emotions through nonverbal emotional vocalizations. *PNAS* 107 (6): 2408–2412. 9 February 2010.

*Sauter, Disa A., Olivier Le Guen and Daniel B. M. Haun. 2011. Categorical perception of emotional expression does not require lexical categories. *Emotion* 11: 1479–1483.

Saville-Troike, Muriel. 2003. *The Ethnography of Communication*. Oxford: Blackwell.

Sbisà, Marina. 1995. Speech act theory. In: Jef Verschueren, Jan-Ola Östman and Jan Blommaert (eds.), *Handbook of Pragmatics – Manual*, 495–506. Amsterdam: John Benjamins.

*——2001. Illocutionary force and degrees of strength in language use. *Journal of Pragmatics* 33: 1791–1814.

——2007. How to read Austin. *Pragmatics* 17: 461–473.

——2010. John L. Austin. In: Jef Verschueren and Jan-Ola Östman (eds.), *Handbook of Pragmatics Online*. Amsterdam: John Benjamins. URL: http://www.benjamins.com/online/hop/

*Scheflen, Albert E. 1964. The significance of posture in communication systems. *Psychiatry* 27: 316–331.

*Schegloff, Emanuel A. 1988. Goffman and the analysis of conversation. In: Paul Drew and Anthony Wootton (eds.), *Erving Goffman – Exploring the Interaction Order*, 89–135. Cambridge, UK: Polity Press.

——1992. Introduction. In: Gail Jefferson (ed.), *Lectures on Conversation Volume I – Harvey Sacks*, ix–lxii. Oxford, UK: Blackwell Publishers.

*——2007. *Sequence Organization in Interaction: a Primer in Conversation Analysis*. Vol 1. Cambridge, UK: Cambridge University Press.

Schegloff, Emanuel A. and Harvey Sacks. 1973. Opening up closings. *Semiotica* 8: 289–327.

Schieffelin, Bambi B. and Elinor Ochs (eds.). 1986. *Language Socialization Across Cultures*. Cambridge, UK: Cambridge University Press.

Schieffelin, Bambi B., Kathryn Woolard and Paul V. Kroskrity (eds.). 1998. *Language Ideologies – Practice and Theory*. New York: Oxford University Press.

*Schmitt, Alain, Klaus Atzwanger, Karl Grammer and Katrin Schäfer (eds.). 1997. *New Aspects of Human Ethology*. New York: Plenum Press.

Schütz, Alfred. 1962. *Collected Papers. Vol. I*. The Hague: Martinus Nijhoff.

Searle, John R. 1965. What is a speech act? In: M. Black (ed.), *Philosophy in America*, 221–239. New York: Cornell University Press [reprinted 1972].

*——1968. Austin on locutionary and illocutionary acts. *The Philosophical Review* 77: 405–424.

——1969. *Speech Acts – An Essay in the Philosophy of Language*. Cambridge, UK: Cambridge University Press.

——1972. What is a speech act? In: Pier Paolo Giglioli (ed.) *Language and Social Context*, 136–154. Harmondsworth, UK: Penguin.

——1975. Indirect speech acts. In: Peter Cole and Jerry L. Morgan (eds.), *Syntax and Semantics Volume 3: Speech Acts*, 59–82. New York: Academic Press.

——1976. A classification of illocutionary acts. *Language in Society* 5: 1–23.

*——1979. *Expression and Meaning: Studies in the Theory of Speech Acts*. Cambridge, UK: Cambridge University Press.

*——1999. *Mind, Language and Society: Doing Philosophy in the Real World*. London: Weidenfeld and Nicolson.

——2006. What is language: Some preliminary remarks. Berkeley: Mimeo [downloadable from John Searle's website: http://socrates.berkeley.edu/~jsearle/articles.html]

*Searle, John R., Ferenc Kiefer and Manfred Bierwisch (eds.). 1980. *Speech Act Theory and Pragmatics*. Dordrecht, The Netherlands: Reidel.

*Searle, John R., Herman Parret and Jef Verschueren (eds.). 1992. *(On) Searle on Conversation*. Amsterdam: John Benjamins.

Senft, Gunter. 1991. Network models to describe the Kilivila classifier system. *Oceanic Linguistics* 30: 131–155.

——1994. Ein Vorschlag, wie man standardisiert Daten zum Thema "Sprache, Kognition und Konzepte des Raumes" in verschiedenen Kulturen erheben kann. *Linguistische Berichte* 154: 413–431.

——1995. Notes from the field: Ain't misbehavin'? Trobriand pragmatics and the field researcher's opportunity to put his (or her) foot in it. *Oceanic Linguistics* 34: 211–226.

——1996a. *Classificatory Particles in Kilivila*. New York: Oxford University Press.

——1996b. Phatic communion. In: Jef Verschueren, Jan-Ola Östman and Jan Blommaert (eds.), *Handbook of Pragmatics, 1995 loose leaf installment*, 1–10 Amsterdam: John Benjamins.

——1997a. Introduction. In: Gunter Senft (ed.), *Referring to Space – Studies in Austronesian and Papuan Languages*. Oxford, UK: Clarendon Press.

——1997b. Bronislaw Kasper Malinowski. In: Jef Verschueren, Jan-Ola Östman, Jan Blommaert and Chris Bulcaen (eds.), *Handbook of Pragmatics: 1997 loose leaf installment*, 1–20. Amsterdam: John Benjamins.

——1998. Body and mind in the Trobriand Islands. *Ethos* 26: 73–104.

*——1999. The presentation of self in touristic encounters. A case study from the Trobriand Islands. *Anthropos* 94: 21–33.

——2001. Frames of spatial reference in Kilivila. *Studies in Language* 25: 521–555.

——2004a. Introduction. In: Gunter Senft (ed.), *Deixis and Demonstratives in Oceanic Languages*. 1–13. Canberra: Pacific Linguistics.

——2004b. Aspects of spatial deixis in Kilivila. In: Gunter Senft (ed.), *Deixis and Demonstratives in Oceanic Languages*. 59–80. Canberra: Pacific Linguistics.

——2005. Bronislaw Malinowski and linguistic pragmatics. In: Piotr Çap (ed.), *Pragmatics Today*, 139–155. Frankfurt am Main: Peter Lang.

——2006. A biography in the strict sense of the term. Review article of the book by Michael Young (2004): *Malinowski: Odyssee of an Anthropologist 1884–1920*, vol. 1. New Haven, US: Yale University Press. *Journal of Pragmatics* 38: 610–637.

——2007. The Nijmegen space games: Studying the interrelationship between language, culture and cognition. In Jürg Wassmann and Katharina Stockhaus (eds.), *Person, Space and Memory in the Contemporary Pacific: Experiencing New Worlds*, 224–244. New York: Berghahn Books.

——2008. The case: The Trobriand Islanders vs H.P. Grice: Kilivila and the Gricean maxims of quality and manner. *Anthropos* 103: 139–147.

——2009a. Sind die emotionalen Gesichtsausdrücke des Menschen in allen Kulturen gleich? In Max Planck Society (ed.), *Max-Planck-Gesellschaft Jahrbuch 2008/09 Tätigkeitsberichte und Publikationen* (DVD) (pp. 1–4). München, Germany: Max Planck Society for the Advancement of Science.

——2009b. Trobriand Islanders' forms of ritual communication. In: Gunter Senft and Ellen B. Basso (eds.), *Ritual Communication*, 81–101. Oxford, UK: Berg.

——2009c. Introduction. In: Gunter Senft, Jan-Ola Östman and Jef Verschueren (eds.), *Culture and Language Use*, 1–17. Amsterdam: John Benjamins.

——2009d. Bronislaw Kasper Malinowski. In: Gunter Senft, Jan-Ola Östman and Jef Verschueren (eds.), *Culture and Language Use*, 211–225. Amsterdam: John Benjamins.

——2009e. Phatic communion. In: Gunter Senft, Jan-Ola Östman and Jef Verschueren (eds.), *Culture and Language Use*, 226–233. Amsterdam: John Benjamins.

——2010a. *The Trobriand Islanders' Ways of Speaking*. Berlin: de Gruyter Mouton.

——2010b. Review of Makihara, Miki and Bambi B. Schieffelin (eds.). 2007. *Consequences of Contact. Language Ideologies and Sociocultural Transformations in Pacific Societies*. Oxford, UK: Oxford University Press. *Paideuma* 56: 308–313.

——2010c. Introduction. In: Gunter Senft (ed.), *Endangered Austronesian and Australian Aboriginal Languages: Essays on Language Documentation, Archiving and Revitalization*, 1–13. Canberra: Pacific Linguistics.

——2012. Expressions of Emotions – and Inner Feelings – in Kilivila, the Language of the Trobriand Islanders: A Descriptive and Methodological Critical Survey. Talk presented at Le Centre d'Etudes des Langues Indigènes d'Amérique, CNRS. Villejuif, Paris. 1 January 2012.

Senft, Gunter and Ellen B. Basso (eds.). 2009. *Ritual Communication*. Oxford, UK: Berg.

Seuren, Pieter A. M. 1994. Presupposition. In: R. E. Asherand J. M. Y. Simpson (eds.), *The Encyclopedia of Language and Linguistics*, Vol. 6, 3311–3320. Oxford, UK: Pergamon Press.

——1998. *Western Linguistics. An Historical Introduction*. Oxford, UK: Blackwell.

——2009. *Language from Within Vol. I.: Language in Cognition*. Oxford, UK: Oxford University Press.

——2013. *From Whorf to Montague. Explorations in the Theory of Language*. Oxford, UK: Oxford University Press.

Seyfeddinipur, Mandana. 2004. Meta-discursive gestures from Iran: Some uses of the 'Pistol Hand'. In: Cornelia Müller and Roland Posner (eds.), *The Semantics and Pragmatics of Everyday Gestures*, 205–216. Berlin: Weidler.

Sherzer, Joel. 1977. The ethnography of speaking: A critical appraisal. In: Muriel Saville-Troike (ed.), *Linguistics and Anthropology. Georgetown University Round Table on Languages and Linguistics 1977*, 43–57. Washington DC, US: Georgetown University Press.

——1983: *Kuna Ways of Speaking. An Ethnographic Perspective*. Austin, US: University of Texas Press.

*——1990. *Verbal Art in San Blas. Kuna Culture Through its Discourse*. Cambridge, UK: Cambridge University Press.

Sherzer, Joel and Greg Urban (eds.), 1986. *Native South American Discourse*. Berlin: Mouton de Gruyter.

Sidnell, Jack. 2001. Conversational turn-taking in a Caribbean English Creole. *Journal of Pragmatics* 33: 1263–1290.

——2009a. Comparative perspectives in conversation analysis. In: Jack Sidnell (ed.), *Conversation Analysis: Comparative Perspectives*, 3–28. Cambridge, UK: Cambridge University Press.

*——2009b. Participation. In: Sigurd D'Hondt, Jan-Ola Östman and Jef Verschueren (eds.), *The Pragmatics of Interaction*, 125–156. Amsterdam: Benjamins.

——2010. *Conversation Analysis. An Introduction*. Oxford, UK: Wiley-Blackwell.

Silverstein, Michael. 1979. Language structure and linguistic ideologies. In: P. Clyne, W. Hanks and C. Hofbauer (eds.), *The Elements. A Parasession on Linguistic Units and Levels*, 193–247. Chicago, US: Chicago Linguistic Society.

Skeat, Walter W. 1984. *Malay Magic – Being an Introduction to the Folklore and Popular Religion of the Malay Peninsula*. Singapore: Oxford University Pess.

Slobin, Dan I. 1991. Learning to think for speaking: native language, cognition, and rhetorical style. *Pragmatics* 1: 7–25.

——1996. From "thought and language" to "thinking for speaking", In: John Gumperz and Stephen C. Levinson (eds.), *Rethinking Linguistic Relativity*, 70–96. Cambridge, UK: Cambridge University Press.

*Smith, Anja. 2010. Phatic expressions in French and German telephone conversations. In: Sanna-Kaisa Tanskanen, Marja-Liisa Helasvuo, Marjut Johansson and Mia Raitaniemi (eds.), *Discourse in Interaction*, 291–311. Amsterdam: John Benjamins.

*Smith, Barry C. (ed.). 2003. *John Searle*. Cambridge, UK: Cambridge University Press.

*Sperber, Dan and Deidre Wilson. 1995. *Relevance: Communication and Cognition*. Oxford, UK: Blackwell (second edition; first published 1986).

*Stam, Gale and Mika Ishino (eds.). 2011. *Integrating gesture: The interdisciplinary nature of gesture*. Amsterdam: John Benjamins.

*Stenström. Anna-Brita and Annette Myre Jörgensen. 2008. A matter of politeness? A contrastive study of phatic talk in teenage conversation. *Pragmatics* 18: 635–657.

Stivers, Tanya, Nicholas J. Enfield, Penelope Brown, Christina Englert, Makoto Hayashi, Trine Heinemann, Gertie Hoymann, Federico Rossano, Jan Peter de Ruiter, Kyung-Eun Yoon and Stephen C. Levinson. 2009. Universals and cultural variation in turn-taking in conversation. *PNAS* 106: 10587–10592.

Strawson, Peter F. 1950. On referring. *Mind*, N.S. 59: 320–344.

*Streeck, Jürgen, Charles Goodwin and Curtis LeBaron (eds.). 2011. *Embodied Interaction: Language and Body in the Material World*. Cambridge, UK: Cambridge University Press.

*Takanashi, Hiroko and Joseph Sung-Yul Park (eds.). 2011. Reframing framing: Interaction and the constitution of culture and society. *Pragmatics* (special issue) 21: 185–286.

Tanaka, Hiroko. 1999. *Turn-Taking in Japanese Conversation. A Study in Grammar and Interaction*. Amsterdam: John Benjamins.

Tannen, Deborah. 1981. Indirectness in discourse. Ethnicity as conversational style. *Discourse Processes* 3: 221–238.

Trask, Robert L. 1999. *Key Concepts in Language and Linguistics*. London: Routledge.

*Tsohatzidis, Savas L. (ed.). 1999. *Foundations of Speech Act Theory: Philosophical and Linguistic Perspectives*. London: Routledge.

*——(ed.). 2007. *John Searle's Philosophy of Language: Force, Meaning, and Mind*. Cambridge, UK: Cambridge University Press.

Verschueren, Jef. 2011. IPrA, the International Pragmatics Association, at 25. *SemiotiX* XN-6: 1–10. URL: http://www.semioticon.com/semiotix/2011/10/ipra-the-international-pragmatics-association-at-25/

——2012. *Ideology in Language Use. Pragmatic Guidelines for Empirical Research*. Cambridge, UK: Cambridge University Press.

*von Cranach, Mario, Klaus Foppa, Wolfgang Lepenies and Detlev Ploog (eds.). 1979. *Human Ethology – Claims and Limits of a New Discipline*. Cambridge, UK: Cambridge University Press.

*Warnock, Geoffrey J. 1989. *J. L. Austin*. London: Routledge.

*Webster, Anthony K. 2008. "Plaza 'g and before he can respond...": Language ideology, bilingual Navajo, and Navajo poetry. *Pragmatics* 18: 511–541.

Weissenborn, Jürgen and Wolfgang Klein. 1982. Introduction. In: Jürgen Weissenborn and Wolfgang Klein (eds.), *Here and There. Cross-Linguistic Studies on Deixis and Demonstration*, 1–12. Amsterdam: John Benjamins.

Weitz, Shirley. 1979. *Nonverbal Communication. Readings with Commentary*. New York: Oxford University Press. [second edition].

*Werner, Oswald. 1998. Sapir-Whorf hypothesis. In: Jacob L. Mey and Ron E. Asher (eds.), *Concise Encyclopedia of Pragmatics*, 799–807. Amsterdam: Elsevier.

Whorf, Benjamin Lee. 1940a. Science and linguistics. *Technology Review* 42: 229–231 and 247–248 [= 1956: 207–219].

——1940b. Linguistics as an exact science. *Technology Review* 43: 61–63 and 80–83 [= 1956: 220–232].

——1941. The relation of habitual thought and behavior to language. In: Leslie Spier (ed.), *Language, Culture and Personality – Essays in Memoriam of Edward Sapir*, 75–93. Menasha, US: Sapir Memorial Publication Fund [= 1956: 134–159].

——1956. *Language, Thought and Reality: Selected Writings of Benjamin Lee Whorf Edited by John B. Carroll*. Cambridge, MA, US: MIT Press.

*Wilce, James M. 2009. *Language and Emotion*. Cambridge, UK: Cambridge University Press

Wilkins, David. 2003. Why pointing with the index finger is not a universal (in sociocultural and semiotic terms). In Sotaro Kita (ed.), *Pointing: Where Language Culture and Cognition Meet*. 171–215. Mahwah, US: Lawrence Erlbaum.

*Wodak, Ruth. 1997. *Gender and Discourse*. London: Sage.

Woolard, Kathryn A. and Bambi B. Schieffelin. 1994. Language ideology. *Annual Review of Anthropology* 23: 55–82.

Wundt, Wilhelm. 1900. *Völkerpsychologie – Eine Untersuchung der Entwicklungsgesetze von Sprache, Mythus und Sitte. Erster Band: Die Sprache. Erster Teil*. Leipzig, Germany: Wilhelm Engelmann.

——1900-1920. *Völkerpsychologie – Eine Untersuchung der Entwicklungsgesetze von Sprache, Mythus und Sitte*. 10 Vols. Leipzig, Germany: Wilhelm Engelmann.

——1973. *The Language of Gestures*. With an introduction by Arthur L. Blumenthal and additional essays by George Herbert Mead and Karl Bühler. The Hague: Mouton.

Young, Michael. 2004. *Malinowski: Odyssee of an Anthropologist 1884 – 1920*. New Haven, US: Yale University Press.

Index